AURORA

By
Andrew Blakemore

COPYRIGHT

First published in 2009
By Authorhouse.

ISBN: 978-1-326-87473-5

CONTENTS

3

61. Aster
62. The daisies and buttercups
63. Bore da
64. If you cannot write a love song
65. This beautiful day
66. Amazon
67. For you did mend my broken heart
68. When love has gone
69. The golden eagle fly
70. A pocketful of dreams
71. Grains of sand
72. I cannot rest
73. As clouds now weep
74. I dreamt about you every night
75. I rest upon this lonely rock
76. Free as I can be
77. This music so sweet
78. Watching the waves
79. The colours of morning
80. The long stone
81. Our love is an ocean
82. Death does hold no fear for me
83. Thank you God
84. I saw the newborn ducklings swim
85. The graveyard
86. The jackdaws are calling
87. I wander through the pasture
88. The daisies stay closed
89. Beneath that fallen rock and stone
90. As cloud now lies upon the hills
91. This morning makes the chaffinch sing
92. A dream I'll always keep
93. I traced the steps of Tennyson
94. Within this old deserted barn
95. Within these walls of stone
96. Now soon the cliff will crumble
97. Haystack
98. I wished I'd lived to see the land
99. Driftwood
100. Ragwort
101. The clover on this hill
102. The buzzard
103. Afterglow
104. Within this rock and stone
105. You were the thorn upon the rose
106. This stone I keep within my hand
107. The winds across the downs
108. On that lonely craggy shore
109. Blossom sky
110. Cattle field

111. The mole
112. Within that stirring cloud
113. The guns forever silent
114. Wildwood
115. Through falling, falling snow
116. There stands the open gate
117. The sweet song of the wren
118. I wrote her name upon the sand
119. Blow winds gently blow
120. To all the loves that passed me by
121. The hammer and the rusting nail
122. Morning rose
123. Leaving footprints on the sand
124. As all day long I toil and strain
125. To Lichfield leads this lonely road
126. Gold Hill
127. I rest my head upon the leaves
128. Derwentwater
129. Hardy's cottage
130. From Eype to West Bay
131. When blossom drapes the orchard boughs
132. Sleep gentle waves
133. Sweet tree of heaven
134. The ghost of the white horse
135. Golden Cap
136. Eventide
137. The song of the wind
138. I'm down by the river
139. Sky
140. The dust now settled gently
141. A lonely leaf
142. The woodland track
143. Wrapped within the petals
144. Parachutes
145. Broken wings
146. The mirror lies broken
147. This sweet little child
148. Rests in God's hands
149. Sleep on gentle night
150. I need you more each day
151. The nights are long and lonely now
152. My heart was made to be in love
153. I long to walk those golden sands
154. The shipwreck
155. The hardest part of loving you
156. The summertime is over now
157. It's only make believe
158. The morning dew
159. Please picture the scene
160. Walsall leather

213. A part of me died with you
214. As from the chalky cliffs so sheer
215. Why I may kiss this scarlet rose
216. Your hand of loving kindness
217. So still was morning's restful air
218. If love could fly upon the wing
219. Please paint me a beautiful picture
220. You are the reason
221. Wind chime
222. From whence that little robin came
223. While this ocean flows
224. A wonderful friend
225. Our lives are entangled
226. For every day without a smile
227. As soft as a snowflake
228. Hurt me most of all
229. For every heart that's found true love
230. Each night I pray unto the stars
231. In the shade of the green wood
232. Live out the rest of my days
233. A crofter's tale
234. A thousand wishes
235. Some days
236. An acorn lies within the snow
237. Arise Sunday morning
238. I gaze at the sky
239. The last kiss I shall ever give
240. Song thrush
241. Your brazen heart shall never feel
242. The wisdom of my youth
243. Upon the shaded river bank
244. A view from the park bench
246. Shannon's Mill
247. I kick the can
248. The son of a fisherman
249. A frosty morn
250. Cathedral bells
251. For forty summers
252. God bless the children
253. As dawn does stir the sleeping night
254. For things will never be the same again
255. Beside the frozen lake I stand
256. I'll walk with God
257. Where art thou pain?
258. Please let me rest
259. Brittle twigs
260. For now as the dawning has ended the darkness
261. Footprints in the snow
262. As autumn leaves keep falling
263. The water wheel

368. That summer evening calm and still
369. And as the breeze now gently blows
370. I wake to see the rising dawn
371. The dawning filled with birdsong
372. Fear not the fate befallen me
373. I've come to see my maiden fair
374. The petals from my fallen rose
375. I saw the newborn lambs that played
376. As softly as the stream does flow
377. When summer fades to autumn
378. I rest beside the golden corn
379. That fateful day
380. Be still the chilly wind that blows
381. My dreams of love may never be
382. My lonely heart shall wait for spring
383. That kiss shall keep you in my dreams
384. As sunrise brings the morning songs
385. As autumn comes with falling leaves
386. A scarlet rose for my true love
387. Farewell to England's pastures green
388. Until he drew his final breath
389. Across the windswept downs I go
390. Within the April woodland grow
391. If I should lose my heart to thee
392. As sheep within their pastures graze
393. The early morning lark did sing
394. Where has the sun of morning gone?
395. Please cease for me o restless breeze
396. The rose now blooms and shines so bright
397. All hope seems gone and lost to me
398. Awake sweet morn to end the night
399. The mist does drape the distant hill
400. While here remains my shattered dream
401. My sweetest love beside me lie
402. I wish I were that butterfly
403. So green the land that I can see
404. I touch the morning of the spring
405. My aching heart does need you so
406. The summer breeze that gently blows
407. I love to walk upon the hills
408. O radiant stars that shine above
409. Your loving hand
410. When swallows grace the morning sky
411. Sweet thrush if I could sing like you
412. My lonely heart can never love
413. The school tree
414. Upon the blackened canvas
415. At the bottom of the garden
416. Summer dreams
417. Love

418. I'm crossing the causeway
419. When frozen streams shall flow once more
420. O lasting love that knows no bounds
421. The sound of wind within the trees
422. The Airston wool shop
423. The rusting old bucket
424. The gift of love
425. If I should find no answers there
426. Getting ready for apple picking
427. Portland stone
428. The washing line
429. The potter
431. The early morning mist and dew
432. To me you are sunlight
433. I feel a joy now spring's begun
434. Till God does find another path
435. All is silent
436. And as the winter's moonlight falls
437. The trawler
438. I found it in the morning
439. On the sixteenth day of August 1977
440. The timber trail
441. The ancient pearl
442. My heart is yours for evermore
443. Put aside your differences
444. A misty light
445. My love shall flow like gentle streams
446. I shall forever think of you

INTRODUCTION

Andrew Blakemore was born on January 1st 1966 in Aldridge, West Midlands and is the youngest of three sons. His parents both worked for Walsall fire service and married in 1959. Andrew was educated locally at Redhouse Junior and Infant Schools (1971-77) and at Aldridge Comprehensive School (1977-84). His childhood was a happy one, in which he formed strong ties with the area where he still lives and works, and which continues to inspire his poetry.

From an early age, Andrew had a passion for the arts, particularly reading, drawing and music. At sixteen, he taught himself to play the guitar and began writing songs, a hobby which was to give him a thorough grounding in the fundamentals of rhyme, rhythm and structure. In 1992, he embarked on a Bachelor's degree in Music with the Open University, graduating with honours in 1999. During this time, he became an accomplished musician, achieving Grade Eight on classical guitar, and also learning to play the piano, violin and clarinet.

However, it was only as recently as 2001 that Andrew began seriously to write poetry. He was asked to contribute a verse to Aldridge Methodist Church Newsletter, and chose *A Child is Born.* It was really a Christmas song written some years earlier but it was well received, and he soon began making regular contributions. Encouraged by this and with the support of those closest to him, Andrew has continued to write prolifically, producing more than 900 poems to date.

Andrew's work has been included in publications from both United Press and Forward Press, and in July 2007, he was voted Forward Press Poet of the Month by a panel of judges for his poem *I wrote her name upon the sand.* In 2006, he self-published *Kaleidoscopes and Rainbows,* followed in 2007 by *The Wonder is You,* an ambitious 452-page volume containing all of his completed works at that time. On a similar scale, *Aurora* demonstrates his continuing development as a writer.

Among his influences, Andrew cites such poets as Frost, Keats, Burns, Tennyson and Wordsworth, and the Romantic connection between nature, emotion and spirituality is evident in much of his work. However, he is also increasingly willing to experiment with new forms and subject matter, and the poems in *Aurora* run the gamut from timeless themes of love, nature and the divine, to the harsh realities of industrial heritage and significant moments in twentieth-century popular culture. By turns poignant, nostalgic and uplifting, they represent Andrew's highly individual view of the world. Expressed in an unpretentious but lyrical style, it is a view that will resonate with a wide range of readers.

Kathy Moore

Aurora

Aurora the dawning
The beautiful morning
As the sun gently shines through the trees,
The clouds lit with gold
Watch their colours unfold
As they sail through the air on the breeze.

Now darkness is ending
The sun is ascending
And casting its light on the land,
What greatness I see
As the day comes to be
And I capture the scene in my hand.

As the birds start to sing
A sweet joy they do bring
To the dawn and its marvellous show,
As I look on this day
And its wondrous display
Where my dreams shall eternally flow.

Aurora the dawning
The beautiful morning
As shadows are lit by the sun,
The chorus of pleasure
I witness its treasure
As the new day has now just begun.

All through the barren winter

All through the barren winter
I have waited for this day,
To see the signs of springtime rise
Across the barren way,
For all the purple crocuses
And snowdrops now in bloom,
Have brought a joy into my heart
And lifted winter's gloom.

To see the golden daffodils
Now bursting into flower,
And blossoms catch the morning breeze
Upon the cherry bower,
The meadows filled with daisies
And the hawthorn dressed in white,
As through the skies the swallows soar
So wonderful their sight.

The days are growing longer
As the air grows warmer too,
Now soon the threat of snow will pass
And frosts will melt to dew,
When bluebells grace the woodland
Like the waves upon the shore,
I'll know that spring has come at last
And winter is no more.

The clouds on the mountains

The clouds on the mountains like smoke are descending
And cloaking the sunlight they gather with force,
A storm is approaching with rumbles of thunder
And flashes of lightning that follow its course,
Ever encroaching the slopes are now hidden
They creep down the valley as dark as the night,
As echoes do tremble and rain begins falling
And I face the wrath of its vengeance and spite.

A strong wind is blowing and trees are now bending
As rain lashes down from the coal coloured sky,
Whilst shaking the branches with gusts unrelenting
And stripping their leaves as it races on by,
The drumming of hail that now covers the landscape
And glistens in silver as skies start to clear,
As a shaft of a sunbeam does shine through the blanket
Yet still distant rolls of the thunder I hear.

The clouds on the mountains are moving away now
Revealing the picture that I wished to see,
So still is the evening so green is the meadow
Now lit by the sunlight as if just for me,
The birds singing sweetly from out of the treetops
A whispering breeze brings a joy to the air,
As arching above there's a rainbow so vivid
That glows on the canvas through clouds of despair.

The leaves are slowly turning

The leaves are slowly turning
As September slips away,
The blue skies of the summer
Now a pallid shade of grey,
When cold winds blow the leaves will fall
And frosts shall grip the night,
Then dawn will wake in silence
And shall wear a cloak of white.

Now as the woodland turns to gold
And sap begins to dry,
The last flames of the autumn glow
That soon shall fade and die,
As nature sleeps and will not stir
While sun too weak to thaw,
Those months ahead shall seem so long
Till spring arrives once more.

When the flowers start to open
And the winter does depart,
Then I shall see the blossomed boughs
A sight to warm my heart,
But yet for now the boughs are bare
And chill winds blow so cold,
While scattered all around my feet
The leaves, a field of gold.

I look upon those ghostly trees
Through freezing mist they peer,
Now snow and ice have gripped the land
And shall not start to clear,
Till winter ends and sun does warm
Those silent skies above,
Till then I'll dream of daffodils
And the season that I love.

This picture is mine

I see all the flowers so pretty before me
Their colours so vivid and bright,
They blend in the meadows so happy together
And fill this sweet morn with delight,
As the pink cherry blossoms are draping the branches
And daffodils glow like the sun,
My heart feels the joy for the winter has passed
And the springtime has now just begun.

I see all the rivers that glisten in silver
Whilst breathing the life into land,
They gently meander through wide sweeping valleys
Their waters so cool to my hand,
The fruit is now growing as summer's upon us
I look to those emerald hills,
And fields of the country so rich and inspiring
With all that their beauty instils.

I see all the trees that do rise from the forest
Which turn as the season goes by,
In beckoning breezes the branches are waving
As leaves gently fall from the sky,
Then slowly they fade to the shades of the season
Now hues of the autumn surround,
November approaches soon boughs will be bare
And a carpet shall cover the ground.

I see all the mountains those ranges before me
Whose peaks are now shrouded with snow,
And gripped by the freeze that's unwilling to yield
As the cold winds of winter now blow,
As ice slowly forms and is touched by the sunlight
The crystallized landscape does shine,
As I stand here alone and I gaze at the scene
I can say that this picture is mine.

A bird is perched upon the gate

A bird is perched upon the gate
And singing sweetly for his mate
So patiently he there does wait
There's no reply at all,
Time again he tries and tries
From perch to post to branch he flies
Not knowing that his mate now lies
At peace beside the wall.

For she was hit by speeding car
Her flecks of blood now stain the tar
She flew but she could not get far
And sadly there did fall,
Within the evening's amber glow
A gentle breeze begins to blow
The time has come for her to go
And leave her grassy shawl.

As there her lifeless body stays
Beside the field where cattle graze
Lit by the sunlight's fading rays
She looks so frail and small,
Her spirit flies into the air
Again the summer skies they share
She sees her mate still singing there
And longs to heed his call.

The dawn was cold as biting winds

The dawn was cold as biting winds
Did blow across the down,
I saw the crows that fed within
Those lowly fields of brown,
As clouds did skim the hilltops there
Like smoke above the ground,
The air was hushed and all was still
I could not hear a sound.

Along the worn and stony path
I headed on my way,
Yet all was lost unto me now
Beneath those skies of grey,
I walked alone with broken heart
With no place left to go,
Whilst longing for the clouds to lift
I prayed the sun would show.

And there I waited for a while
Till rain began to fall,
I tried to find some shelter then
But none was there at all,
I turned my collar to the wind
And knew I must go on,
With nothing left to call my own
For everything had gone.

I felt bereft and empty
As I reached the bitter end,
And looked across the ocean
Where the sea and sky did blend,
So drab the view and yet I heard
The waves upon the shore,
That once did fill my life with cheer
Yet gave me joy no more.

So joyful the sight

So joyful the sight of the woodlands that glow
In the hues of the fall like the sun sinking low,
A tapestry woven such pleasure to see
This joy I am feeling forever shall be,
The morning so peaceful now day has begun
The ground gently warmed by the warmth of the sun,
While touching the fields and the fruit on the vine
Each picture complete as the colours do shine.

So joyful the sight of the meadows I pass
Where flowers emerge from the long waving grass,
This place is my love as I walk hand in hand
With nature as one through this wonderful land,
The stream trickles by with its water so clear
A melody pure that's so sweet to my ear,
The sound is so soothing I long it to play
Wherever I wander this beautiful day.

So joyful the sight of the mountains that rise
And touching the clouds as they soar to the skies,
So tall and imposing so mighty and strong
They beckon me closer to where I belong,
The pathway is stony yet shall lead me there
To stand on the summit and breathe in the air,
And gaze at the landscape so rugged and true
My heart shall belong here forever with you.

God's hand was surely here

When rolling fields and pastures green
Light England's countryside,
When hills do rise in harmony
And clouds above them glide,
When shining in the summer sun
The view I hold so dear,
So wonderful there is no doubt
God's hand was surely here.

What joy does live within me
When the trees are dressed in gold,
Within the autumn woodland
As the season does unfold,
When leaves then turn and start to fall
Until they disappear,
So wonderful there is no doubt
God's hand was surely here.

When snowfalls of the winter
Leave the land all frozen white,
When the scenery does glisten then
My heart sings with delight,
When frosts lie on those misty dawns
And starry nights so clear,
So wonderful there is no doubt
God's hand was surely here.

When snow and ice begin to thaw
And springtime comes again,
When bluebells dance and bowers bloom
And blossoms fall like rain,
When the colours glow around me
And the songbirds bring me cheer,
So wonderful there is no doubt
God's hand was surely here.

The ash tree

That mighty ash a friend to me
A lifetime known it there,
I've seen it when all clothed in green
And when its branches bare,
So often last to gather leaf
And then the first to fall,
But like a rock it's always stood
And shone there over all.

I've watched it grow so wide and broad
Each day since I was born,
And there beside its burly form
I've seen each breaking dawn,
When snow clad boughs of crystal white
Lay still against the skies,
'Twas like a dream that had come true
And stood before my eyes.

I've seen it bending in the gale
And yet remain so strong,
Found peace within its cooling shade
And rested there so long,
I've listened to the winds that blew
Like waves upon the shore,
And I again would be so glad
To hear that sound once more.

That mighty ash a friend to me
Gave shelter from the rain,
So many times I've waited there
Till sunlight shone again,
I watched the birds that built their nests
Until they flew away,
No better place I thought to live
No better place to stay.

The forest of old

I treasure those moments I keep in my heart
Of my love and the life we did share,
You'll stay in my dreams and you never shall leave
Yet I wish God would answer my prayer,
For as September nears and the winds start to blow
They shall fill me with sorrow and pain,
As the forest of old slowly turns into gold
How I long to be with you again.

For there through the summer when leaves were all green
And I rested alone in the shade,
I remembered the joy and the times that we shared
They are memories that shall never fade,
Yet now I'm so lonely as October nears
And the sunlight has turned into rain,
As the forest of old is now burning in gold
How I long to be with you again.

As leaves gently fall from the branches above
And I capture one there in my hand,
So fragile it feels and will soon turn to dust
Now a carpet does cover the land,
I gaze at the treetops as November nears
And I know that my love shall remain,
As the forest of old slowly loses its gold
How I long to be with you again.

The General in his tunic red

The General in his tunic red
Unto their deaths so many led
Obeying orders that he said
Were lions ruled by mice,
His tactics hard to understand
While bodies lay upon the land
All killed by his uncaring hand
They paid the sacrifice.

His orders met with great dismay
Within the lines so far away
In muddy fields and sodden clay
He ordered to attack,
His men through hell of spitting fire
Were caught within the razor wire
Or choked by gas amid the mire
The General turned his back.

No sense of feeling nor regret
No heart had he to get upset
And in peace he always slept
Far from the bloody fight,
Those medals on his chest he wore
Were never earned and nothing more
Than tokens yet awarded for
His errors he thought right.

When he knew the end of war was near
From country mansion did appear
And seemingly he had no fear
To visit the front line,
Although the General never brave
He took the accolades they gave
And basked in glory to his grave
And drank the victor's wine.

Barr Beacon

From the crown I now gaze at this wonderful view
As the heart of my homeland does shine,
The hills in the distance, the fields and the country
Where a patchwork of colours entwine,
The morning is clear as the scenery reaches
Across the horizon so wide,
Now lit by the sunlight it gleams in its glory
Such joy I am feeling inside.

Alone save the breeze of the summer which blows
And caresses the grass that does bend,
While hedgerows alive with the sparrows that sing
And I live for the message they send,
As they fill the air with their songs of the morn
Which now carry me forth to the shade,
Of the evergreen trees with their old wizened boughs
Where I feel that my fortune is made.

As slowly I climb the memorial steps
Then I rest by the plinth where I dwell,
As I look to the skies all my memories return
For there's so many tales I could tell,
Of lingering evenings and sunsets I've seen
When the clouds were all burning with gold,
Then under the starlight until the dawn rose
When I watched the new morning unfold.

As now I do walk by the ribbons of gorse
With the bushes so newly in flower,
The scrubland and heather where I used to roam
And I'd pass away many an hour,
So little has changed as I now carry on
For I'm lost to the joys of the land,
Each touching my heart with the pleasure I feel
That is leading me on by the hand.

I look to the city so grey and imposing
Its tower blocks reach to the sky,
With a layer of haze that does stubbornly cling
To its form as the morning goes by,
Yet here there is peace and serenity thrives
In my heart and my soul for this day,
As I leave with a sense of fulfilment and cheer
And I wish I had longer to stay.

The cold days of winter

The cold days of winter and long nights together
When sharing the bond of a close family,
The memories so clear of the home I was raised in
It's so long ago now but I can still see.

The fire gently burning and lighting the darkness
Each warming our hands from the harsh winter's cold,
We talked and then listened to gramophone music
So happy we were on those long nights of old.

We watched as the snowflakes did gather on ledges
Then crept up the window as soft candle light,
Did glow on the walls of the room where we lingered
And burned through the evening and into the night.

So little we had and yet we were so lucky
For we'd got each while others had none,
Huddled we sat by the warmth of the fire
And there we did stay till the last flame had gone.

Then falling in slumber and sleeping in armchairs
With eyes feeling heavy and resting our heads,
Then climbing the staircase as embers were glowing
And bidding goodnight as we went to our beds.

Those cold days of winter and long nights together
Shall never return for those years have gone by,
Those memories won't fade I will always remember
Just watching those flames slowly flicker then die.

The Sherbrook Valley

As over the hills of September there lies
A rich carpet of heather so fine,
That sweeps across slopes in the valley of violet
And in the pale sunlight does shine,
For the mist of the dawning that hung like a shroud
Has now drifted away on the breeze,
That stirs the soft shadows and carries the clouds
As it sails through the boughs of the trees.

I follow the path as it winds its way down
To the river that gently flows by,
While the conifers stand like a ribbon of green
As they reach to the glorious sky,
The bracken grows wild and the ferns are adorned
By the thickets of bramble and gorse,
As I roam through the land I am under its spell
And amazed as I follow its course.

For a peace fills the air and I listen with joy
To the tunes that the songbirds do sing,
As the late summer fades I do treasure each day
That the swallows still soar on the wing,
For this palette so rich is a picture to savour
A tapestry blending as one,
Yet the call of the autumn now draws ever closer
And summertime soon will be gone.

And then this sweet valley shall wither to brown
And the hush of the winter descend,
Yet for now I'll enjoy all these sights and the sounds
Till they sadly all come to an end,
As over the hills of September there lies
A rich carpet of heather so fine,
That sweeps across slopes in the valley of violet
And in the pale sunlight does shine.

Will you pray for me?

Will you pray for me?
My friend I need a helping hand,
To lead me to the sunlight
That does shine upon the land,
For so much I have suffered
And in darkness I have dwelt,
I need someone to free me
From the pain that I have felt.

For all around lies emptiness
A void does fill my mind,
And skies are grey with misery
And days to me unkind,
I head alone nowhere to go
In search of hidden gold,
As rain falls down upon me
And the chilly wind blows cold.

Now while the winter does remain
The spring will never bloom,
Nor shall the flowers rise again
To lift the air of gloom,
If I was blessed with fortune
That has always been denied,
Then love may find a way to me
And then no longer hide.

Will you pray for me
For I'm a lonely soul in need
Who sought a life of happiness
But never did succeed,
Your prayers may go unanswered
Yet the hope does still remain,
That love one day shall come to me
And dry my tears of pain.

The new dawn

The new dawn is rising from out of its slumber
And stirring the morning to wake,
As the whispering clouds in the skies slowly drift
Such a marvellous picture they make,
I feel I'm in heaven surrounded by beauty
A gift only God could bestow,
For life now has meaning and speaks to me clearly
Within this most wonderful show.

So bright is the sunlight that glistens through branches
And beams of its glory it sends,
To the land there before me absorbing its riches
Caressing the garden it tends,
Now filling my soul with a passion that flows
Like the river that's running with grace,
While the threads in the hedgerows are shining in silver
For spun there with fine silken lace.

The new dawn is rising and shadows are lifting
I've waited so long for this day,
For the spring has arrived and awoken the flowers
And the winter has now passed away,
The daffodils wave and are lit now in gold
And their petals are sprinkled with dew,
As the blossoms are glowing from hedgerow and bough
I shall dream of this wonderful view.

I'll walk with my head held up high

Such hurt I now feel but I won't let it show
And I'll try to smile at the people I know,
I'll wait for the sunlight to shine up above
As I dream for that moment of love,
And yet I don't know if it shall come to me
If it be my fate or my true destiny,
I'll still carry on for my hopes shall not die
And I'll walk with my head held up high.

Yet love never found the right way to my heart
When life dealt its cards I was doomed from the start,
If I was a bird then I'd fly on the wing
But I haven't a song I could sing,
Yet when I was young I had so much to give
But as I grow old I just don't want to live,
For time's been so cruel as the years passed me by
Still I'll walk with my head held up high.

I long for the day when I can feel inside
A sense of achievement some honour and pride,
But sadly I fail in whatever I do
And sweet happiness I never knew,
For nothing I have all I get I do share
Except for my soul and the clothes that I wear,
Yet still I do suffer I'll never know why
But I'll walk with my head held up high.

A love so deep

A love so deep it shall not fade
For there in heaven it was made,
No wedge could prise our souls apart
You'll always live inside my heart.

As I hear the waters flow
While evening falls and clouds aglow,
There's nowhere else I'd rather be
Than by your side eternally.

I carve your name upon the bark
While high above the soaring lark,
Does call your name upon the breeze
That gently strokes the woodland trees.

I see the sunset then unfold
And like the wheat it shines in gold
Watching as the fading light
Then slips unto the waiting night.

So glad to be a part of this
I seal the moment with a kiss,
Into our souls this day shall pour
A time to save for evermore.

So still the evening not a sound
As shadows creep across the ground,
But while the distant hills do shine
I know you'll be forever mine.

Light trickles now like falling tears
The clouds forlorn as twilight nears,
Which wander just like far off dreams
To find another home it seems.

I know with you my heart shall stay
As time does pass and years decay,
I will recall this evening sweet
That came and made my life complete.

A love so deep we'll always share
The stars above at which we stare,
Upon this still and peaceful night
For you and I they glow so bright.

In verses just for you

So hard to say I'm sorry
For those words I cannot speak,
I long to find some comfort now
For happiness I seek,
I take a pen and paper
And each word I say so true,
As I write down the love I feel
In verses just for you.

If I could change the things I said
If I could change the past,
And hold you in my arms again
This time I'd make it last,
I need you there for evermore
I want the life I knew,
As I write down the love I feel
In verses just for you.

I can't go on without you now
Alone too much to bear,
I wish that you were with me
And that God would hear my prayer,
My paper's stained with tears that fall
I know my hopes are few,
Yet I write down the love I feel
In verses just for you.

I dream about you every night
I think of you each day,
You'll be forever in my heart
And there you'll always stay,
I'll wait for you eternally
I'll count the seconds too,
As I write down the love I feel
In verses just for you.

Orca

The orca so peaceful
Are singing together,
They glide through the ocean
So placid and blue,
And gracefully move
As they shear through the wave tops,
A sight so inspiring
That's calling us too.

They speak and we listen
They guide and we follow,
But knowing not where
Or the secrets they keep,
For they're ours to discover
To learn of their wisdom,
As they wander on
Through the waters so deep.

Their spumes like a cloud
As they rise to the surface,
Their spray like the rain
From the heavens above,
As they head on their journey
A trail they are making,
Embracing our souls
With their passion and love.

The orca so peaceful
Are singing together,
At home in the ocean
So natural and free,
Their tails send a greeting
So warm and so gentle,
For they are our kindred
The gods of the sea.

A child of the mountains

My home is the valley a child of the mountains
Their silver-capped peaks in the sunlight do shine,
So picture a scene now and let your thoughts wander
This can be your dream for it surely is mine,
I gaze at the ranges that reach unto heaven
And touch all the clouds as they slowly pass by,
The calm mirrored lakes lying still and so peaceful
Reflecting the art of this wonderful sky.

My home is the meadow so fresh and inspiring
For here by the river the flowers do grow,
Which dance in the breeze and do carry a promise
Where waters of life shall eternally flow,
I walk in the foothills each step an adventure
And I long to stay here the rest of my days,
So wild and so natural their undisturbed treasure
That's rising before through the soft misty haze.

My home is the country the land of my fathers
I'll follow their footsteps wherever they lead,
They rose with the dawn and they slept under starlight
And farmed all these pastures and planted the seed,
I stand now in awe of these rocky cathedrals
That tower before me so hard to forget,
For here they do shine on this beautiful morning
And glow in the evening as sun starts to set.

Melting ice

I am a mighty polar bear
Who never did do wrong,
I raised a family of my own
And once my will was strong,
I liked to wander far and wide
Across the caps I'd roam,
But every year things seem to change
It feels no longer home.
My world is falling to the sea
I've had to pay the price,
I have nowhere that I can live
My land is melting ice.

I am an Emperor penguin
And I have a tale to tell,
I raised a family of my own
Together we did dwell,
Each egg I cradled carefully
While bitter winds did blow,
But every year things seem to change
I watched it slowly go.
My world is falling to the sea
I've had to pay the price,
I have nowhere that I can live
My land is melting ice.

I am a lonely Arctic seal
Who's resting on the shore,
So many of us used to come
In years that passed before,
But sadly now I'm all alone
My friends no longer here,
Yet still I wait in yearning
That one day they will appear.
My world is falling to the sea
I've had to pay the price,
I have nowhere that I can live
My land is melting ice.

The train within the station stands

The train within the station stands
The passengers with bags in hands,
Upon the crowded platform wait
To board the train that's running late,
The carriage doors are opened wide
And so they make their way inside,
The doors are shut the whistle blows
A flag is waved and there she goes.

Now slowly down the well-worn track
So dark within the tunnel black,
To reach the end where sunlight shines
Upon the sleek and silver lines,
The train now gently gathers speed
Beside the rusting tracks and weed,
For there unused in sidings by
The broken trucks and wagons lie.

Pass over points at pace go past
And down the line now moving fast,
Beneath the bridge of blackened brick
A gush of air that is so quick,
Past sidings filled with rolling stock
From side to side the train does rock,
Some people then with cups in hand
Do sway as they can barely stand.

They make their way back to their seat
As wheels upon the tracks do beat,
A rhythm that is loud and clear
That gently slows as stations near,
Past houses on the bleak estates
The empty yards and factory gates,
Then through the land of urban sprawl
And by the flats that stand so tall.

A speeding shooting sudden sound
As swiftly by and northern bound,
The racing wind with mighty force
Another train upon its course,
Graffiti sprayed A.V.F.C
Beside the church and cemetery,
The terraced rows with slated tiles
Which seem to spread for miles and miles.

Now racing by the hills and fields
With all the power the engine yields,
As through the cuttings straight and deep
Where trees do line the banks so steep,
Then over works canal and barge
And through the towns both small and large,
Then by the school the walls and fence
Where thickets grow so dark and dense.

Then over road and under bridge
Across the river and the ridge,
And by the meadows rich and green
The countryside looks so serene,
Where all the cows and sheep do graze
Within the pastures spend their days,
So peaceful in its rural charm
The antiquated rustic farm.

And on towards the smoky town
The scrap yards and the fields of brown,
As pylons tower above the blight
The drabness of this sorry plight,
Where buildings crumble into dust
And metal roofs are holed by rust,
The warehouse with its empty yard
That's left to rot with disregard.

Then past the roads all choked with cars
The fast food and the all night bars,
Exist within that living hell
In which so many have to dwell,
The taxis queuing in a row
The buses and the coaches slow,
For people as they disembark
Congested and so hard to park.

Now having reached its destination
The train does roll into the station,
And then beside the platform stands
While passengers with bags in hands,
Then all step off and make their way
Towards the city stark and grey,
And after hours of toil and strain
They'll make their journey home again.

Sister Dora

Upon "The Bridge" her statue stands
A Saint to all who knew her well,
Her memory lives and shall not fade
Although the years go by,
Forever she will dwell with those
Who welcomed her with open arms,
Into the town she called her home
And now at peace does lie.

For she became a friend to all
The humble folk of Walsall town,
She helped the poor and destitute
And tended those in need,
She fought against authority
To end the hardship of the poor,
And gave her life to help the cause
A kindly soul indeed.

She cared for those who were bereaved
When all those local miners drowned,
Within that dark and flooded seam
And dried their falling tears,
They came to know and love her more
An angel in a nurse's guise,
As if from heaven she was sent
To ease the people's fears.

She nursed the injured and the maimed
And worked so hard to cure the sick,
She persevered with everyone
So many lives did save,
Until the time she lost her strength
And closed her eyes upon the world,
Then Sister Dora thousands mourned
As she went to her grave.

On the streets I do decry

It's growing dark I'm running scared
I need to get back home,
For everyone's deserted me
Alone I now do roam,
Past empty homes and alleyways
Where danger lurks at night,
My hastened steps do quicken
As I move towards the light,
I feel that someone's watching me
I sense a prying eye,
And hurry through the shadows
On the streets I do decry.

The rats do scurry by me
From the bin bags that are torn,
The terraced windows boarded up
Shan't see the light of dawn,
I hear some footsteps follow me
That sound not far behind,
I turn but I see no one there
Which feeds my anxious mind,
The siren and the flashing lights
A squad car races by,
I hurry through the shadows
On the streets I do decry.

A cat does hiss a can does roll
Into the littered kerb,
Upon the wind that whistles loud
And silence does disturb,
The curtains twitch and close again
A gang is grouped ahead,
I cross the road and walk away
Ignoring what they said,
And as the rain starts falling
In my effort to keep dry,
I hurry through the shadows
On the streets I do decry.

The raven in the skies

Upon these rugged peaks that rise
The sun does gently shine,
It falls upon those mirrored lakes
So too the emerald pine,
Then through the silence of the morn
A lonely voice now cries,
As high above the mountain soars
The raven in the skies.

This moment I do share its world
Its secrets now revealed,
This stony path shall lead me on
Through all that was concealed,
I walk the verdant valley
Where the breeze now softly sighs,
As high above the mountain soars
The raven in the skies.

As like a falling shadow
So majestic in its flight,
Its silhouette familiar
And its form as dark as night,
I too could make my home within
These rugged peaks that rise,
As high above the mountain soars
The raven in the skies.

Down the mine

Down the mine through tunnels dark
They walk towards the jagged seam,
Where carbide lamps and lanterns shine
To guide the way ahead,
Their families wait their safe return
They fear the danger of collapse,
Where many lives been lost before
Their days are filled with dread.

With hands of steel and ground in dirt
The miners go with trusted picks,
They rest them on their shoulders strong
Ignoring all their fears,
The empty trucks upon the rail
Are waiting to be filled again,
Beside the rich and fruitful seam
They've worked for many years.

As heavy swings begin to fall
Familiar sound of steel on coal,
The splinters then do break away
And roll onto the floor,
Then shovelled up and loaded on
Those waiting trucks that rumble loud,
And echo through the darkness
As they start to roll once more.

Along the old and twisted track
As miners take a welcome rest,
And lean upon their picks and spades
In dirty clothes they wear,
With sweat upon their arms and brows
So warm and cramped they cannot stand,
With lungs of dust they wheeze and cough
While gasping for some air.

A band of brothers side by side
With burdens that do weigh them down,
But aches and pains forgotten
For they have a job to do,
Each one of them a family man
And yet their thoughts are far from home,
For they must always concentrate
To make it safely through.

Again, again they swing their picks
And chip away with all their strength,
Upon the hard and chiselled wall
They work throughout the morn,
Then stop for lunch of bread and jam
And take a swig of water too,
Then back to work upon the seam
To earn their daily corn.

While singing songs they laugh and joke
To keep morale and spirits high,
And thus forget the danger
Of their cruel and sorry plight,
They swing and swing their heavy picks
To break the coal that stands before,
With faces black and eyes that gleam
They work with all their might.

Until their shift is over then
They slowly leave the jagged seam,
Exhausted and in need of rest
They make their weary way,
But soon they will return once more
With all their trusted picks in hand,
Then resting on their shoulders strong
To start another day.

Valentine's Day

Nobody does remember me
Or seems to care that much,
My friends have left and gone away
And never kept in touch,
In all the years that I have lived
I've never felt this bad,
This wretched day I always say
Was made to make me sad.

I dread this time and what it means
For those who can't find love,
Whose hopes and dreams have all been lost
Within the clouds above,
I doubt if luck will change for me
I've tried all I can do,
This wretched day I'll always say
My wishes won't come true.

And so I wait here all alone
Just like the year before,
It never seems to bring me joy
Or laughter anymore,
As sadness fills my lonely heart
I have no sympathy,
This wretched day I'll always say
Was never meant for me.

Berry Head

On Berry Head where grasses wave
Beneath the sunlit sky,
I feel a peace within me
As I watch the day go by,
While there I stand upon its peak
And look upon that view,
The ships do rest at anchor there
Upon the sea of blue.

Beside the yellow flowered gorse
Upon the slopes I roam,
And there the meadow butterflies
Have made this place their home,
While from the sheer and jagged cliffs
The guillemots do soar,
As through the air they deftly fly
The rolling waves do roar.

The crowns of regal goldilocks
Adorn the windswept heath,
Across the wild and waving scrub
With rocky crags beneath,
I stay until the sun does fall
And skies of amber burn,
Then look upon its majesty
And know I shall return.

To see again those wondrous sights
And breathe that giving air,
I'll not forget the things I saw
As I did wander there,
And when I rest my weary head
I'll dream about this day,
And I shall live that time again
To pass the night away.

Mothers Pride

When I was young I still recall
I stood beside our wooden gate,
And there I waited for so long
Just gazing up the street,
Until the baker's van appeared
Familiar in its red and white,
That stopped at almost every house
Until the round complete.

When Betty Hardman used to chat
To all the friendly people here,
So glad to share her company
And pass the time of day,
Upon the doorstep loaf in hand
A ray of light to lonely folk,
But conversation's over now
There's nothing left to say.

Come rain or shine would always come
To bring our daily loaf of bread,
Those times forever gone alas
It's such a desperate shame,
As one by one the orders fell
Until so few of us remained,
It wasn't worth the effort
And the van no longer came.

So now the street is hushed and still
The doors are closed and no one speaks,
The supermarket won the fight
And killed the Mothers Pride,
I pity all who never saw
Those times that shall not come again,
Such happy days of long ago
Which sadly now have died.

With all my heart

Your kindness speaks unto me
Through the earth in which we share,
Whilst walking through the countryside
We find such comfort there,
Both living dreams and knowing
That our lives shall be as one,
And forever through eternity
Our spirits carry on.
Together we shall always stay
Not live a day apart,
For I love you like the world in which we live
With all my heart.

When we walk along the riverside
And see the water shine,
Or step amongst the bluebells
Of the woodland so divine,
I capture every moment
As your loving hand I hold,
Within the flames of passion burn
That never will grow cold.
Together we shall always stay
Not live a day apart,
For I love you like the world in which we live
With all my heart.

Where'er I see the colours
Which do sweep across the land,
Through all the fields and meadows
To the mighty hills that stand,
And rolling down the valleys
On the gentle breeze that blows,
I see the sights of wonder there
In every flower that grows.
Together we shall always stay
Not live a day apart,
For I love you like the world in which we live
With all my heart.

I watch the waves of sadness

Those days we spent together
That I never thought would end,
Now vanished on the wind that blew
Away my only friend,
And how I long for yesterday
As rain begins to pour,
I watch the waves of sadness
As they fall upon the shore.

For now the sense of loneliness
Is just too much to bear,
My spirits fading with the light
Now you're no longer there,
As I look unto the future
And to all it holds in store,
I watch the waves of sadness
As they fall upon the shore.

As mist does drift across the sea
And clouds are rolling by,
I know that I shall love you now
Until the day I die,
As shells do rest just like my dreams
All shattered on the floor,
I watch the waves of sadness
As they fall upon the shore.

I wish you were beside me
As I walk along the sand,
For many times we'd been this way
Together hand in hand,
You left me broken hearted
Now I'll stay for evermore,
To watch the waves of sadness
As they fall upon the shore.

I wish I was with you

I wish I was with you to share in this moment
Reliving those memories so precious to me,
I'm casting aside all the thoughts of the future
And things that I'd longed for that weren't meant to be.

I wish I was with you and watching the sunrise
To greet the new morning now each day it rains,
For I am alone and so nothing else matters
I don't want to wake while this heartache remains.

I wish I was wish you to walk through the country
To hear all the songbirds which so sweetly sing,
For gone is the joy and the times here together
Their voices sound lost and no pleasure they bring.

I wish I was with you to witness the sunset
The fires in the sky and its warm amber glow,
For there in the evening where we used to linger
We kissed in the twilight a long time ago.

I wish I was with you my hope never ceases
One day you'll return and then you shall be mine,
I'll sleep though in peace for in dreams we're together
Where love never fades and the stars always shine.

Rusting spade

So many hands have held the shaft
Worn smooth from days of toil,
Passed down the line of family tree
From fathers to their sons,
And no one knows what age it is
Unused it now does stand,
The rusting spade
With blunted blade,
Once turned the sacred land.

As time preserved a relic
Of that golden age gone by,
When man did work within the fields
And cut the emerald turf,
It dug the furrows straight and long
Unused it now does stand,
The rusting spade
With blunted blade,
Once turned the sacred land.

The plough replaced the need for it
First horse and then machine,
Much quicker than the hand of man
And so was cast aside,
No longer did it need to dig
Unused it now does stand,
The rusting spade
With blunted blade,
Once turned the sacred land.

When everyone deserted me

When everyone deserted me
You gave me love and sympathy
From loneliness you set me free
When no one else did care,
I turned a corner, looked ahead
Believing every word you said
And saw the hope I thought was dead
And now my life you share.

When I was lost no home had I
And joy had always passed me by
You dried the tears that I did cry
Then took me by the hand,
And soon the sun began to rise
The clouds did clear within the skies
When once a fool you made me wise
So I could understand.

My heart remains forever true
You're with me now in all I do
For so much I depend on you
My dear eternal friend,
As years do come and years do go
And seasons change like winds that blow
The greatest gift I'll ever know
Is love that has no end.

Above the peaks of mountains high

Above the peaks of mountains high
The clouds do roll across the sky,
And as they pass their shadows fall
Upon their rugged stone,
To cloak the crack and crevice deep
And scree that lies on slopes so steep,
The boulders at the foothills rest
Where I now walk alone.

The river down the valley flows
The water sparkles as it goes,
And slowly heads unto the sea
Upon its endless way,
Like rushing wind its gentle sound
As it does cross this rocky ground,
And shining in the morning sun
The ripples dance and play.

The lichen stains and moss of green
Mark every stone where I have been,
While fragments of the blackened slate
Rest on the path I tread,
From when they mined the quarries here
That one by one did disappear,
Now closed and gone for evermore
And silence reigns instead.

Above the peaks of mountains high
The clouds do roll across the sky,
And as they pass their colours change
As evening starts to fade,
And from this rocky valley floor
I climb the slopes that lie before,
To see the sunlight setting
On the land that God has made.

I hear thy voice it speaks to me

I hear thy voice it speaks to me
Like music through the air,
That sails across the land and sea
And tells me you still care,
Alas that song is in my mind
And soon away shall blow,
Upon the wind that's so unkind
And pains and hurts me so.

I often wonder where you are
Each moment is a strain,
If wishes now could travel far
I'd be with you again,
I call your name I hope it flies
And finds its way to you,
Then love shall fill the evening skies
And dreams will then come true.

I hear thy voice it grows so weak
And then it starts to fade,
For joy to me so hard to seek
While sadness tailor-made,
If only love could make its way
Unto this lonely shore,
Where I now wait upon this day
To be with you once more.

I seek another lonely soul

I seek another lonely soul
For life has been so cruel,
No riches gained nor I deserve
What has befallen me,
The darkest skies do follow now
And rains do never cease,
My spirit weak I cannot fight
And so must let it be.

I wish to lock myself away
So I could not be seen,
For pity brings such sorrow now
The pain too much to bear,
I cannot face the world alone
Its trials are far too great,
I'm restless in my solitude
And find no comfort there.

I seek another lonely soul
To share my emptiness,
Who's lost it all and struggled so
And needs a brand new start,
I lift my eyes towards the sky
And wish the sun would shine,
And pray that fate will change for me
Then joy shall fill my heart.

Look around

Look around to see the dawning
Of the brand new day,
For you are here within my arms
And dreams were made this way,
The love we share together now
Will live and never die,
And soar unto the clouds above
Like songbirds in the sky.

Look around at all the beauty
Of the flowers that grow,
A scene so rich with pleasure now
As April colours show,
For spring's arrived and brought us love
We both had waited for,
Which as we breathe the morning air
Shall last for evermore.

Look around at all the greatness
Of the setting sun,
As day is slowly ending now
Our life has just begun,
And watching as the sunlight falls
As clouds of fire unfold,
Then hand in hand we look upon
The skies that turn to gold.

Look around at all the wonder
Of the stars above,
Which grace the skies in heaven
And do spell the word of love,
So picture now this happiness
For memories we shall keep,
And dream about this day we shared
Within our precious sleep.

The bright golden sunlight

The bright golden sunlight is filling the morning
And shines on the dew that does rest on the leaves,
It glistens on cobwebs adorning the hedgerows
For summer has passed and the autumn now grieves.

Its teardrops are weeping from trees in the woodland
And fall to the ground like soft droplets of rain,
The hushed amber carpet forlorn and so peaceful
That longs for the bluebells to rise once again.

The silhouette shadows where colours keep changing
And move with the motions of branches and breeze,
Now yielding the scenes of this picturesque moment
As framed here the beauty of October's frieze.

The bright golden sunlight is filling the morning
With songs so enriching from birds up above,
Their melodies capture the skies with their sweetness
And call to the dawn and the springtime of love.

At the edge of the field

The meadow so tranquil with hills in the distance
Where sunlight is shining on emerald green,
As I make my way through the heart of the country
I gaze at the sight of the land so serene,
So glad to be part of this beautiful morning
For here I can see all its glory revealed,
I lean on the fence where I watch the sheep grazing
That borders the path at the edge of the field.

As daffodils dance in the breeze of the springtime
I'm floating on clouds and I'm carried away,
So far unto heaven for peace does belong here
And it shall remain through this wonderful day,
For here I do listen to songs of the morning
Where birds sing for joy yet remain so concealed,
I stand in the shade of the leaves and the branches
From trees that do grow at the edge of the field.

The hedgerow in blossom like snowflakes have fallen
And gathered on bushes now painted in white,
So pure and so pretty they bloom in their glory
With sweet scented perfume and shining so bright,
I feel I am drawn to the call of the morning
That's filling my senses with all it does yield,
I stand on the verge in the thickets of flowers
Now lining the way at the edge of the field.

I'll never let you go

Throughout the mists of darkness came
When hope deserted me,
I stood alone but for my thoughts
Of endless misery,
No will had I to carry on
Days came and then did pass,
But nothing seemed to ever change
Just like my luck alas.

A faint and empty shadow
For my heart and soul were bare,
Was searching for an answer then
But no one heard my prayer,
Then through the clouds a light did shine
That warmed against the chill,
And showed to me the way ahead
My destiny and will.

As if a burden lifted
From my shoulders then so weak,
It seemed to me I'd found at last
The joy that I did seek,
I heard the words I longed to hear
"I'll always love you so,
And I shall be forever yours
And never let you go".

My Lord did save me from myself
I wished my life to end,
But then within my darkest hour
I knew I had a friend,
And now I want to live each day
No better place to be,
Than with my Lord and saviour now
Through all eternity.

So peaceful is the river

I hear the sounds of morning
And the sweetness of its song,
I'm home amidst the scenery
To which I now belong,
Where hills so green in majesty
Are rising to the sky,
So peaceful is the river
As I watch it flowing by.

I see the sights of morning
As I walk along the way,
The sunlight falls upon me
As it shines upon this day,
Where willows line the bank ahead
And bow their heads and cry,
So peaceful is the river
As I watch it flowing by.

I feel the breeze of morning
As it sweeps across the land,
Amongst the fields and meadows now
While leaves are gently fanned,
As swallows soar so high above
With grace they deftly fly,
So peaceful is the river
As I watch it flowing by.

I hear the songs of morning
As they float upon the air,
Each graceful note a note of joy
Upon this day so fair,
As there amidst the cooling shade
Beneath a tree I lie,
So peaceful is the river
As I watch it flowing by.

I touch the flowers of morning
Now the springtime has begun,
For there the daisies welcome me
And bloom within the sun,
I walk amidst the country
Where my dreams shall never die,
So peaceful is the river
As I watch it flowing by.

Camellia

The smoke clouds are drifting above the horizon
The first light is rising I hear the sweet call,
Of a voice in the woodland that's breaking the silence
The blackbird is singing a welcome to all.
So still,
The song of the dawn,
Camellia shines
As a new day is born.

In the beams of the morning the colours are glowing
The shadows of darkness are fading to grey,
The warm air of springtime a river that's flowing
The frosts of the winter have melted away.
So still,
The song of the dawn,
Camellia shines
As a new day is born.

A soft breeze is stirring the leaves gently glisten
The pink petalled flowers are sprinkled with dew,
Whilst weeping they shed silver tears of emotion
Which fall to the ground as the skies turn to blue.
So still,
The song of the dawn,
Camellia shines
As a new day is born.

For no one should have suffered

For no one should have suffered
In the way I suffered so,
Was blamed for all the problems
And absorbed each mortal blow,
But none of them did I deserve
And turned the other cheek,
Yet still I never found relief
Or joy that I did seek.

So many times my lonely heart
Did long to be with you,
So many times I tried to love
Yet nothing could I do,
Through all those days of sadness
I still wore a smile with pride,
To stop my tears from falling
When I hurt so much inside.

Your promises were hollow
Yet back then I couldn't see,
Was blinded by the romance
That was never meant to be,
That burden I did carry
But the weight too much to bear,
For you my love I gave my all
But still you didn't care.

Although my wounds shall never heal
I love you just the same,
For still the fact we broke apart
Does fill my soul with shame,
And since that time of bitter hate
I've nothing but regret,
Your image stays within my mind
I never shall forget.

Aster

Aster your star of the morning is shining
As sunlight now rests on your lavender blue,
As all through the winter the frosts and the snowfalls
My heart felt so empty in longing for you,
I dreamt of the day that your petals would open
I planted your seed and I then watched you grow,
I prayed every day you would rise with the dawning
And longed for the time that your colours would show.

Aster your star of the morning is shining
With all of your secrets I've waited to share,
Which have been revealed in your moment of glory
And I am so happy to know you are there,
So reach for the sunlight you sweet flower of heaven
And look to the skies and its greatness above,
For there you were made by the hand of my father
That blessed you with beauty and gave you his love.

Aster your star of the morning is shining
Your florets a picture all furnished in gold,
I watched as you rose there from out of the darkness
And saw your sweet petals as they did unfold,
As you stand beside me I'll always remember
And treasure each minute of pleasure you give,
For soon you shall fade and your petals shall wither
Yet my joy is your joy as long as you live.

The daisies and buttercups

The daisies and buttercups so freely entwine,
For there in the meadow those sweet flowers shine,
As oaks in the distance are casting their shade,
The sheep rest beneath them till sunlight does fade.

The blackbird above is now singing with glee,
His song fills the morning as pure as can be,
The hawthorn's in blossom so lovely its sight,
Adorning the country while all dressed in white.

The blue skies revealing the joy that is here,
Awaiting the swallows and swifts to appear,
My prayers have been answered I look on this day,
And know God has blessed me with nature's display.

The daisies and buttercups now herald the spring,
A fanfare of colour such beauty they bring,
For there in the meadow like snowflakes and gold,
Their flowers are blooming to end winter's cold.

Bore da

The peaks of Snowdonia rise to the sky
And they sink to the ribbons of pine,
As the pastures of green and the ranges before me
Now glow as the sunlight does shine,
As I say bore da to the land of such beauty
For my friends are each mountain and field,
Good morning to all of God's creatures and flowers
And to all of the glory they yield.

The lakes are a mirror so still and inspiring
The breeze over water now sails,
Through the moorlands of heather in violet September
Which climb on the slopes of the vales,
As I say bore da to the land of such treasure
For my friends are the forests that grow,
Good morning to all of God's creatures and flowers
In nature's most wonderful show.

I walk through the meadows enchanting and peaceful
My heart is now lost to their grace,
And I shall not forget all these sights I have witnessed
For my thoughts shall remain of this place,
As I say bore da to the land of such wonder
For my friends are the valleys and streams,
Good morning to all of God's creatures and flowers
For this is the home of my dreams.

If you cannot write a love song

When you can't express yourself
And words come hard to you,
When feelings you can't capture
And you don't know what to do,
When rhythms and the melodies
Are lost in clouds above,
If you cannot write a love song
Then you've never been in love.

When your heart just can't be touched
Emotionless like stone,
When only joy does fill your soul
You've never been alone,
When all the lines just fail to rhyme
And each one seems a strain,
If you cannot write a love song
Then you've never felt the pain.

When pages blank in front of you
With nothing left to say,
When you're lost within the darkness
And you cannot find your way,
When years have gone with chances passed
And dreams have floated by,
If you cannot write a love song
Then you've never learned to cry.

When memories now are all you have
For love you could not save,
When restless days and sleepless nights
Do haunt you to the grave,
When skies above forever bleak
And tears like raindrops fall,
If you cannot write a love song
Then you've never cared at all.

This beautiful day

From out of the darkness the morning is rising
The clouds in the sky are now coloured in gold,
I can't wait to breathe the sweet air of the springtime
And smell all the flowers as petals unfold,
My heart longs to sing for the love that has found me
And all of the wonders the coming of May,
The whisper of dawn that's so soft and so gentle
Yet I hear its call on this beautiful day.

And so let me walk through the arbours of roses
Then under the blossoms which hang from the bough,
And then through the woodland where I hear the calling
Of emerald meadows which beckon me now,
My heart longs to sing for the love that has found me
The fine painted pictures of nature's display,
As I gaze at the skies and the clouds slowly passing
I feel I belong to this beautiful day.

I head to the sunset as evening is falling
A heavenly ceiling now skies are aglow,
As the soft fading embers do yield to the darkness
I walk in the moonlight with nowhere to go,
My heart longs to sing for the love that has found me
As stars gleaming brightly are guiding my way,
I'll always remember the sights I have witnessed
So glad I was part of this beautiful day.

Amazon

The forest enchanting with mystical spirit
It's yielding its magic and life-giving air,
So precious its riches that lie there before us
A God-given gift we are grateful to share,
The birds now are calling from heaven so sweetly
For this is their home where they truly belong,
Its creatures do sing from the boughs of the treetops
The call of the wild is this Amazon song.

The parrots so vivid and bright are their colours
The scarlet macaws and the aracari,
The osprey does glide through the air of the morning
And follows the river that winds to sea,
Their sight is a picture majestically soaring
As there on the wing they so gracefully fly,
And long may they rule as the masters of greatness
Forever they reign in the Amazon sky.

So ancient the trees which are broad and so mighty
And dense yet the orchids do shine through the shade,
They burst into flower like flames in the darkness
A race against time for so quickly they fade,
Their scent then is carried on blossoming breezes
Their petals of springtime like pockets of snow,
While butterflies flutter and feed on their nectar
So deep in the heart of the Amazon glow.

The heart of the forest is beating so strongly
Within this great wilderness nature's alive,
The skinks and the geckos and sloths of the jungle
Where ocelots, monkeys and jaguars thrive,
Their home's rich in wonder the finest cathedral
The jewels of the forest such joy to behold,
And now as the sun sinks towards the horizon
So witness the sight of the Amazon gold.

For you did mend my broken heart

Those empty days and empty nights
I now have left behind,
For since you came into my life
The times have been more kind,
You gave me warmth when I was cold
And took away my pain,
For you did mend my broken heart
And let me love again.

Those lonely days and lonely nights
That seemed to have no end,
Are now no more for I have found
A true and lasting friend,
For through the clouds the sun appeared
That dried the falling rain,
For you did mend my broken heart
And let me love again.

Those wasted days and wasted nights
Now seem so long ago,
So too the years that I have lost
More than I care to know,
You took away my burdens
But you helped me bear the strain,
For you did mend my broken heart
And let me love again.

Now happy days and happy nights
Have come to me at last,
And now I know I can forget
About my troubled past,
The future seems much brighter now
My dreams shall never wane,
For you did mend my broken heart
And let me love again.

When love has gone

When love has gone and sadness reigns
Within your shattered heart,
Such emptiness you feel inside
When dreams are torn apart,
You cannot seem to find a way
And weep at every song,
Just think of me for I've been there
And suffered for so long.

When love has gone no happiness
Each morning as you wake,
You feel you have no future
And your past a big mistake,
You cannot seem to find a way
In which to smile again,
Just think of me for I've been there
And so I share your pain.

When love has gone the things you try
Just never turn out right,
No matter what you do attempt
You face the same old plight,
You cannot seem to find a way
To break that wretched spell,
Just think of me for I've been there
And know the hurt so well.

When love has gone no sympathy
From others you do get,
For everyone seems happy
While you're feeling so upset,
You cannot seem to find a way
And joy does never call,
Just think of me for I've been there
And know the best of all.

The golden eagle fly

The silence of the hunter
Like a whisper through the air,
As he scans the heath and heathered moor
And rocky cliffs so bare,
An eyrie built of branch and twigs
Upon an outcrop high,
The greatest sight of all to see
The golden eagle fly.

For there his mate with hungry chicks
Is waiting on the nest,
She keeps them sheltered from the wind
Beneath her feathered breast,
She calls across the valley
With a shrill and piercing cry,
And there before my eyes I see
The golden eagle fly.

He glides across the wilderness
With sunlight on his wings,
He soars above the mountains tops
Unto his prey he clings,
Then swoops along the river
Where the rocks and boulders lie,
The greatest sight of all to see
The golden eagle fly.

He leaves the nest and rides again
Upon the wind that blows,
Across the wild and rugged land
And calling as he goes,
With grace he turns and circles there
The master of the sky,
The greatest sight of all to see
The golden eagle fly.

A pocketful of dreams

I head alone with broken heart
Not knowing where to go,
The autumn leaves have fallen
Now the winter winds do blow,
Yet I've a pocketful of dreams
I carry all the while,
For when I'm sad I pull one out
And each one makes me smile.

They're all I've got within this world
No money left to spend,
I walk without direction
For the pathway has no end,
I never reach my destiny
Nor find a place to stay,
With no one there to guide me now
I know I've lost my way.

My love no more I have no one
To take away my pain,
Nor lift me from my misery
And share my life again,
Yet I've a pocketful of dreams
I carry all the while,
For when I'm sad I pull one out
And each one makes me smile.

Grains of sand

Now love has gone there seems no end
To all the hurt I feel,
There's no one there to dry my tears
The wounds will never heal,
I don't know if I'll love again
It's left me in such doubt,
As grains of sand are slipping by
My time is running out.

Now all is lost there is no light
There's darkness everywhere,
For now I cannot find my way
And no one seems to care,
I don't know if I'll love again
It's left me in such doubt,
As grains of sand are slipping by
My time is running out.

My dreams have faded out of view
No hope is left for me,
There's no one there to change my course
My fate or destiny,
I don't know if I'll love again
It's left me in such doubt,
As grains of sand are slipping by
My time is running out.

I cannot rest

I cannot rest I'm all alone
So long this lonely night,
I wish that you were with me now
To make the world seem right,
For you could keep me company
And free me from this pain,
For now my sleep is empty
Yet I long to dream again.

I lie awake and think of you
And of the love we shared,
But now I know it's useless
How I wish that you still cared,
You're far away and moving on
While I am left behind,
I wish like you I could forget
And clear my troubled mind.

I cannot rest nor close my eyes
I feel the bitter cold,
Without you there beside me now
I have no one to hold,
As stars do shine in sympathy
Within the solemn skies,
I'll lie awake till dawn does come
Then watch the morning rise.

As clouds now weep

As through the winter's rain I go
And facing chilly winds that blow,
As I do wander here alone
Along the paths of cobbled stone,
The walls are steep on either side
No home in which I can abide,
For hopes of love have passed me by
As clouds now weep and gently cry.

Within the alley that I walk
The feral cats begin to stalk,
From bins upturned they follow me
As if it is their territory,
They see me off into the road
They hiss and scratch and then they goad,
For hopes of love have passed me by
As clouds now weep and gently cry.

Along the faceless streets of hate
I walk along and cannot wait,
Or stop and talk to those who dwell
The people I once knew so well,
Who now don't give me time of day
But simply look the other way,
For hopes of love have passed me by
As clouds now weep and gently cry.

As darkness falls I carry on
My spirit's weak my will has gone,
Yet in my dreams I think of you
The only love I ever knew,
Against the arch I rest my head
And slowly make my sodden bed,
For hopes of love have passed me by
As clouds now weep and gently cry.

I dreamt about you every night

I dreamt about you every night
Within my deepest sleep,
The thought of you within my heart
Your memory I did keep,
I couldn't wait to hold you tight
To ease my hurt and pain,
Then look into your eyes once more
And love you once again.

I dreamt about you every night
And wished that you were there,
I thought about the fun we had
And joy that we did share,
I couldn't wait to see you then
Those days were such a strain,
I tried so hard to reach you
And to love you once again.

I dreamt about you every night
I slept just like a stone,
And felt you there beside of me
But woke and was alone,
My thoughts of you were endless then
And never did they wane,
I hoped my wishes would come true
To love you once again.

I dreamt about you every night
You never left my mind,
Those days were cold and empty
For I'd left my world behind,
With every minute that did pass
My sadness did remain,
Until I found my way back home
To love you once again.

I rest upon this lonely rock

I'm counting every wave that rolls
Onto this endless shore,
I'm thinking of tomorrow
And to what it holds in store,
With echoes of the calling birds
As hungry seagulls fly,
I rest upon this lonely rock
And watch the day go by.

I think of what I left behind
And wish that I were there,
My heart shall always rest with her
But now I feel despair,
No clouds above to hide the sun
So clear the summer sky,
I rest upon this lonely rock
And watch the day go by.

The time does pass so quickly now
And soon I'll be with you,
Then love shall find a way again
Across the seas of blue,
I'm waiting for that day to come
My solemn tears won't dry,
I rest upon this lonely rock
And watch the day go by.

My thoughts are many miles away
Upon that distant land,
I wish that I could touch you
Like the waves do touch the sand,
Yet know within my aching heart
I'll love you till I die,
I rest upon this lonely rock
And watch the day go by.

Free as I can be

Somewhere within this wilderness
I found a place to stay,
It's miles and miles from anywhere
And I came from far away,
To settle where the sun did shine
With many sights to see,
So I belong to no one now
I'm free as I can be.

Somewhere within this wilderness
I found a place to live,
That now I never want to leave
For joy this land does give,
The hills within the countryside
Were calling out to me,
So I belong to no one now
I'm free as I can be.

Somewhere within this wilderness
I found a place so sweet,
With meadows rich and beautiful
Have made my life complete,
Where'er I look there's beauty
That does fill my heart with glee,
So I belong to no one now
I'm free as I can be.

This music so sweet

This music so sweet
That does sing through the morning,
Whilst holding my dreams
As the sun starts to rise,
My heart full of joy
As it tells me a story,
Those phrases speak softly
And float through the skies.

This music so sweet
That I hear on the breezes,
Those melodies dancing
And sailing away,
Please open your window
And you too can listen,
To harmonies endless
To welcome the day.

This music so sweet
Every song it does carry,
Far over the treetops
And never shall rest,
They roam and they drift
Through the heart of the country,
Northwards and southwards
To east and to west.

This music so sweet
Let it play on forever,
Its sound reassuring
Wherever I go,
Refrains of the summer
Are yielding such pleasure,
This music so sweet
Shall eternally flow.

Watching the waves

Sea breezes enrich me
They're crossing the water,
And filling my senses
With joy evermore,
I wait on the coastline
And gaze at the ocean,
I'm watching the waves
As they roll to the shore.

The sunlight is shining
And dancing on water,
As over the shingle
The white surges draw,
Which then disappear
And like dreams are forgotten,
I'm watching the waves
As they roll to the shore.

The seagulls are shearing
High over the coastline,
And skimming the crests
As the mighty seas roar,
They're moving so swiftly
And call through the silence,
I'm watching the waves
As they roll to the shore.

The evening is falling
And skies are now glowing,
Through vast clouds of scarlet
The sunbeams do pour,
And lighting with gold now
A path to the ocean,
I'm watching the waves
As they roll to the shore.

The colours of morning

The colours of morning are lifting from shadows
And caught in the sunbeams as dawn starts to rise,
That shines through the branches and lights up the darkness
And touches the clouds as they float through the skies.

How softly they fall on the cherry white blossoms
And rest on the hedgerows of hawthorn like snow,
A picture so peaceful for so long I've waited
To gaze at the springtime's most wonderful show.

An ocean of bluebells now flow through the woodland
As emerald hills in the distance do stand,
So sweet are the meadows which lie there before me
The fields are a patchwork adorning the land.

The colours of evening the palette of scarlet
That's blending with amber a beautiful sight,
The skies are now filled with a heavenly glory
That fades to the stars and the dark of the night.

The long stone

With clouded skies above me I do climb this winding pathway,
And yet I feel that I am not alone,
So many years have passed and yet its secrets still remain there,
Within the place they laid that ancient stone,
I look upon the rolling downs that reach into the distance,
And then I gaze across the mirrored sea,
So calm and yet disturbing for it lies a ghostly grey now,
As if the sailors' souls are warning me.

And yet I'm drawn still further by the power that it is yielding,
I follow those who've passed this way before,
As now a bitter wind does blow a fine mist from the water,
That's creeping ever closer to the shore,
As over now the fields it drifts and seems so unrelenting,
And casts a shroud upon the open ground,
A winter chill descends amidst the land so unforgiving,
The air is hushed I cannot hear a sound.

I turn the corner then I see the stone before me waiting,
Then sense a restless presence drawing near,
I feel I am not wanted and it makes me feel uneasy
But still I carry on so full of fear,
And as I place my hands upon the rock so strong and mighty,
I close my eyes yet pictures come to mind,
Which fill my heart with darkness so I pull my hands away now,
And leave that long and ancient stone behind.

Our love is an ocean

Throughout my whole life I have longed for this moment
You came when I thought all my chances had died,
Now I'll never leave you for nothing else matters
I'd cross over waters to be by your side,
I want to be with you this day and forever
You capture my feelings bring joy to my heart,
I know what we have here is truly amazing
Our love is an ocean and can never part.

I cannot believe all my sadness is over
I so want to hold you and never let go,
My dream everlasting and always about you
Where rivers of joy shall eternally flow,
For once I was lost and was heading to nowhere
And I was alone yet I found a new start,
I've left all my woes and my sorrows behind me
Our love is an ocean and can never part.

I'll never look back but instead to the future
And treasure each minute together we spend,
Our story was written above in the starlight
I pray that this chapter shan't come to an end,
Please let it continue with words of such beauty
For I shall be with you to share nature's art,
As dawn comes again let our journey continue
Our love is an ocean and can never part.

Death does hold no fear for me

So beautiful the garden grows
The pathway lined with gold,
The beauty that shall lie before
Its glory to behold,
I'll greet departed loved ones
And shall live in one accord,
So death does hold no fear for me
For I will see my Lord.

So many seen a glimpse of it
When they were old and frail,
And felt the love and shared the joy
Yet lived to tell the tale,
They told me not worry
As the way they have explored,
So death does hold no fear for me
For I will see my Lord.

So wonderful is paradise
For souls so lost as I,
A place where I can find myself
A home when I should die,
Whatever creed or colour
Every soul there is adored,
So death does hold no fear for me
For I will see my Lord.

Thank you God

Thank you God for giving me
A chance to live this day,
So glad am I to look upon
The fields that gently sway,
Within the breeze that carries dreams
As clouds go floating by,
And as they pass the sunlight shines
Amidst the April sky.

Thank you God for giving me
The chance to see again,
The blossoms form upon the boughs
And petals fall like rain,
When flowers stir from slumber
To adorn the barren ground,
The calling of the season
Is to me the sweetest sound.

Thank you God for giving me
The chance to breathe this air,
As nature all around me grows
There's nothing can compare,
So sweet the scent that softly drifts
Across the waiting land,
And sails unto those emerald hills
Which in their greatness stand.

Thank you God for giving me
The chance to see once more,
The beauty of this season
And the sights that I adore,
For I so love this time of year
When songbirds start to sing,
So glad to be a part of this
And all that is the Spring.

I saw the newborn ducklings swim

I saw the newborn ducklings swim
Upon the lake so calm,
They trailed their parents closely
So they wouldn't come to harm,
The mallards and the moorhens there
With coats of down they wore,
Were calling out so softly
As they led them to the shore.

They rested there upon the bank
Within the cooling shade,
Of reeds and weeping willows
And a haven there they made,
As there they dwelt together
Safely hidden from my sight,
Within the shadows they did blend
Amidst the fading light.

I waited till the evening
When they left their sheltered shore,
And swam upon the waters there
Just like they'd done before,
And as I headed on my way
The geese above did fly,
As I looked unto the setting sun
That glowed within the sky.

The graveyard

The stones are bent and leaning
On this land unkempt so long,
Some shattered, prone and broken lie
Where once stood proud and strong,
The lichen stains and time have made
Those names so hard to read,
Yet there the robin makes its perch
Amongst the bush and weed.

Where willow herb and ox-eye thrive
Around each cross and stone,
As no one tends or visits now
Those spirits rest alone,
But there the crow with deathly stare
Does gaze across the way,
Within the yew of twisted boughs
The reaper there does stay.

As his callous cry and cackles call
The birds take to the wing,
For it echoes through that weeded ground
Where nettles densely cling,
Those holy walls fell long ago
Forgotten now it stays,
There are no prayers of comfort
Nor no hymns of Godly praise.

Now silence sails across the land
Upon this Sunday morn,
As a cloud of mist does gently rest
To greet this ghostly dawn,
The skies are grey, the raindrops fall
Which drown the hallowed cry,
Of all those lonely souls who passed
And in the graveyard lie.

The jackdaws are calling

The jackdaws are calling from out of the woodland
They lurk in the branches where hidden from sight,
While scanning the ground where the food now is scattered
Yet covered they rest in the shade of the night.

They swoop in a flash and it's gone in a moment
With stealth and with cunning pass almost unseen,
Then again to the treetops to dwell in the shadows
To peer to the ground through the leaves that are green.

They stare at the scrub at the thickets and bushes
Like thieves of the darkness now ready to steal,
Their cloaks are of black and with grey hoods concealing
Their image and features no shame do they feel.

They swoop once again in the safety of numbers
And into the open they land on the floor,
In silence they stalk and then gather like reapers
The scraps in their beaks as they head off once more.

To return to the peace and the shade of the woodland
With rustle of branches to which they now cling,
As they then fly away in the skies far above me
And soar to the clouds as they sail on the wing.

Like gypsies they travel and head on their journey
Not seeming to settle nor finding a home,
From pillar to post they go constantly searching
As over the land and the country they roam.

I wander through the pasture

I wander through the pasture
Where a gentle stream does flow,
And daisies rise to light the path
Like freshly fallen snow,
I know where'er I care to walk
That I will surely see,
God's wonderful creation
And his greatest gift to me.

I climb the rolling hills of green
So gracefully they stand,
While patchwork fields adorn the way
And dress the rural land,
The view is calling out to me
As wheat does turn to gold,
And tossed like waves upon the sea
As autumn days unfold.

I roam amongst the woodland trees
And feel their cooling shade,
As sun between the branches shines
My dreams will never fade,
Within the boughs the birds do sing
Their songs so sweet to hear,
Each graceful note upon the air
So pleasing to my ear.

I wander on the coastline
Where the mighty waves do roar,
I see them crashing on the rocks
And rolling to the shore,
So grateful I to live this day
My memories shall remain,
Of all the sights that I have seen
And long to see again.

The daisies stay closed

The rain is now falling
The streets are all empty
The clouds up above are so dark and so grey,
And I wait in longing
For sunlight to find me
Yet daisies stay closed and won't open today.

My heart is now broken
Such sadness I'm feeling
I've nothing to live for no luck comes my way,
For all of my joy now
Is lost to the darkness
While daisies stay closed and won't open today.

I'm watching the raindrops
Which run down my window
Like tears as my heartache forever will stay,
And as I look out
On the scene so depressing
The daisies stay closed and won't open today.

The rain is still falling
No end is forthcoming
With no one to hear all the words that I say,
My life is in pieces
My dreams have been shattered
As daisies stay closed and won't open today.

Beneath that fallen rock and stone

Now as the cliffs do crumble
And they fall into the sea,
Just like the ruins of my life
There's no escape for me,
Although I try I know that I
Can't face this world alone,
My broken heart lies crushed beneath
That fallen rock and stone.

Now battered by the forces
Of the waves upon the shore,
By fierce and unrelenting winds
And heavy rains that pour,
I feel so lost without you now
You're all I've ever known,
My broken heart lies crushed beneath
That fallen rock and stone.

The hand of fate so cruel to me
It dealt a bitter blow,
And now I am a lonely wreck
With nowhere else to go,
I've nothing left within the world
I've lost all I did own,
My broken heart lies crushed beneath
That fallen rock and stone.

And there it shall lay buried
Till the day we meet again,
With no hope for the future
And each day I live a strain,
I wish we were together
Yet so far apart we've grown,
My broken heart lies crushed beneath
That fallen rock and stone.

As cloud now lies upon the hills

As cloud now lies upon the hills
That cuts their peaks like scything blades,
Engulfing then the emerald slopes
And turning them to grey,
The distant land now cloaked afar
And hidden is its shape and form,
I can but dream of times before
Now lost unto this day.

And as the light does slowly fade
As clouds do roll across the sea,
Upon the gusts of wind that blow
The bringers of the rain,
Like smoke they're drifting through the air
While shrouding every hill and field,
A chill descends a ghostly hand
Does grip this scene of pain.

It shan't let go until the front
Has passed to let the sunlight shine,
Upon the peaks and emerald slopes
That once did greet me there,
And yet for now there seems no end
No beam to break the drizzle skies,
That sweep across the latent land
And fills it with despair.

This morning makes the chaffinch sing

This morning makes the chaffinch sing
Upon the blossomed cherry bough,
Awakes the day with cheerful song
And fills it with such wonder now,
As he doth wake me from my sleep
And from my window open wide,
I see upon the branch below
The little bird that sings with pride.

I smell the rose its perfume sweet
Its petals in the sunlight shine,
So warm the feeling that does touch
My spirit and this soul of mine,
And so I walk down country lane
And through the woodland's deepest shade,
Yet still the song does follow me
And never does it seem to fade.

I see the view across the fields
The downs within the distance stand,
Which rise and fall with slopes of green
So picturesque this pleasant land,
This morning makes the chaffinch sing
And as he flies from tree to tree,
Within the sky of deepest blue
My heart shall always rest with thee.

A dream I'll always keep

As somewhere through the darkness
All my thoughts do drift away,
I wish that they could reach you now
And there forever stay,
For now I am so far from home
But know that in my sleep,
I'll dream about you every night
A dream I'll always keep.

My thoughts pass through the moonlight
And are led by every star,
Whilst searching for a place to rest
To find just where you are,
I hope that they will make it now
But know that in my sleep,
I'll dream about you every night
A dream I'll always keep.

And when my thoughts do find you there
Then joy shall fill my heart,
And break the spell that kept us both
So many miles apart,
And how I long to be with you
But know that in my sleep,
I'll dream about you every night
A dream I'll always keep.

I traced the steps of Tennyson

I walked along the chalky path
Upon the burrowed way,
I passed the gorse that swept before
And reached unto the bay,
As I did roam and wandered free
On England's precious crown,
I traced the steps of Tennyson
Across the windswept down.

I watched the clouds above that sailed
Across the summer sky,
Which scored the blue and hid the sun
Until they drifted by,
I walked through bush and heather then
The shade of dusty brown,
And traced the steps of Tennyson
Across the windswept down.

A yellowhammer sang above
And flew from post to post,
He followed me where'er I went
Along that wondrous coast,
I heard his sweet and gentle song
The gusts tried hard to drown,
As I traced the steps of Tennyson
Across the windswept down.

As I stood upon that verdant brow
The sea before me shone,
Its ebbing waves were calling out
I had to carry on,
I walked above those rugged cliffs
That wore an emerald gown,
And traced the steps of Tennyson
Across the windswept down.

Within this old deserted barn

The walls have cracked and crumbled
And the roof of slate now holed,
Through which the rain does slowly seep
So too the bitter cold,
The rafters creak and groan inside
Through savage winds that blow,
Away those memories and the tales
Of times of long ago.

Yet by an empty bucket lies
A pitch fork and a spade,
Behind that old and battered door
A scythe with blunted blade,
A plough that once did turn the earth
Within that fallow field,
Where trees and bush in scrubland grow
And no more corn will yield.

The farmer's tractor stands forlorn
And shall not move again,
Its scarlet paint has lost its shine
Yet there it does remain,
With nettles growing by the wheels
And motor seized with rust,
Within this old deserted barn
It wears a coat of dust.

Where walls have cracked and crumbled
And now soon will disappear,
So too the land on which it stands
As now the end does near,
The fields then lost forever
With the trees and hedges too,
And never shall I see again
This calm and peaceful view.

Within these walls of stone

So far away my heart now lies
My wishes cannot bring her back,
For days gone by and chances lost
The stormy skies are dark and black,
Throughout my life I never wished
To face the future all alone,
My dreams shall now forever rest
Within these wretched walls of stone.

Those bitter thoughts now haunt my sleep
For filled with memories of the past,
My mind can think of nothing else
But love that sadly could not last,
If only I could find a way
But through the years my sorrow's grown,
My dreams shall now forever rest
Within these wretched walls of stone.

For as I wake at morning rise
Each day to me now merge as one,
And never seem to bring me joy
Nor lift me now my love has gone,
The sun will never shine again
And while the winds of winter moan,
My dreams shall now forever rest
Within these wretched walls of stone.

Now soon the cliff will crumble

The savage waves with crests of white
Now pound against the stone,
Pushed by the wind that cruelly blows
And wails a deathly moan,
No respite from their mighty force
They crash relentlessly,
Now soon the cliff will crumble
And will fall into the sea.

The thunder clap of every wave
That slaps against the base,
Each one is like a hammer blow
Upon that chalky face,
They fling the rock and pebbles
With the shingle and the scree,
Now soon the cliff will crumble
And will fall into the sea.

The spray that flies with foamy surge
Is tossed upon the air,
It scours and scrubs the headland now
The strain so hard to bear,
Each mortal thud another crack
Sends splinters working free,
Now soon the cliff will crumble
And will fall into the sea.

Haystack

As shadows lift upon the land
And skies above do shine in gold,
To light the slopes of distant hills
As morning sun does rise,
Within the field now cut and reaped
As August sinks into the fall,
And summer's drawing to a close
The farmer's haystack lies.

Beside the hedgerow thick and dense
From where the birds do sing with cheer,
It waits to be collected
To provide the winter feed,
For all the cows that graze within
The meadows of the countryside,
This field shall then be turned and ploughed
And planted with the seed.

In spring the shoots of corn will grow
And yet it seems so far away,
Through all the hardship and the cold
Till it shall come again,
And yet for now the day so still
Within the field a gentle hush,
The combine rests its work complete
To gather in the grain.

As shadows lift upon the land
Another day has come to be,
I look upon the view before
As morning sun does rise,
And know that soon the leaves shall fade
Then fall unto the autumn ground,
As there within that lowly field
The farmer's haystack lies.

I wished I'd lived to see the land

God made the world for all to share
When wonders it did yield,
Before man scarred the landscape
And its fate was cruelly sealed,
When forests stretched for miles and miles
Mature and broad did grow,
I wished I'd lived to see the land
So many years ago.

For then the world lay undisturbed
Untouched by blade or plough,
And all the birds did sing for joy
Yet they are silent now,
When peace did reign upon the earth
That now is filled with woe,
I wished I'd lived to see the land
So many years ago.

It must have been so beautiful
But now so much has gone,
Some species lost for evermore
This pillage can't go on,
We have to change to save the world
Or reap the things we sow,
I wished I'd lived to see the land
So many years ago.

Driftwood

My heart was made for loving you
But now the love has gone,
My arms were made to hold you close
But now I have no one,
Yet still the waves keep rolling
And I'll hurt for evermore,
As driftwood floats upon the sea
Then washed unto the shore.

My mind was made for kindly thoughts
But now those thoughts are dead,
My hands were made for touching you
But they were both misled,
Yet still the waves keep rolling
And their comfort I implore,
As driftwood floats upon the sea
Then washed unto the shore.

My dream was made in heaven
But my dream did fade away,
My eyes were made for seeing
Now they only weep each day,
Yet still the waves keep rolling
And the rain begins to pour,
As driftwood floats upon the sea
Then washed unto the shore.

My soul was made for hoping
But my hope did disappear,
My lips were made for kissing
Not to speak the words I fear,
Yet still the waves keep rolling
And the pain I feel so raw,
As driftwood floats upon the sea
Then washed unto the shore.

Ragwort

This bleak barren wasteland with ruinous rubble
Where buildings and shelters are slowly reclaimed,
By ragwort that clings to the crack and the crevice
On concrete carpets abandoned and framed,
By old rusting fences and gates that are padlocked
A perilous prison of damp and decay,
But soon it shall yield to the forces of nature
As slowly these remnants now crumble away.

As flowers do spread and then cross over borders
And sprinkle with gold with such freedom of will,
Where once was alive with the sounds of the foundry
The steel and the furnace but now it lies still,
For there undisturbed all the weeds shall develop
And mask the harsh lines as the seeds are then cast,
On winds that will blow through this old blackened brickwork
And there they shall thrive with industrial past.

The years will go by but the ragwort shall linger
And grow ever denser with bush and with tree,
When walls will all tumble then drowned by the thickets
No more shall remain of this shell I now see,
So shine on sweet flowers and cover this wreckage
Let this be a place then in which we can share,
For I long to witness the land in its glory
And hear the hushed songbirds again singing there.

The clover on this hill

One day my life shall end upon
This earth on which I tread,
I've found the place I wish to rest
And make my final bed,
As on this cliff above the shore
So peaceful and so still,
I'll lie amongst the flowers
Of the clover on this hill.

Where I shall always see the waves
And view the countryside,
The sights that always filled my heart
With joy and so much pride,
This peak shall be my garden then
My wish it shall fulfil,
To lie amongst the flowers
Of the clover on this hill.

No scar upon the landscape
Nor a cross that bears my name,
Yet friends shall know I lie there
And remember me the same,
For here I'll find eternal peace
It is my lasting will,
To rest amongst the flowers
Of the clover on this hill.

The buzzard

The buzzard now circles and glides on the thermals
So graceful it moves on the currents of air,
Alone it does fly with the courage of freedom
While silently drifting it roams without care.

It sails over water the valleys and mountains
To climb to the heavens it spirals so high,
Its wings in the sunlight are shining before me
As there it ascends through the glorious sky.

Majestically rising on winds that are blowing
It clings to the clouds as above it does soar,
Then heads to the ocean as blue as a sapphire
To gaze at the waves as they roll to the shore.

The buzzard now growing so faint in the distance
As further and further it fades from my sight,
Its beauty that shone through the skies of the evening
Now heads for the sunset and into the night.

Afterglow

Now as the sun does sink behind
Those dark and distant hills,
A halo of its afterglow
Does light the evening skies,
A golden crown before me now
And over land adorned,
That shines throughout its kingdom far
Before the moon does rise.

As stillness of the dusk now brings
A hush upon the air,
A sense of peace that shall prevail
Throughout the coming night,
For there the silken clouds do shine
In scarlet as they pass,
And float upon the gentle breeze
To catch the fading light.

Horizon burns with passion now
Yet soon the fire will fade,
And then shall yield to darkness
When the moon and stars appear,
The sun begins its journey far
And bids a sad farewell,
Now as the evening fades away
And night will soon be here.

Within this rock and stone

Although I shall be leaving soon
And heading on my way,
My dreams last with my memories
That I so long want to stay,
I walk towards the sunset now
And find myself alone,
Yet my spirit and my soul remain
Within this rock and stone.

No words can say just how I feel
So hard to say goodbyes,
And leave behind the countryside
With tears within my eyes,
Farewell to all the happiness
For me the weeks have flown,
Yet my spirit and my soul remain
Within this rock and stone.

I'll miss the fields I roamed within
The trees that were my friends,
With all the joy that I had found
But now so sadly ends,
For as my home is calling me
It chills me to the bone,
Yet my spirit and my soul remain
Within this rock and stone.

The love I have inside my heart
Of waves upon the shore,
And seas that kept me company
Shall last for evermore,
I face a weary journey now
Where time is not my own,
Yet my spirit and my soul remain
Within this rock and stone.

You were the thorn upon the rose

You were the thorn upon the rose
Such beauty yet you brought me pain,
Within my heart I can't forget
Those scars I'll always bear,
And each one shall remind me of
The day our love did end with tears,
And so my wounds shall never heal
While I feel such despair.

Your scarlet lips once spoke to me
With graceful words but say no more,
For silence cast its muting spell
And now we do not speak,
A frost has glazed the petals once
So vibrant in the flush of youth,
But as they fade and crumble now
The memories grow so weak.

Each one a kiss once soft and sweet
As velvet yet lie frozen now,
No love could thaw the bitter chill
That's standing in our way,
And melt the rift that's grown so deep
Or bridge the gap that widens with,
Each moment that we are apart
And every passing day.

They soon shall fall unto the ground
Then blow away upon the wind,
And scatter far across the land
Until they are no more,
The rose shall never bloom again
But rest within the shaded nook,
And thus remain forgotten
As it withers to the floor.

This stone I keep within my hand

I watch the gently rolling waves
Upon the shingle shore,
And there a stone shines brightly
On the beach that lies before,
I pick it up and hold it tight
I'll never let it go,
This stone I keep within my hand
Is all I've left to show.

Like you the stone did catch my eye
I plucked it from the wave,
And I shall keep it safely now
Then take it to my grave,
So smooth the shape unto my touch
So soothing it does feel,
This stone I keep within my hand
Will help my wounds to heal.

For it shall keep me company
Now everything has gone,
No reason left for me to live
So hard to carry on,
My dreams of you go floating by
Lost in the clouds above,
This stone I keep within my hand
Reminds me of our love.

As days begin and days do end
And years shall pass me by,
But still your name I shan't forget
Until the day I die,
For all the love that we did share
Was never meant to be,
This stone I keep within my hand
Shall last eternally.

The winds across the downs

I saw the fields of green before
Where hanging mist did lie,
The sun though weak was breaking through
And beams shone from the sky,
They lit the peaceful landscape there
So too the sleeping towns,
As clouds were sailing high upon
The winds across the downs.

I saw the vetch and daisies
And the golden fields of corn,
While gorse adorned the sweeping slopes
And dressed that summer's morn,
I gazed in awe upon that view
And watched those silken gowns,
As clouds were sailing high upon
The winds across the downs.

I saw the dancing meadows
As I looked across the way,
The sapphire sea so peaceful
As it rolled into the bay,
Then the rising sun of morning
Touched those rich and verdant crowns,
As clouds were sailing high upon
The winds across the downs.

On that lonely craggy shore

As winds do blow across the seas
And chill me to the bone,
No respite does it bring to me
As I stand there alone,
I watch the waves come rolling in
As love could last no more,
My tears shall fall forever
On that lonely, craggy shore.

For there the rocks and boulders lie
All battered by the swell,
That rages through both day and night
And there shall always dwell,
I watch the waves come rolling in
So wild the ocean roar,
My tears shall fall forever
On that lonely, craggy shore.

Those rocks resist the forces yet
I cannot do the same,
Each wave that falls a hammer blow
That fills my heart with shame,
I watch the waves come rolling in
As rain begins to pour,
My tears shall fall forever
On that lonely, craggy shore.

Blossom sky

I look upon the blossom sky
Like spring afar the colours shine,
Above the darkened summits
Of this wild and rugged land,
The hush of dawn yields silence here
But for the breathless breeze that blows,
Across the far and distant hills
Which in their greatness stand.

The valleys catch the morning beams
Which sink upon their sweeping slopes,
As they absorb those amber rays
They glow like burnished gold,
As shadows lift upon the ground
Sweet music flows within the air,
As birds now sing with joyful cheer
To melt the morning's cold.

While heather flows across the heath
Their flowers blend there into one,
Where violet sprigs and yellow gorse
Adorn the grassy shawl,
As carmine clouds do slowly pass
And pale as they then touch the sun,
I look upon the blossom sky
And watch the petals fall.

Cattle field

Upon a winter's morning cold
The frosted grass lies crisp and white,
Amidst the field where cattle graze
Their warm breath making clouds.

A lonely blackbird sweetly sings
His joyful song does carry far,
While perched within that barren tree
With branches now so bare.

The cattle bow their heads to feed
They tug and pull the brittle blades,
And chew the cud with all their might
Like there's no time to lose.

They stand beside the wooden gate
Where mud had frozen through the night,
And puddles iced like glass within
Those deeply rutted prints.

I stand alone and watch the dawn
As all the colours fill the sky,
Upon the hills the hanging mist
Like smoke across the land.

That soon shall clear now sun does rise
And shimmers through the distant trees,
To melt the frost within the field
And lift the shadows long.

The mole

The mole does dig with spade-like hands
Within the cloak of night he works,
For in the darkness goes unseen
And wears his black disguise,
He burrows with his sharpened claws
And feeds upon the worms he finds,
The hunter toils and does not rest
Until the dawn does rise.

And as the sunlight gently falls
Upon the ground it does reveal,
The hills of which this creature built
Within the field before,
Which scar the landscape of the morn
A curse to all those hapless souls,
Who must repair those earthy mounds
And tread them in once more.

While then the mole does soundly sleep
Until the eve again does fall,
And sun does set within the west
From slumber wakes alone,
Can barely see for almost blind
And yet he seems to know the way,
By touch and smell he tunnels on
Around the rock and stone.

Within that stirring cloud

No more the skies of summer blue
Where once I felt I did belong,
When sun did shine and I received
Such joy in love and song,
For me those days were always bright
But now the thunder rumbles loud,
Where hope and all my passion ends
Within that stirring cloud.

For now the days of darkness come
And rain shall fall like river tears,
As I await with bated breath
For God to end my years,
The hills now cloaked and colours fade
Where once they stood so tall and proud,
But now are lost and go unseen
Within that stirring cloud.

I cannot find a shelter now
My longing dreams all washed away,
And as the ground grows thick with mud
So ends another day,
My soul grows ever weaker while
The skies above an evil shroud,
No strength to fight my will does drift
Within that stirring cloud.

The guns forever silent

It'd so hard to see the suffering
That those soldiers had to face,
Now fields of mud are lush and green
And a calm befalls that place,
Yet there so many lives were lost
And many crosses stand,
The guns forever silent now
And peace does fill the land.

It's so hard to imagine
How they fought against the cold,
For now the sun is shining down
On buttercups of gold,
No shells or flying bullets
And no screams of dark despair,
The guns forever silent now
And peace does fill the air.

The trenches lying empty
Where the rows of soldiers stood,
And there the scarlet poppies grow
No longer stained with blood,
The cries of pain extinguished
And hushed the battles roar,
The guns forever silent now
As peace did end the war.

Wildwood

There stands the wildwood touched by God
And left in peace to grow,
Its beauty undisturbed now dwells
With trees so broad and strong,
Amidst its cloak of deepest green
Its spirit there does rise,
And clinging to my lasting dreams
Just like the birds in song.

The graceful fern in dappled light
From shade of broken branch,
A carpet rich of fallen leaves
Lies furnished there in gold,
As boughs do reach to skies above
And try to touch the clouds,
To catch the early sunrise there
As morning does unfold.

There stands the ancient woodland tall
With gnarled and pitted trunks,
Their twisted talons reach and bend
And grip the timber claw,
They wear the scars so proudly now
From many storms gone by,
No fence to hold or thus confine
Shall live for evermore.

Through falling, falling snow

As from my frozen window pane
I looked upon that winter's day,
The snow was drifting deep and crisp
And skies were darkest grey,
I did not wish to leave the warmth
Of home but knew I had to go,
And walk towards those factory gates
Through falling, falling snow.

I headed down those empty streets
Within the early morning light,
So hard each step I had to take
Through all life's bitter spite,
I longed to go back home again
As freezing winds did cruelly blow,
But headed to those factory gates
Through falling, falling snow.

I wondered where it all went wrong
Those thoughts remained within my mind,
As I did languish in the drifts
My eyes were almost blind,
I could not see the way before
And yet the way I seemed to know,
That led unto those factory gates
Through falling, falling snow.

And so towards that bleak estate
Past houses that I knew so well,
I thought that I would rather starve
Than face that day of hell,
I fought against my apathy
But soon my tears began to flow,
As then I saw those factory gates
Through falling, falling snow.

There stands the open gate

A way to find my love again
To rid me of my endless pain
And give me shelter from the rain
There stands the open gate.

A way to walk through meadows green
And see the hills that stand serene
To visit lands I've never seen
There stands the open gate.

A way to leave this smoky town
Where all my hope did sadly drown
Far from the life that dragged me down
There stands the open gate.

A way to leave my misery
And find a place I can be free
To live in peace and harmony
There stands the open gate.

The sweet song of the wren

As darkness lifts upon the land
And summer sun does rise,
The scarlet clouds above me
Slowly drift across the skies,
Just as the night is fading
And the morning comes again,
I listen to the dawning
And the sweet song of the wren.

His voice so pure it carries me
To places yet unseen,
Far over hills and meadows
And the pleasant pastures green,
As shadows fade and light does shine
I sit and ponder then,
To listen to the dawning
And the sweet song of the wren.

I hear within the woodland now
His joyful melody,
That floats upon the summer wind
And fills my heart with glee,
For there the sound so beautiful
As morning comes again,
I listen to the dawning
And the sweet song of the wren.

I wrote her name upon the sand

I walked along the shoreline
And the ocean looked so blue,
The seagulls called upon the wind
Above me as they flew,
So far across the waters there
I knew my love did stay,
I wrote her name upon the sand
But waves washed it away.

I watched the clouds and dreams go by
With happiness we shared,
As I looked out across the sea
And wished that she still cared,
I'd lost all hope of loving
And I could but only pray,
I wrote her name upon the sand
But waves washed it away.

Around her name a heart of love
That wasn't meant to be,
A symbol of the time we shared
Yet did not comfort me,
For there it looked so empty
And I shan't forget that day,
I wrote her name upon the sand
But waves washed it away.

Blow winds gently blow

Blow winds gently blow
And send my love to you,
Please carry dreams into the sky
Until they reach your heart,
For only hope can shield me now
From all the hurt I feel,
And offer me a shelter
As I face a life apart.

Blow winds gently blow
A way into your soul,
My wish is that you shall return
Your love is all I've known,
Please come to me I need you so
And let me hold you near,
I cannot face another day
Too hard to bear alone.

Blow winds gently blow
And carry dreams afar,
Please head across this barren land
And lead the way before,
Bring colour to the emptiness
And make the flowers bloom,
So I can then relive the past
And be with you once more.

To all the loves that passed me by

To all the loves that passed me by
And drifted to infinity,
Then lost forever to my heart
I bid a sad farewell,
For in my dreams I loved you all
But let each chance slip through my hands,
And now regrets do fill my days
For now alone I dwell.

And with no end to lonely nights
I lie awake until the dawn,
Where sun does light my window
But it never lights my door,
I can't look forward only back
To where my precious memories lie,
But soon I know they too will fade
Then I will see no more.

Yet I shall hope eternally
My luck will change just like the wind,
And fortunes shine on me again
To end these bitter years,
One day the rose may bloom for me
And as I touch its petals red,
My love shall come into my life
And dry my lonely tears.

The hammer and the rusting nail

The hammer and the rusting nail
Lay on the shelf within the shed,
They did not speak or even glance
Each day for them a strain,
The hammer knew he had the strength
To bend and break the rusting nail,
Or drive it firmly into wood
To not be seen again.

The rusting nail so small in size
Was sure he was no match for him,
And lived in fear that one day soon
That he would meet his end,
He prayed that day would not arrive
And would be left to live in peace,
To look out of the window there
And one day be his friend.

The hammer longed for him to go
And wanted all the wooden shelf,
To call his own and not to share
Yet all he tried did fail,
Each day he left and did return
And after toiling many hours,
Was placed upon the same old spot
Beside the rusting nail.

One day a man did take the nail
From off the shelf where it had lain,
So many years there undisturbed
And held it to the wall,
He drove it hard into the frame
Beside the window in the shed,
And hung the hammer on it then
So that it would not fall.

From that day on in harmony
The hammer and the rusting nail,
Lived side by side and made a vow
Of friendship strong and true,
The hammer knew without the nail
That he would fall down to the ground,
The nail free to live in peace
To gaze upon the view.

Morning rose

The freshness of the morning rose
So soft the petals small and frail,
And there within its flower holds
The sweetness of my love,
To feel its passion deep inside
Where hearts entwine for evermore,
With beauty that is heaven sent
From God so high above.

And as I smell the morning rose
It fills my senses with desire,
I long to hold your loving hand
Then kiss you once again,
My thoughts now flow in silken dreams
And rivers that shall lead to you,
That wind within the valleys deep
Across the barren plain.

And as I hold the morning rose
I wish so much that it were you,
So we could rest together here
And watch the clouds go by,
I hope that soon you shall return
To fill my days of emptiness,
And kiss again my wanton lips
Beneath the summer sky.

Leaving footprints on the sand

I'm beckoned by the calling wind
And waves that fall upon the shore,
For there the lonely seagull flies
Across the waters evermore,
The sun now shines through passing cloud
And lights the cliffs upon the land,
With empty heart I walk alone
Just leaving footprints on the sand.

The salt that blows within the air
Does leave a bitter taste to me,
For all the times I knew not when
That I should meet this destiny,
For now I'm at my lowest ebb
I'll never reach your loving hand,
With empty heart I walk alone
Just leaving footprints on the sand.

The ocean lies between us now
So distant from the days I knew,
For all is lost there is no path
To part the seas and lead to you,
Within this life I left no mark
For not a trace or fraying strand,
With empty heart I walk alone
Just leaving footprints on the sand.

Still beckoned by the calling wind
I hear your name each time it blows,
There to remind I shan't forget
Till lasting peace before me grows,
And still I watch the rolling waves
That washed away my future planned,
With empty heart I walk alone
Just leaving footprints on the sand.

As all day long I toil and strain

As all day long I toil and strain
With honest sweat on honest brow,
And in a rut so deeply grooved
There's no escape for me,
I stare upon my faithful watch
And count each minute passing by,
While longing for the shift to end
For then I can be free.

Through wind and rain through ice and snow
And through the summer's beating sun,
No help or sympathy I get
Just left to fend alone,
For such a wretched life I lead
I wonder where it all went wrong,
Some seem to think I do not care
And have a heart of stone.

As all day long I toil and strain
Lord spare me from these days of woe,
Please take my hand I offer now
And lead me to the light,
I need you in my darkest hour
Yet if this be my destiny,
I must accept it like a man
And face the bitter night.

To Lichfield leads this lonely road

To Lichfield leads this lonely road
Surrounded by the fields of green,
As there within the distance stand
The spires that steeply rise,
And reach unto the clouds above
Those wondrous ladies of the vale,
Majestic in their shape and form
Against the city skies.

As ever closer they appear
I feel that they are calling me,
Towards my goal and journey's end
Then I shall want no more,
I look upon those figurines
At all the Prophets, Kings and Saints,
Which grace the ancient facade there
Above the open door.

I enter in the subdued light
Where for a moment I am blind,
But then my eyes adjust to see
The great cathedral there,
The evensong so soft and sweet
Does lead me to the altar steps,
Where candles burn and people kneel
So silently in prayer.

While deep inside these holy walls
A presence now that I can sense,
A heavenly peace that lives within
The spirit of the stone,
Before the cross I bow my head
For now I feel my God is here,
And while his love does fill my soul
I'll never be alone.

Gold Hill

This ancient cobbled street that climbs
So steeply through this Dorset town,
Belongs to ages long ago
And yet it does remain,
When horse and cart once made their way
And hooves did scrape upon the stones,
To reach the top of this old hill
A life of toil and strain.

Yet in the quaint and rural charm
Of England's rich and pleasant land,
I walk with joy within my heart
Beneath the summer sky,
It seems that I am lost in time
So little changed throughout the years,
I close my eyes and dream a while
Of days that have gone by.

I carry on and as I climb
Past humble homes of slate and thatch,
And ruins of the Abbey walls
To share what those have seen,
The beauty of this heavenly vale
That lies adorned with woodland trees,
And countless fields that dwell amidst
Those wondrous downs of green.

I rest my head upon the leaves

September days have drifted by
And winter now does near,
The green of youth has turned to gold
And soon shall disappear,
No birds to sing upon the boughs
As now the trees do sleep,
I rest my head upon the leaves
Of autumn and I weep.

For trees can never speak the truth
Nor can they tell a lie,
Yet hope has gone like all my dreams
That blew across the sky,
And all around there's emptiness
But memories I shall keep,
I rest my head upon the leaves
Of autumn and I weep.

For here we met in springtime
And we kissed so tenderly,
Then shaded from the summer sun
Beneath our favourite tree,
I carved your name within a heart
The love we shared so deep,
Yet rest my head upon the leaves
Of autumn and I weep.

Derwentwater

Upon Derwentwater the sunrise of morning
Is lighting the surface a mirror of gold,
A scene of reflections now blending together
And painting a picture as colours unfold,
The peaks in the distance so deep and mysterious
So soft are their shadows which gracefully fall,
They wake from their slumber as dawn is now breaking
Yet shrouded in mist as they rise over all.

The blue Derwentwater where sun is now shining
And so captivating it yields such delight,
The hills and the valleys are cast now in emerald
They reach to the heavens so wondrous the sight,
Just like a dream yet it's real as can be now
A memory to treasure as long as I live,
To look on its greatness as God had intended
With so much to offer and so much to give.

So pure Derwentwater is lit by the evening
As now it does glow under Cumbrian skies,
The clouds pass in amber and scarlet before me
Whilst burning like flames till the fire slowly dies,
Asleep now it glistens so calm and so gentle
As still as the moonlight that rests on the lake,
The boats on the shoreline are tied to the jetty
And there they will stay till the dawn shall awake.

Hardy's cottage

I came to the hamlet of Lower Bockhampton
And watched as the corn in the breezes did sway,
As I crossed the bridge that was spanning the river
The sunlight was shining that beautiful day,
It shone on the Frome flowing silver beneath me
The music it played brought a joy to my ear,
As it danced over stones and the pebbles that lay there
The trees cast their shadows on waters so clear.

I saw then before me the cottage of Hardy
His birthplace and home at the brow of the hill,
With roof newly-thatched for its straw was so golden
A place of such beauty so peaceful and still,
What words must have flowed as he sat at that window
And gazed at the downs and the garden he knew,
Inspired by the flowers the lupins and roses
I too saw those dreams in that wonderful view.

For set in the heart of the green pleasant country
Alive with the birdsong from boughs reaching high,
That sailed over heath land upon summer breezes
And drifted like clouds that did float in the sky,
The stonewalls kept secrets from times in the distance
So many years passed yet those memories live on,
As if I belonged to the year eighteen hundred
I stepped back in time to the ages now gone.

From Eype to West Bay

I stand upon this shingle shore
As evening starts to fall,
While in the fading skies above
The passing gulls do cry,
Beside the upturned fishing boats
The lobster pots and nets,
And crates that held their morning catch
Which now are left to dry.

I cross the gentle stream that flows
Then climb the hill of green,
Through waving grass so steep the rise
That seems to have no end,
The wind does blow so strongly
From the ever restless sea,
And wails an errant ghostly song
As thickets shake and bend.

I reach the peak where I survey
The town that lies below,
Its lowly beach deserted now
So too the sleeping bay,
And there the cliffs do shine like gold
Within the setting sun,
That's slowly swallowed by the waves
Until it slips away.

I walk amidst the twilight
To the peaceful harbour there,
And see the stranded trawlers
Resting on the drying sand,
Now waiting for the morning tide
So they can sail again,
To brave the seas and cast their nets
And then return to land.

As darkness falls a chill descends
Upon this Dorset town,
While windows from the tavern glow
I hear the ocean roar,
As moonlight shimmers on the sea
That shines in silver now,
I watch the crests which ebb and flow
And roll unto the shore.

When blossom drapes the orchard boughs

When blossom drapes the orchard boughs
Like freshly fallen snow,
When sleeping lands begin to rouse
And slowly start to grow,
When daffodils do grace the way
And shine like burning gold,
It is indeed a fine display
When springtime does unfold.

When bluebells light the woodland floor
No better sight to see,
Than when that ocean sweeps before
In all its majesty,
And when the hawthorn's dressed in white
And borders every field,
It fills my heart with such delight
To see it there revealed.

When daisies in the meadow rise
Then open in the sun,
When swallows swarm the April skies
I know that spring's begun,
And when the birds shall sweetly sing
From every branch and tree,
Each joyful note that they will bring
Shall mean so much to me.

When blossom drapes the orchard boughs
Like freshly fallen snow,
When sleeping lands begin to rouse
And slowly start to grow,
When winter's cold is at an end
And browns then turn to green,
Those precious gifts the spring shall send
The greatest ever seen.

Sleep gentle waves

Sleep gentle waves let me rest on the shoreline
And look to the stars that are shining above,
So peaceful and still let me share in your wisdom
For heaven's the home of the one that I love.

Sleep gentle waves as the moonlight does glisten
For there on the waters my dreams ebb and flow,
And then sail away to the land of my fathers
Where love may await me I'll watch as you go.

Sleep gentle waves as the chill air is falling
The sky is my blanket but can't warm this cold,
Nor can I find hope in the stones and the shingle
As I long for the first light of dawn to unfold.

Sleep gentle waves let me hear the sweet music
That calls to me softly from so far away,
Forever I'll listen till your love shall find me
And here I'll be waiting to meet you one day.

Sweet tree of heaven

Sweet tree of heaven that stands there so proudly
A sunset of evening, a dream passing by,
A picture of beauty that speaks through its colours
While shining in red like the September sky.

Its branches of fire are embracing the morning
And lift from the shadows and glow like the sun,
Each leaf like a flame that shall burn through the season
And will not extinguish till winter's begun.

My hope springs eternal with joy it is yielding
A palette so rich in its majesty flows,
The artist's conception the brush carries meaning
So freely it wanders wherever it goes.

It waves in the breeze that does blow through the branches
The onset of autumn does tenderly call,
Through sorrow and sadness of cold days approaching
And soon shall be lost when the leaves start to fall.

The ghost of the white horse

The ghost of the white horse that dwells on the hillside
And leaps from the grassland and gallops through fields,
So strong is the figure an image of beauty
It heads through the country such power it yields.

It rides on the wind with its long mane a-flowing
And sails through the clouds and the sunset of fire,
For there it ascends on its journey to freedom
And carries its rider to lands of desire.

Over the mountains the lakes and the oceans
It races at speed to the lands far away,
Its sound like a rumble of thunder approaching
That causes the treetops to bend and to sway.

It heads through the heavens past stars that are shining
And travels so fast with the knight at its rein,
As dawn is approaching it moves to its homeland
And then at the sunrise it rests once again.

For there on the hillside it stays through the daytime
To look on the meadow's most wonderful sight,
And yet in the evening when darkness is falling
Once more it shall rise and will run through the night.

Golden Cap

Golden Cap views from its peak so enchanting
Across the blue waters to Lyme Regis bay,
The fine pearl of Dorset her Cobb and the harbour
Her colourful houses are lining the way.

I walk through the grass on this heavenly hillside
That's rising so steeply to Corsican Pines,
I stand there and gaze at the south coast of England
The land and the ocean where beauty entwines.

Crowned by the sandstone that shines in the sunlight
Where nature's alive and forever will be,
The wild flowers that grow on the slopes gently waving
And bend on the breeze that does blow from the sea.

The call of the country is singing so loudly
The song of the seagulls that soar through the sky,
A place full of dreams and my heart is so joyful
To dwell there in peace as the day passes by.

Golden Cap views softly melt to the sunset
With clouds glowing amber as daylight does fade,
The silhouette shoreline that sinks to the darkness
Till beauty I saw there is lost to the shade.

Eventide

So peaceful the breeze as it sails over hilltops
And beckons the starlight to shine,
On clouds that are floating of scarlet and crimson
With colours that merge and entwine,
The dark growing shadows as sun gently sets
Then beneath the horizon does slide,
The silhouette trees on the canvas of gold
In the glow of the cool eventide.

I hear gentle waves as they fall on the shore
And I watch as the seagulls do fly,
They call to the night as they head on their journey
Across the vast ocean and sky,
The daylight is fading and yielding to darkness
The clear panorama so wide,
That soon shall be sleeping and lying so still
In the glow of the cool eventide.

The cloak of the night is so quickly descending
And breaking the spell of the day,
Soon stars up above shall be shining so brightly
And then will be guiding my way,
The waters are dousing the flames that are sinking
As moonlight on wave tops does ride,
So graceful it moves as it ebbs and it flows
In the glow of the cool eventide.

The song of the wind

Far over the hills of this wilderness landscape
So deep in the soul of the beautiful dales,
Now calling me softly the voice of the morning
With all of its stories and magical tales,
I gaze now in awe at this wonderful country
And know to this land I shall always belong,
I hear the sweet tune as it floats and it whispers
The strong wind is blowing and yielding its song.

The soft changing shades of the light that is falling
Creating this vision like orbs through the sky,
They roll on the slopes with the clouds slowly passing
And shine on the shadows then fade till they die,
So glad to be part of this wonderful country
The sound of its pulse now is beating so strong,
And racing away on a symphonic journey
The strong wind is blowing and yielding its song.

The green painted pastures are rising before me
From out of the darkness its path does await,
It beckons me forward my destiny certain
To walk on in wisdom and open the gate,
That heads to the heart of this wonderful country
As ten thousand angels are singing along,
Their voices from heaven are filled with emotion
The strong wind is blowing and yielding its song.

I'm down by the river

I'm down by the river a feeling so peaceful
To gaze at the water that slowly flows by,
Whilst heading downstream on a tide of emotion
It mirrors the sight of the beautiful sky,
While there from the bridge I can see in the distance
The ancient Cathedral that proudly does stand,
Through treetops of emerald is rises before me
To dwell in the heart of this wonderful land.

The gentle reflections that fall on the surface
Are casting their shadows that softly do rest,
Then merge with the diamonds that dance in the sunlight
And ride on the breeze to their heavenly quest,
The silver white swans by the shoreline are gathered
As river boats waiting are tied to the quay,
And ready to sail for they're crowded with people
Embracing the views that are calling to me.

I'm down by the river as evening's approaching
I watch the sun falling and shadows that grow,
The silhouette skyline upon the red canvas
All blending as one as the skies are aglow,
The church bells are ringing from over the water
Their sound is so soothing and sweet to my ear,
I watch as the sun slowly yields to the twilight
Then look to the sky as the stars do appear.

Sky

Daybreak the dawning of a new day beginning
As colours now lift from the cloak that it wore,
For lit now in gold it does merge with the backdrop
And meeting the mist that does lie on the shore,
As blue as the ocean it sails far above me
The thin wisp of cloud like the wave tops that roll,
And ride on the wind as they reach the horizon
The shoreline of prayers which exists in my soul.

The clouds rolling in for the bringers of darkness
Moving above in the grey slated mass,
They're charged and they gather together in union
Seeping and blending in palettes they pass,
The hammer of anvils the roll of the thunder
The flashing of lightning the hail and the rain,
All is then still now the storm has gone over
And heads to the distance so peace lives again.

The beams of the sunlight that warm my emotion
And touching my heart in the land that I see,
The rainbow of hope as I look to the future
A gate to the truth and my own destiny,
As evening is fading the glow of the sunset
The embers are burning the clouds are on fire,
As smoke drifts across all the shadows are falling
And lost to the twilight my longing desire.

The moon sleeping low as it flickers through branches
Yet soon it shall rise and will shine from above,
Although far away it does speak in its wisdom
While lighting the way to the pathway of love,
The stars are so bright making wishes to heaven
So peaceful it seems as the night does descend,
The cold air surrounds me no warmth does it offer
I look to the sky now in search of a friend.

The dust now settled gently

The bricks that made these shattered walls
Were laid by honest toil,
That bonded the community
When here they built their homes,
But cracks appeared and dreams did die
Then walls began to lean,
And now a deathly silence yields
A wind that cruelly roams.

The terraced streets lie empty now
Where many lives were shared,
The shattered windows boarded up
Those sites shall soon be cleared,
No children play within the roads
Deserted and so still,
For families there were torn apart
When jobs then disappeared.

The chimney stacks stopped smoking
And the factory gates were closed,
So many had to move away
To seek a life elsewhere,
And memories died with people
Who no longer had a trade,
They felt they'd been forgotten
As nobody seemed to care.

For now the mines and mills have gone
The land has lost its soul,
The workers' hands lie idle
And no future can they see,
A wasted generation
Who had so much left to give,
The dust now settled gently
On the town that used to be.

A lonely leaf

The tree does bend as winds do blow
This chill December day,
And yet a lonely leaf remains
Upon the dormant bough,
It's withered dry yet still it clings
By thread that's growing frail,
That soon will break it cannot last
Its end is nearing now.

For there it hangs so limply yet
Keeps moving back and forth,
And sympathy does fill my heart
It could be me that's there,
When in the autumn of my life
And best days all behind,
With nothing to look forward to
Its loneliness I share.

I rest against the mighty trunk
And look towards the sky,
Through dark and twisted talons
That cast shadows on the land,
Yet still the lonely leaf remains
And bravely lingers on,
Yet I shall wait for it to fall
To catch it in my hand.

The woodland track

The woodland track was muddy
And some puddles stained the path,
The boughs were hushed no birds did sing
My steps the only sound,
The early morning rain had made
The day seem fresh and new,
As winds did blow the fallen leaves
That rested on the ground.

The sun was peeking through the clouds
Then hidden by the grey,
As time again the light and shade
Formed patterns that did merge,
It shone between the branches
Where the silver droplets fell,
Upon the nettles and the ferns
That lined the lowly verge.

'Twas fading there to amber yet
It caught the morning light,
And lined the course on which I went
As if a guide for me,
Beneath the strong and mighty oaks
The acorns there did lie,
And scattered far across the land
As far as I could see.

As autumn's fall was drawing close
And trees would soon be bare,
I knew that then I'd not return
Until the coming spring,
When once again the bluebells came
To grace the barren floor,
My heart should then be filled with cheer
With all the joy they'd bring.

Wrapped within the petals

My love is drifting through the sky
With every cloud that passes by,
My hope does fade a little more
As rain does gently fall,
No end to winter can I see
While skies do shed no sympathy,
No flowers will light the waiting land
And spring shall never call.

Her name upon the rushing air
And yet it is my longing prayer,
That I should find a joy at last
For then the clouds would clear,
But as for now the flowers hold
The pain and angst of winter's cold,
Yet maybe when they open
All my hurt shall disappear.

For when the sun does shine so bright
The flowers may yield a great delight,
For wrapped within the petals
Are my dreams and tears I cried,
When colours sweep across the ground
I'll hear the dawning chorus sound,
For then I'd give my all to have
My lover by my side.

Parachutes

As seeds blow from the dandelions
Across the fallow field,
They sail upon the autumn breeze
Like parachutes they go,
Whilst floating through the chilly air
To some place far away,
And then shall rest upon the ground
When in the spring they'll grow.

To spread their mark upon the land
And furnish it with gold,
To every corner they shall dwell
Then rise in majesty,
And colour England with their grace
In every nook and verge,
Though some shall fall to stone and stream
And meet their destiny.

Alas my heart does feel for those
Deprived the chance to live,
Who never bloomed within the sun
And lost for evermore,
I stand alone and watch them go
And bless them as they rise,
To seek the breeze and fly afar
Then wait for snow to thaw.

Broken wings

I was born within the countryside
And learned to love the land,
I saw the seasons passing by
And tried to make a stand,
Where I was raised I made my home
But cut down in my flight,
I can no longer circle high
From dawn unto the night.

For once I was a songbird
And I flew within the sky,
Across the fields and peaceful hills
Until my dream did die,
I saw the world so beautiful
Found freedom in the air,
But can no longer ride the wind
Or find some comfort there.

My feathers dull and lifeless now
I'm in a sorry state,
No joy to fill my empty days
And now await my fate,
For here beneath the shaded bush
The sun will never shine,
I can no longer feel its warmth
Within this heart of mine.

My friends have left and gone away
And yet I am still here,
To contemplate on all I've lost
And all that I held dear,
As all alone I face the cold
And pain each day now brings,
I can no longer touch the clouds
Or use my broken wings.

The mirror lies broken

The mirror lies broken and so much misfortune
Is coming my way and I cannot break free,
I long to escape but I know it will follow
Wherever I hide it shall always find me.

I'm lost in a wilderness dark without corners
And trapped in a circle that's drowning my soul,
That's breaking my spirit and crushing my longing
I haven't a purpose nor have I a goal.

No light is appearing from out of the darkness
No hope I can cling to for everything's gone,
I reach for salvation and pray God can hear me
And give me the strength so that I can go on.

The mirror lies broken and luck has deserted
I'm left all alone and no future have I,
The days come and go but there's never an ending
I'm wasting my life as the days trickle by.

This sweet little child

This sweet little child had his whole life before him,
Could be what he wanted the pathway was clear,
Each place that he went to did welcome him gladly,
But as he grew older his joy turned to fear,
As he was rejected and no one would take him,
Or give him a chance that he so much deserved,
Nor offer their hand when he needed protection,
His life was so cruel and a penance he served.

This sweet little child always searching for freedom,
For he longed to soar and to fly like a bird,
He looked to the clouds but the sky had no answers,
He prayed to his God but his prayer went unheard,
So he lived all alone with no friends or no family,
To wipe away tears that he wept every day,
They fell to the earth and were dried by the sunlight,
Where no one could guide him or show him the way.

This sweet little child then did hide in the darkness,
Where sun never shone and he couldn't be found,
And flowers never opened nor bloomed in the springtime,
Where he made his bed on the hard frozen ground,
For hope was a dream that he could see no longer,
As now he was blind to the life he once led,
He so loved the world but the world he belonged to,
Had changed like the seasons and soon would be dead.

Rests in God's hands

I have searched to discover the wisdom of earth,
It's a long tiring journey from the moment of birth,
Till the time that I leave here and then fly away,
Through the clouds unto heaven I long for the day,
For there I'll find peace and in joy I will live,
And all that I long for I know he shall give,
As my future is written in stone on the lands,
And my life always rests in God's hands.

I know he'll be with me each step that I take,
And will act as my guide with the choices I make,
He'll always bring comfort when I'm in despair,
And I know he will listen and answer each prayer,
Without him I'm nothing nowhere I belong,
My body is weak yet he makes me so strong,
I'll bow down before him like waves on the sands,
For my life always rests in God's hands.

The rock that I cling to that never shall fall,
And in times when I'm lonely his love conquers all,
He'll never desert me my master and friend,
For he is my saviour on whom I depend,
Like the sun in the sky and the land and the sea,
The hills and the mountains forever shall be,
In all of creation his epitaph stands,
And my life always rests in God's hands.

Sleep on gentle night

Sleep on gentle night as your stars shine so brightly,
So peaceful the air as the darkness lies still,
Please carry my loved one upon your sweet shoulders,
And rise in the dawning to answer my will.

I hope she'll be with me to share in the beauty,
As each morn I wake and I face the new day,
For then I shall hold her and savour each moment,
I've missed her so much there's no more I can say.

So come to me softly and whisper your secrets,
In prayers I have begged that our love shall not die,
As moon through the treetops does flicker so gently,
And casts down its light from the heavenly sky.

I still dream of her and I wish she was with me,
For I feel so empty my soul wracked with pain,
I'm lost in a world where nobody can find me,
My heart is so longing to love her again.

Sleep on gentle night rest your head until morning,
As frost is now forming upon the cold ground,
And when the sun rises and shines through my window,
I hope that tomorrow my love I have found.

I need you more each day

I need you more each day we spend apart I cannot go on,
Just dwelling on the love that could've been,
I want to live again the times that we did share together,
As far too many lonely days I've seen,
I hope that in your empty heart you still have feelings for me,
But now I fear they've drifted far away,
For I have tried so hard and yet my effort's all been wasted,
And now it seems my loneliness will stay.

For when you walked away and you just turned your back upon me,
I never thought that it would be for good,
But now so many years have passed it seems that it's for certain,
And I have tried just everything I could,
My letters go unanswered and you cannot hear me calling,
I know that I must face the world alone,
I must accept that things have changed and it is surely over,
And yet I thought our love was carved in stone.

But still my tears are falling though I know you do not want me,
I cannot face the fact that it's the end,
There's no one that compares to you and second best is pointless,
And now I feel so lost without a friend,
I watch the waves upon the shore and wish they'd bring you to me,
And breezes blow your love upon the air,
I look toward the sunset far away into the distance,
And wonder of the life you're living there.

I need you more each day we spend apart it's getting harder,
To live without you and to carry on,
My strength of will grows weaker now with every day that passes,
And all the joy and happiness has gone,
For sadness now resides in me and only you can end it,
My longing dreams may never be fulfilled,
Yet I will wait with open arms and long for your returning,
For then these troubled waters shall be stilled.

The nights are long and lonely now

The nights are long and lonely now
And never seem to end,
With no one I can turn to
Or on whom I can depend,
I'm left with my misfortunes
All my burdens and my fears,
How I so wish that you were here
To dry my falling tears.

A thousand times I tried so hard
To win your heart once more,
And yet I knew it was too late
To live just as before,
The rift too wide and so we went
Upon our separate ways,
And now the truth so hard to bear
As are these empty days.

Within the glow of candlelight
Your picture in my hand,
As I now hold it to the flame
I'll never understand,
Why we did part I can't forget
Until all trace has gone,
And as it burns my hopes shall die
For now I must move on.

My heart was made to be in love

My heart was made to be in love but feels so cold and empty,
And lonely days have never felt so bad,
I wish that I could find a way to make my life seem better,
Instead of being so bitter and so sad,
For now I feel like giving up there's nothing left to live for,
And somewhere else I may find joy at last,
Within the blossom sunrise as the brand new dawn is breaking,
I wish that I could now forget the past.

My heart was made for loving yet in pieces it lies broken,
As sunny skies are turning into rain,
For in my mind I've searched so long but couldn't find the answers,
And no one now could rid me of this pain,
For everything seems hopeless and in truth I've stopped believing,
No comfort can I get in shattered dreams,
As the colours of the springtime have all faded into autumn,
No end to all the bitterness it seems.

My heart was made for loving not to carry this resentment,
Sometimes I know I can do nothing right,
For everything I try I fail and I grow ever weaker,
So now I feel I've no more strength to fight,
Nobody wants to know me or to dry the tears I'm crying,
Nobody wants to take a chance with me,
For when the dealer dealt my cards they were so unforgiving,
The hand I got I did not want to see.

I long to walk those golden sands

I long to walk those golden sands
And gaze across the sea again,
To live those days of happiness
Which now are lost to me,
To hear the cry of hungry gulls
As they do shear above the waves,
Which roll onto the endless shore
Would fill my heart with glee.

I'd made a vow that I'd return
Yet I am trapped nowhere to go,
Imprisoned by the life I lead
Within these blackened walls,
The chains that bind me hard to break
But if I could I'd leave this day,
For there my home shall always lie
Yet I ignore her calls.

I carry on through darkened times
Where streets run wild unsafe to go
For feral youths have gathered there,
Like rats within the night,
The violence breeds in empty rows
Where idle hands make devil's work,
For they are drawn unto them now
Like moths unto the light.

I long to walk those golden sands
And leave behind this crime and smoke,
To see again the ocean blue
And waves upon the shore,
But now it seems a distant dream
For in the urban skies above,
The clouds have gathered overhead
And rain begins to pour.

The shipwreck

The shipwreck lies upon the shore
And will not sail the seas no more,
Nor will her bow cut through the wave
Now stranded on her rocky grave,
Her twisted hull is sliced in two
The breakers now are crashing through,
Her plated steel is red with rust
And soon will crumble into dust.

Her barnacled and battered form
The victim of that evil storm,
So long ago yet still remains
With every wave she creaks and strains,
The bitter wind does never cease
To offer her a moment's peace,
It howls just like sad lament
As if from hell each gust was sent.

The wreck no longer bears her name
She proudly wore but now with shame,
She shakes with every forceful blow
That strikes her down and wounds her so,
Beneath the jagged cliff so tall
Still pounded by the waves that fall,
Since on a stirring sea of white
She floundered on that stormy night.

The hardest part of loving you

The hardest part of loving you is now you are not with me,
I think about you every night and day,
And long to hold you near me and to share our lives together,
But now it seems my heartache's here to stay,
I wish that I could a find a way but each road leads to nowhere,
For now I know you never will return,
So I must face my destiny however hard and lonely,
And from mistakes I made I now must learn.

I'll not take love for granted for it's then that it starts fading,
Until it's gone completely and for good,
The pleasure's always matched with pain there's no way of preventing,
For I have tried just everything I could,
In fairy tales it never seems to end and lasts forever,
But in reality it's not the same,
It hurts you time and time again and when your tears start falling,
Then all that's left is bitterness and shame.

And when you find yourself alone nobody wants to know you,
For friends can't bear a loser or their ways,
And when you need them most of all they haven't got the time then,
To listen or to share your empty days,
For now I'm feeling helpless and my future is uncertain,
Although I try I don't know where to go,
The rain is falling on me and the sun will never shine now,
And winds of fate shall always cruelly blow.

The hardest part of loving you is knowing that it's over,
There's nothing I could do to make it last,
I wish I could forget you but your memory shall remain here,
As now I'm left just dwelling on the past,
I watch the glowing sunset as its embers now are fading,
So closing yet another chapter there,
I'll turn the page and hope the dawn will bring a change of fortune,
And free me from this burden that I bear.

The summertime is over now

The summertime is over now
September cannot stay,
The autumn wind is blowing strong
As trees now bend and sway,
The evening's growing colder
As the sun sinks in the sky,
And soon the frosts of winter's chill
Upon the ground shall lie.

For as the flowers wither
And the colours start to fade,
I see the barren landscape
That the cold days now have made,
And pray for spring to come again
With golden daffodils,
When sheep will graze so happily
Upon those distant hills.

As one by one the leaves do fall
And each seems like a tear,
As if to bid a sad farewell
To end another year,
Now soon the boughs shall all be bare
And cloaked by winter's snow,
Then I'll recall the summertime
That seems so long ago.

It's only make believe

It's only make believe
So I will have to stop pretending,
There's someone in this lonely world for me,
For all the times I've dreamed of love
But dreams just never happened,
I'm feeling it was never meant to be,
As I stumble down the highway
I feel lost without direction,
The view from every road just looks the same,
I rest within the gutter now
To watch my life that's passing,
And wonder why my fortune never came.

I never found the one I love
And yet I'll go on searching,
For someone who could make my life complete,
The journey is so hard and long
I don't think I can make it,
I have to rest my tired and aching feet,
As now the rain is falling
There's no end to all my sadness,
And clouds now hide the sunlight out of view,
A chilly wind does blow so strong
It saps my fading spirit,
And now I feel there's nothing I can do.

I wish that I could find a way
And wish I knew for certain,
There's someone there who longs to be my friend,
I drown within my sorrow
As I head into the distance,
Not knowing where this winding road shall end,
I look towards the heavens
And I pray for inspiration,
I hope that God can free me of this pain,
And tell me what I have to do
To make my life seem better,
And show the way to happiness again.

The morning dew

The morning dew like tears that fall
So softly on the rose,
And settles there like sadness now
That's how my story goes,
As sunlight rises in the sky
And mist begins to clear,
With all my heart I now do wish
That my true love was here.

The wren does sing so joyfully
Upon the autumn bough,
And tries to cheer me with his song
But yet he fails for now,
For I can't see no end in sight
To hurt I have to bear,
My life is one of emptiness
And filled with deep despair.

The air is cold I see my breath
Along this lonely way,
I know I must forget the past
And face another day,
But everywhere that I do go
Her memories still remain,
Reminders of the heartbreak
I must live time and again.

The morning dew like tears that fall
And shine as day does start,
So brightly but they cannot light
The way back to her heart,
And so my dreams that slowly fade
Will soon be lost to all,
For in the end it matters not
That leaves do gently fall.

Please picture the scene

Please picture the scene of the hills and the valleys
Now rolling before you a patchwork so fine,
The cornfields of gold and the pleasant green pastures
And capture this moment as sunlight does shine,
Sail like the wind as you rise in the morning
And into the blue of the sky up above,
Please see it forever and live for its beauty
And follow me onward to share in its love.

Please picture the scene of a calm flowing river
That's winding before you and showing the way,
So cool and so fresh as the ripples are dancing
For each is a heartbeat of joy that will stay,
So taste the pure water its life giving spirit
That's filling your soul and its peace you now feel,
Please see it forever and live for its beauty
And follow me onward where dreams become real.

Please picture the scene of the flowers in the meadow
The blossoms of springtime where colours surround,
Now draping the land and are painting the country
And always remember the sight and the sound,
As petals start falling like snowflakes from heaven
And forming a carpet of white where you go,
Please see it forever and live for its beauty
And follow me onward then God you shall know.

Walsall leather

'Twas born on the riches of iron ore and lime
From the quarries they mined there to feed this great trade,
In smoke-ridden buildings of Walsall it grew there
Thus shaping the landscape where leather was made,
The stitch of the seam and the cutting and shaping
Within cobbled backstreets those workshops did thrive,
There curriers fashioned with tanning and dubbing
From dawn until dusk all those workers did strive.

The loriners' hands were so skilled with the making
Of spurs and the stirrups and buckles for belt,
With bridles and saddles they served the great Empire
In the heart of Victorian England they dwelt,
Those thousands of people who toiled in its hardship
With wages so poor in this labour of sweat,
The women who suffered on piecework went hungry
Were slaves to the needle and always in debt.

They worked for their children to keep them from gutters
So many long hours their hands rough and sore,
Just to provide a few scraps for the table
They earned such a pittance and hungered for more,
So little remains save the memories of elders
The buildings now cleared yet their souls do remain,
And live on forever in graves of the workers
The times and the likes we shall not see again.

A boy was born with innocence

A boy was born with innocence
His heart was kind and good,
So pure the gift from heaven lay
A flower in new bud,
The focus of attention
And his eyes so deep and blue,
When cradled in his mother's arms
A loving home he knew.

He grew to walk then run and play
Beneath the summer skies,
He went to school and studied hard
And learned to be so wise,
But saw his life so quickly change
His joy then turned to pain,
Then sunny days he loved the most
Were rarely seen again.

He dreamed of being someone
But he ended up alone,
When all his friends deserted him
He wept upon his own,
He tried his hardest to succeed
But everything went wrong,
And so he hid himself away
Then suffered for so long.

He turned to God when no one else
Had time for him or care,
He prayed for joy and happiness
To end his dark despair,
His spirit then was lifted
And his deep blue eyes could see,
The beauty of the world around
And all that he could be.

He saw the blossoms of the spring
The flowers of delight,
He smelt their sweetest perfume
And he marvelled at their sight,
He tasted water from the stream
That led him to the shore,
He felt God's love within him grow
And never asked for more.

He saw the mountains and the hills
The peaceful countryside,
Those sights he would remember there
Until the day he died,
He saw the sunsets in the sky
And autumn forests glow,
He saw the glory all around
Wherever he did go.

He saw the winter snowfalls lie
Upon the ground so deep,
And found a place to call his own
Where he could rest and sleep,
But when he woke he roamed again
To greet the brand new day,
And took the time to look around
As he went on his way.

A boy was born with innocence
Yet grew so strong and tall,
He then embraced the scenery
And shared a love for all,
He gazed unto the stars above
Then watched the breaking dawn,
And knew that he was lucky
And so grateful he was born.

Please let me be the one

Please let me be the one
That you've been searching for so long now,
And let me fill your lonely heart with love,
For as the clouds of darkness
Roll across the skies so quickly,
I pray the sun will rise again above,
To show the way to happiness
So we can be together,
And lift the waves of sadness that I feel,
Then dry my tears I often cried
In loneliness and sorrow,
And maybe then my wounds shall start to heal.

The patterns of our destiny
Have all been too familiar,
We seemed to share that suffering and pain,
Throughout the years of solitude
When everything seemed hopeless,
But now we've found a chance to love again,
Let's take this opportunity
To know each other better,
And share the secrets we have kept so long,
Forget the bitter times we had
And leave them all behind us,
And hope this time that nothing shall go wrong.

We've nothing left to lose because
We've lost it all already,
And would be fools to throw this chance away,
And watch our dreams just float upon
The clouds into the distance,
Forever then we would regret this day,
Please let me be the one
That you've been searching for so long now,
So take my hand and say you will be mine,
And let us share a future
Full of joy that's never-ending,
Then every day the sun will always shine.

I cannot stop the rising tide

I cannot stop the rising tide engulfed by my emotions,
I'm drowning in self-pity and in shame,
I cannot save myself from all the pain that does surround me,
And since you've gone now nothing seems the same,
My days are always empty there's no end to all the sadness,
With nights so cold and lonely I can't bear,
Just gazing at the stars that shine so brightly high above me,
So deep into infinity I stare.

While wishing you were with me but there's many miles between us,
For now my prayers of longing go unheard,
And silence fills the darkness that is growing ever deeper,
For lost in time and space my every word,
I think of all those good times and I wish we could relive them,
So long ago I never will forget,
The years have passed so quickly yet I always will remember,
The precious time and moment we first met.

Those memories now are all I have and all I've left to cling to,
But as the time goes by my dreams will fade,
And then I shall have nothing with no strength to go on living,
The future's bleak and I feel so afraid,
The trees all stand forlornly as the moonlight now is falling,
And frost descends upon the winter's ground,
I stare out of my window but the picture never changes,
The image of my joy just can't be found.

The morning is rising

The morning is rising the blackbird is singing
From out of the shadows of branches and leaves,
His song rides the breeze and is breaking the silence
As into the springtime his melody breathes.

New life through the stillness as skies are now glowing
And colours awaken as night fades away,
The sunlight is peeping above the horizon
And casting its warmth at the start of the day.

With blossoms so pretty like snowflakes are falling
As daffodils shine in their glory like gold,
And waving before me they greet the new dawning
An ocean of beauty to douse winter's cold.

The morning is rising the blackbird is singing
And filling the air with his sweet notes of love,
As echoes of joy now envelop the woodland
The sunlight does shine from the blue skies above.

Sandcastles

Down on the beach and within the warm sunlight
The children are playing and laughing with glee,
With buckets and spades they are building sandcastles
Then watching them crumble and fall to the sea.

A girl collects shells as she walks by the water
Whilst dodging the waves as they roll to the shore,
She gathers each one in her hand for safe-keeping
Until it is full and can carry no more.

The mother and father are calling their children
They've ice-creams and lollies for them to all share,
With joy they come running so quickly towards them
Then rest in the shade of the parasol there.

And when they have finished their faces and fingers
Are sticky so wipe them and then head away,
To pick up their buckets and spades they'd abandoned
And there they remain for the rest of the day.

When the sun starts to fall as the evening approaches
They pack their belongings and then they do go,
The tide is retreating as shadows now lengthen
As over the water a cool breeze does blow.

Wallflower

Wallflower you carry my hopes for the future
Your beauty brings joy to the new day begun,
That captures my spirit with kindness endearing
And warming my soul like the warmth of the sun.

My hand longs to touch you I reach out to feel you
As if I were living my dream of all dreams,
With you I belong and I shall now forever
My happiness flows like the rivers and streams.

For you are my world you mean everything to me
And all of my wishes have come true this day,
So come let us sail on the breeze unto heaven
And ride on the clouds to a place far away.

Wallflower my lover my long search is over
For now I have found you I'll never let go,
And share all my days with you always together
From dawn until dusk I shall watch our love grow.

Brixham harbour

As seagulls now ride on the breeze from the ocean
They call to the clouds as they soar through the air,
While cliffs in the distance of bridal white limestone
Adorned in the cloak of the emerald they wear,
While outside "The Strand" there are some painting pictures
The townsfolk are viewing those works on display,
While others relax drinking tea at the tables
With families and friends and enjoying the day.

The boats in the harbour are casting reflections
Upon the still water they peacefully lie,
For sheltered they rest in a haven of beauty
And shine in the sunlight as morning goes by,
Majestic and graceful the Golden Hind lingers
A ghostly reminder of ages now passed,
When Drake sailed the world to new lands and horizons
And wind filled her sails as they hung from the mast.

The trawlers lie idle yet soon they'll be sailing
And shearing the waves as they head out to sea,
The fishermen ready to board their own vessels
Are gathered together and talk on the quay,
I look to the shop fronts the buildings and houses
Which dwell on the hillside and roll to the shore,
A paint-box of colour in harmony blending
The sight so enchanting and one I adore.

For broken hearts and fairy tales

For broken hearts and fairy tales have never gone together,
And yet this is the way that it must be,
I feel a sense of sadness that is tearing me apart now,
No one can break this spell of misery,
Each chapter that has gone by in my life has had no meaning,
And everything I've tried has turned out wrong,
There's nothing else I could've done to change it for the better,
And now I have no place where I belong.

But as the pages turn there seems no end to all the sorrow,
I wish a wand could take the pain away,
And magic dust could bring me joy and dry the tears I'm crying,
But now I feel my heartache's here to stay,
I cannot cut a path through all the thorns that now surround me,
I'm tangled up and lying on the floor,
My princess tired of waiting has now left and gone forever,
And nothing seems to matter anymore.

With broken hearts and fairy tales there is no happy ending,
The book is closed and resting on the shelf,
Nobody wants to read it for the storyline is hopeless,
And I brought every word upon myself,
The truth lies hidden out of sight and I don't want to share it,
It's best that it remains there out of view,
And my advice that I now give, don't follow in my footsteps,
And try to find the one who's meant for you.

Landfill

Where once the green and rolling hills
Lay in the midst of England's heart,
The scars she wears unsightly
As they spread across the land,
They ripped and tore the beauty from
The scenes that once belonged to all,
And took away serenity
That once inspired the hand.

For now the brown and littered mounds
Do dominate the views of old,
And pungent stench of filth and waste
Is carried on the breeze,
Where scavengers now make their home
To seek the comfort of its mire,
And hungry gulls do swarm the skies
So distant from the seas.

With every week that passes by
It grows and grows and hides the sun,
And casts an ugly shadow
Where the children once did play,
But now the field is silent there
No laughter now but only tears,
Deserted save the slide and swings
Which slowly rust away.

How God must weep when he does see
His great creation in this state,
A time bomb of destruction
In his garden once divine,
The flowers have all wilted now
And trodden flat within the mud,
Where spring shall never come again
Or vivid colours shine.

I'll find the road to happiness

I'll find the road to happiness
Though it may take a lifetime,
I hope somewhere that joy does wait for me,
All through the barren years I've lived
I've never found my way there,
And waited long to change my destiny,
But nothing seems to happen
Every day seems never-ending,
I battle through the dark clouds of despair,
Just waiting for the sun to shine
But skies are full of teardrops,
And when they fall nobody seems to care.

My friends have all deserted me
And I am on my own now,
I call for help but they just walk on by,
I'm left within the gutter
And I can't go on much longer,
While watching every dream just fade and die,
I'm heading to the drain now
With the leaves of autumn falling,
And soon I shall just disappear from view,
As still the rain is pouring down
I long to find some shelter,
And know there's nothing else that I could do.

I'll find the road to happiness
I hope I'm getting closer,
And maybe then the sun will start to shine,
And love shall warm my heart again
That feels so cold and empty,
Then lift me from the sorrow that is mine,
And so I'll go on walking
As I head into the distance,
The pavement's cracked and worn beneath my feet,
So many souls have trod before
I hope they found the answer,
I'll follow them until my life's complete.

I feel reborn

I feel reborn as the morning is breaking
And wind is now blowing the blossoms of spring,
The petals are falling like snowflakes around me
The flowers and rainbows with songbirds that sing,
My heart is now beating with life and the living
To see all the colours that shine in the sun,
The winter is over my spirit is rising
And heads from the cold for a new day's begun.

I feel reborn as I witness this beauty
My eyes cannot close to the glory before,
I gaze at the sky with its apricot layers
The glow of the dawn that has opened the door,
To brand new adventures the past is behind me
I look to the future the way lies ahead,
A journey of promise I so long to follow
That captures my wishes in tulips of red.

I feel reborn as I breathe the new morning
For blessed by the hand of my Saviour I know,
I'll walk through the arbour of sweet scented roses
And follow the pathway wherever I go,
I dance through the meadows and capture each moment
The joys and emotions are rolled into one,
I pray that this moment and time last forever
For while I believe it shall always live on.

The sweet joy that the summer shall bring

I long for your coming to see you and touch you
And know that you love me forever I pray,
That time will come quickly then all of my sorrows
Will melt in the sunlight and brighten my day,
When flowers are blooming with colours that blend
In my soul and my senses all nature will sing,
For there in its midst I know that you'll be waiting
And with the sweet joy that the summer shall bring.

As winter is ending and spring is approaching
The buds on the branches begin to appear,
The day is now nearing when you shall be with me
I long for the time I will welcome you here,
As warm breezes blow the May blossoms like snowflakes
You shall fill my dreams for you mean everything,
And while you exist in my mind I'll be happy
To feel the sweet joy that the summer shall bring.

To share in the peace of this beautiful morning
I live for the moment that you shall be mine,
When graced by your presence I will be so lucky
I'll wait for your coming and search for a sign,
When we'll meet again it will feel like the first time
For love shall then fly like a bird on the wing,
And sailing so softly with hope for the future
With all the sweet joy that the summer shall bring.

Sycamore seeds

The sycamore seeds through the air gently falling
They spiral in circles then rest on the floor,
In the grave of the autumn, a blanket of sadness
That weeps for the passing and summer no more.

The golden leaves blend with the chorus of amber
Through old wizened branches the sunlight does shine,
I look to the skies that are blue as a sapphire
Framing the picture where colours entwine.

A warm breath is thawing the frost of the darkness
The mist of the dawn slowly fading away,
The silver jewelled cobwebs are dressing the hedgerow
Laced in their gowns of an October day.

The sycamore seeds through the air gently falling
They spiral in circles then rest on the floor,
In the grave of the autumn, a blanket of sadness
That weeps for the passing and summer no more.

October morning

This October morning the bright shafts of sunlight
Now shine through the trees like a prism of gold,
And lighting the leaves that remain on the branches
Which hang there forlornly and gripped by the cold.

A lingering mist like a cloud slowly drifting
That grows ever fainter until it does pass,
Revealing the way through the heart of the woodland
Where puddles lie still and are frozen like glass.

The blue skies above of the autumn revealing
The frost of the night and the cold of the day,
And cloaking the spirit of summer now fading
As greens turn to brown and will soon float away.

The soft-dappled beams that are dancing around me
Like diamonds and gemstones adorning the land,
The pathway now sparkles with crystals of silver
All cast in the night by the chill winter's hand.

This October morning I walk in the sunlight
As frost starts to melt on the trees all around,
Through woodland I tread on the chill crispy carpet
As teardrops are falling and rest on the ground.

I'm burning all my bridges

I'm burning all my bridges though it wasn't my intention,
For one by one my friends have disappeared,
And now I'm isolated from the world that didn't need me,
Beneath the cloudy skies that never cleared,
And now the only company I have this lonely shadow,
That stands forlorn and etched upon the wall,
And doesn't know which way to turn for avenues are closing,
As now it seems that I have lost it all.

No one have I to share my thoughts or think about tomorrow,
And so I'm only living for today,
So many things I now regret and could have done much better,
But second chances never came my way,
And now I don't know what to do my destiny seems certain,
It seems that I will spend my life alone,
My broken heart will never mend and lies in many pieces,
I'm left to face the future on my own.

I'm burning all my bridges and the flames are growing stronger,
I know that soon they'll lie beyond repair,
So no one then can reach me I'll be left with my misfortune,
And all those thoughts of sadness and despair,
I thought I was the life and soul but I was so mistaken,
The truth is now so very plain to see,
All through the smoke and charred remains which crumble to the water,
That no one ever really cared for me.

Inspiration

Wherever I look I can find inspiration
For it flows through the country like rivers and streams,
The flowers and the rainbows, the seasons and changes
Are part of my growing and part of my dreams.

I see it in skies, in the clouds and the sunlight
From dawn until nightfall it shall never fade,
I see it in stars and the moon that is shining
For it lies all around in the world God has made.

I see it in hills, in the meadows and mountains
In oceans and waves that do roll on the sand,
I see it in valleys, in carpets of heather
And in heavenly pastures that sweep through the land.

I see it in forests, the birds in the branches
The scenes of serenity filled with delights,
I see it in wheat fields, the hedgerows and bushes
My eyes never tire of these magical sights.

Wherever I look I can find inspiration
For it flows through the country like rivers and streams,
For the blossoms of springtime and snowfalls of winter
Are part of my growing and part of my dreams.

Sands of time

As I gaze unto the stars
I know that all is lost,
For I sacrificed my heart to you
And paid a bitter cost,
You were my all and everything
My soul mate and my friend,
As sands of time slip through my hands
I know that it's the end.

I long to hold you in my arms
And feel your warmth again,
But as the evening gently fades
I'm left to bear this pain,
I prayed that we could work things out
That hope did disappear,
As sands of time slip through my hands
I know the end is here.

Now every star that shines so bright
Within the skies above,
Reminds me of the nights we shared
And memories of our love,
I gaze into the universe
The deep and dark unknown,
As sands of time slip through my hands
I find myself alone.

The sunlight on the water

The sound of the waves now caressing the shoreline
The bleak seas of promise awaiting the dawn,
A cool wind is blowing as starlight is fading
The ribbons of moonlight look sad and forlorn.

As they now succumb to the wandering shadows
Which tired and so weary do rest on the sand,
The lights on the quayside now flicker before me
And fall on the water that reaches the land.

The night is now ending and colours emerging
Upon the horizon a halo of gold,
That holy aurora a breathtaking moment
That shines on the ocean a sight to behold.

Now lifting the darkness that lies all around me
As clouds in the distance are touched by the sun,
And flecked there with crimson and burgundy furrows
The morning is breaking a new day's begun.

The warm fires of sunrise a prism before me
Awakens with glory so blinding the light,
Reflects on the surface so calm and inspiring
The seas still and placid are burning so bright.

A picture of beauty the skies are absorbing
The brush strokes of scarlet that sweep all around,
My heart filled with awe at God's wonderful ceiling
For there in its greatness all wishes are found.

I stand there alone as I watch them unfolding
And swirling and moving in motions of fire,
In circles of hope as the flames are now drifting
Through skies that are yielding all that I desire.

I watch as the reds slowly turn into ambers
And then into primrose the seas are aglow,
With sepia silence and hush of the morning
It then turns to blue as the waters do flow.

The sea now a mirror of secrets and passion
That shines like a sapphire as hungry terns cry,
They soar up above and then dive in the shallows
Then moving so quickly they gracefully fly.

As boats in the harbour are rocking so gently
And sway to the flow of the incoming tide,
Their rippled reflections are cast on the water
While sheltered and safe on the current they ride.

The waves softly glisten and sparkle in sunlight
They're rising and falling then rising once more,
And stirring emotions hypnotic and tranquil
So restful the sound as they roll to the shore.

The warm breeze of summer caresses the beaches
And carries my dreams that forever shall be,
The surge of the swell is now masking my footsteps
That I left behind and are lost to the sea.

The afternoon falls to a warm summer evening
The shadows are growing as light starts to fade,
And as the sun sets on the western horizon
Then deeper and deeper it sinks to the shade.

As high up above me the picture keeps changing
From primrose to amber and then into red,
Igniting the clouds in the distance that linger
And lighting the seas and the sand where I tread.

A pathway of scarlet that crosses the ocean
That grows ever fainter until it has gone,
The sun bids farewell and is lost to the water
And colours grow fainter as evening draws on.

The afterglow peaceful the day now is ending
And seeking the twilight the moon starts to rise,
A still solemn hush as it touches the water
And shines on the waves from the heavenly skies.

Who now can I call my friend?

When sunlight filled my every day
Now seems so long ago,
For through the rocks of turmoil then
My humble life did flow,
Those dreams of joy that touched my heart
Have crumbled into dust,
So who now can I call my friend
When no one can I trust?

I never meant to cause no harm
But words were harsh and cruel,
From those I thought did care for me
I must have been a fool,
For now I know their feelings
I shall have to carry on,
To live my life the best I can
Until the pain has gone.

I thought that I was kind to all
And yet how wrong was I,
To think it could've been that way
I never shall know why,
Some thought it right to wound me so
And break my heart in two,
I doubt that I shall see again
Those wondrous skies of blue.

This scarlet rose

This scarlet rose I offer now
'Twas freshly cut this very morn,
And holds my love in petals frail
For on this day my dream was born.

I ask you now that you'll be mine
I long to hear you say I do,
For then my heart would sing for joy
If I could spend my life with you.

For like the skies of dawn it glows
With all its beauty plain to see,
Reminds me now so much of you
A symbol of your purity.

This scarlet rose I offer now
More than a thousand words can say,
My precious gift I can but hope
You'll share my love upon this day.

Seasons keep changing

All through the springtimes the summers and autumns
The winters that come and then melt once again,
The warm of the sunlight the cold and the snowfalls
With winds that keep blowing the bringers of rain,
As time passes by all the seasons keep changing
And flowers will bloom and then fall to the ground,
As years disappear and we slowly grow older
To reflect on the joys and the sorrows we found.

Then rest with the memories we've taken there with us
In different directions our lives may have gone,
But at journey's end we shall come back together
To share in the glory and live then as one,
As time passes by all the seasons keep changing
And we shall grow wiser yet weaker as well,
Some will gain riches and some will grow poorer
And yet everyone will have stories to tell.

For heaven now waits for the souls of believers
And we shall be judged by the lives that we led,
But if we repent all our sins are forgiven
There's no need to fear for the future ahead,
As time passes by all the seasons keep changing
And some will have families and some left alone,
Some will have fortune while others have nothing
And yet in the end we are all flesh and bone.

Buttermilk skies

As buttermilk skies of the sunset are warming
My soul to its grace as it seeps to the land,
As evening approaches the dark clouds do whisper
And speak of the loss of my sweet lover's hand.

As light is now fading and shadows are falling
From trees of the woodland now losing their green,
I walk through the meadow where once she was with me
So many years passed since this way I have been.

Now scattered with leaves that do dwell in their sadness
And silently rest on the cool solemn ground,
For once they had meaning, direction and purpose
But now to the pain of the autumn are bound.

I too share their grief cast away and unwanted
And tossed by the wind as they wrinkle and die,
Then crumble to dust in the earth there unnoticed
And while I live on I shall never know why.

The flower of love was cut short when it bloomed there
And yet it's still living so deep in my heart,
My steps are now lonely yet carry the memory
Of dreams we both shared and yet tore us apart.

As buttermilk skies are now lost to the darkness
I wish for my lover to welcome me here,
For I'll never rest nor will ever find comfort
While passion grows stronger with each passing year.

A new star in heaven

Each life is a blessing that doesn't last long,
For it passes so quickly it all seems so wrong,
Yet hope keeps me going through all of my pain,
That one day I can be with you once again,
For I know that a new star in heaven does shine,
Yet I wish you were with me and you were still mine,
But sadly I know that it can never be,
Yet your spirit remains here forever with me.

My heart lies so broken no future have I,
For I'm lost in a void as I gaze to the sky,
I'll never forget you as long as I live,
I've so much to offer so little to give,
But I know that a new star in heaven burns bright,
Amidst all the darkness a beautiful sight,
Yet I long to hold you and never let go,
If wishes came true it would always be so.

My tears go on falling such hurt I now feel,
My soul has been wounded and never will heal,
The blossoms of love that we shared blown away,
I live with the cold of the winter each day,
Yet I know that a new star in heaven does gleam,
And you are still with me each night that I dream,
Your memory lives on and I won't let it fade,
And I'll keep to the promise of love that I made.

My words

My words unread and went unseen
Until my ink ran dry,
I poured my soul in every line
Yet still my dream did die,
My name is naught to you I know
For so long tried in vain,
Alas the chance for me has passed
No comfort can I gain.

My words could never touch your heart
Yet my intentions sweet,
The journey was so hard and long
That I could not complete,
I tried to find a way to you
And someday you may see,
My loving hand could yield no more
To win your sympathy.

My words they fell like falling stones
Each one caused you to bleed,
And yet I only sought your love
You were my every need,
But as the skies of evening rest
And day comes to an end,
I shan't forget the times we shared
When you were once my friend.

I stand beneath the starlit sky

I stand beneath the starlit sky and look towards the heavens,
And wonder if my wishes will come true,
For up to yet they've floated far away into the darkness,
So many times I've wished to be with you,
Yet shattered dreams the only things that I have ever found here,
No sign of love to shield me from the cold,
Yet still I wait alone with so much hope and expectation,
That soon my life of hurt will turn to gold.

The stars are shining brightly as I gaze into the distance,
Those endless constellations that I see,
Remind me of the love we shared I thought would last forever,
But sadly it was never meant to be,
The moonlight through the restless trees now flickers for a moment,
And falls upon the hard and frozen ground,
I feel the chill of winter and there's no one here to warm me,
Although I've searched no happiness I've found.

I stand beneath the starlit sky that yields to me no answers,
I try to find the secrets that they keep,
And wish that they could speak and guide my way into the future,
But now it seems for me they only weep,
Yet soon the dawn will rise again with dreams of new beginnings,
And stars will fade within the skies above,
Then sun shall warm my empty heart and let me feel the morning,
And maybe light the way towards my love.

I know how it feels to be free as a songbird

I know how it feels to be free as a songbird
To ride on the winds and to soar through the sky,
And over the meadows the rivers and valleys
So far above woodlands and mountains I fly.

I'm skimming the waves as I'm crossing the ocean
New lands and horizons and places to go,
For this is the moment I'm living my wishes
I head where my dreams shall eternally flow.

Over the blossoms and colours of springtime
And rainbows and pictures to keep in my mind,
That shall never fade and I'll always remember
The scenes of such beauty in all that I find.

As skies are aglow such a magical feeling
To fly to the fire of the fast setting sun,
Then watch as it sinks and does fade to the darkness
As daylight is ending my joy has begun.

My home is the woodland

I walk through the bluebells that herald the spring
A magical feeling of joy they do bring,
I'm watching them wave as the fresh breezes blow
As they line the footpath on which I now go,
My home is the woodland a place of my own
Through which I can wander I'm never alone,
With trees that are mighty with branches so strong
A place of such beauty I feel I belong.

I walk in the summer and rest in its shade
And look on its wonder and greatness displayed,
To hear all the songbirds that sing from the bough
And know that I've reached my true destiny now,
My home is the woodland where peace I can find
Its open arms waiting to bring peace of mind,
With sights so familiar a family to share
And where I can live in serenity there.

I walk in the autumn as leaves turn to gold
A palette of colour that yields to the cold,
I watch as they fall from the branches above
And all through the seasons this place I do love,
My home is the woodland I live for each day
Whenever I come here I so long to stay,
And cherish each moment within it I spend
Where hope's everlasting and dreams never end.

The coal miner

Thirty years in darkness
Felt no sun upon his brow,
He toiled to earn a living there
By chipping at the seam,
Within the pit of choking hell
Where no one wished to be,
The freedom for his children
Was his everlasting dream.

He hoped they would not suffer so
Or follow in his steps,
To don the lantern helmet with
The dwellers of the cave,
Or sweat and strain for pittance
Where the beams did creak and bend,
Or witness old friends buried there
Then weeping by their grave.

And yet his sons did have no choice
No jobs within the town,
So many generations passed
The pickaxe down the line,
Nor ever left those terraced rows
With bleak and blackened walls,
Beneath the reaper's winding wheels
That towered above the mine.

Nor never lived to see old age
For breaths grew short and weak,
That dreaded emphysema
Gripped the lungs of every soul,
The dust the hidden killer lurked
So deeply underground,
Within the wretched confines there
Before the seam of coal.

The stars were my blanket

I gazed at the sunset and watched as it faded
From gold into scarlet and then disappear,
Beyond the horizon felt chills of the evening
And saw how the skies then all started to clear,
Revealing the heavens a picture of splendour
I'll always remember that glorious sight,
I stood there in awe for the scene was amazing
The stars were my blanket that beautiful night.

The edge of the woodland where branches cast shadows
Like claws as they reached across November's ground,
So crisp as I stepped on the now frosting landscape
In hush of the night time there wasn't a sound,
As I carried on through the heart of the country
I watched the moon rising and shining so bright,
And felt so at home and was one with its wonder
The stars were my blanket that beautiful night.

The comfort I gained from this greatness surrounding
The scenery glistened as temperatures fell,
I'll never forget all those scenes and their greatness
And I made a promise this story I'd tell,
As I climbed the brow that was urging me onward
I dwelt on the hillside now covered in white,
I wanted to fly to the heavens above me
The stars were my blanket that beautiful night.

A window to your heart

Fate took away the joy we shared
But I cannot forget,
Each day a lasting memory now
That leaves me so upset,
For I will never understand
Just why two lovers part,
I'll search for evermore to find
A window to your heart.

I tried my best to please you yet
It was to no avail,
For everything I did for you
Then only seemed to fail,
And how I wish I knew a way
To go back to the start,
I'll search for evermore to find
A window to your heart.

But now it seems I've lost the chance
For everything has gone,
My dreams were never meant to be
And yet they linger on,
For as the glowing sunset shines
Within that work of art,
I'll search for evermore to find
A window to your heart.

If love should fill my lonely heart

If love should fill my lonely heart
And take this pain away,
I'd make it through the darkness
And the sun would shine this day,
For if the light of morning rise
Should bring some hope to me,
And bless the dawn with joyful song
A better soul I'd be.

If love should fill my lonely heart
And end my sad despair,
And make my days worth living then
A lifetime we could share,
For then I'll see the colours shine
All hidden for so long,
Thus give me chance to make amends
For dreams that all went wrong.

If love should fill my lonely heart
And greet the budding rose,
Its petals soon shall open
As my passion overflows,
Where dew now rests with tears I cry
And shall for evermore,
Until I find the one I love
The one whom I adore.

Beech wood

Beech wood the hush of the morning surrounds me
I'm cloaked from the sunlight by ceiling of green,
Yet flashes appear through the gaps of the branches
Which shine on the land with a heavenly sheen.

At peace I now feel in this shaded cathedral
With pillars imposing and reaching so high,
Silent and still save the whisper of treetops
Which move with the breeze like a soft breathless sigh.

Where autumn leaves fell they remain on the pathway
Now dry and so dusty a carpet of gold,
With root undulating and twisting and turning
The serpents that slide through this woodland of old.

No flowers or fern just the graves of the fallen
Deserted of life on this featureless plain,
Yet I see an archway a window of brightness
And there I can feel the warm sunlight again.

Beech wood the hush of the morning surrounds me
Where beauty shall thrive while this woodland does stand,
There's no finer sight than its hues of October
When I shall return to this magical land.

God is the artist

God is the artist the painter of petals
Which rise in the springtime with blossoms of snow,
The tulips surrounding the daffodils dancing
A palette of colour wherever I go.

The red skies of morning that soar into sapphire
Which fade into amber and sunsets of fire,
To starlight that shines in the heavens above me
My eyes to its majesty shall never tire.

The fresh fallow fields and the green pleasant pastures
Are sprinkled with daisies where buttercups lie,
All meeting and blending and filling the meadows
With sights of the summer that shall never die.

The hillsides of heather a carpet of violet
Enriching the slopes of this wonderful land,
To soft shaded mountains in stone covered pastels
Which rise to the clouds and so gracefully stand.

The hues of the autumn the trees of the forests
Which turn and then change as they melt into gold,
As leaves gently fall and are carried on breezes
Preparing the way for the harsh winter's cold.

If we could live forever

If we could live forever
How much wiser would we be?
Would we have grown accustomed
To the suffering we see?
And would the world be of one mind
United then in love?
Would we be non-believers
Or have faith in God above?

Would people still be starving
On the scorched and barren plain?
And sadly still forgotten
Waiting for the season's rain?
Or would we show compassion
To the poor and those in need?
Or learn to look the other way
To fuel our selfish greed?

Would we have learned to live in peace
Or learned to count the cost?
Of all the maimed and wounded
And of those whose lives were lost?
In life we only get one chance
To do the things we should,
So if your life is long or short
Just try to do some good.

Our love's like an ocean

As blue as the morning a wonderful feeling
The view of the water brings joy to my heart,
So wide and enchanting so deep and enriching
Our love's like an ocean and shall never part.

We're watching the movement the rising and falling
While seagulls on breezes above us now fly,
Yet here as we rest on this undisturbed shoreline
Our love's like an ocean and shall never die.

A picture of peace as serenity glistens
The sunlight so warming now skies are aglow,
Horizons of fire slowly yield to the darkness
Our love's like an ocean and shall always flow.

As moonlight is cast and the wave tops are shining
And ebbing in silver so graceful the sight,
A mirror that moves to the pulse that is beating
Our love's like an ocean this beautiful night.

If you have a voice

If you have a voice
Then use it and sing,
And if you can fly
Then soar on the wing.

If you have talent
Don't hide it away,
Let everyone see it
And live for the day.

If you are a teacher
Teach knowledge to all,
And solve every problem
And answer each call.

If you are an artist
Can paint and can draw,
Then express all your feelings
Your visions and more.

If you can play music
Let everyone hear,
And all that do listen
Shall lend you their ear.

If grass should grow upon my grave

If grass should grow upon my grave
So wild untamed and hide my name,
And moss should clad my resting stone
Beside that lowly church,
Where branches droop and bushes rise
Within a darkened corner there,
Where blackbirds shall not sing for me
Nor find a place to perch.

If no one should lay flowers there
Nor speak some kindly words to me,
And damp my stone with falling tears
Nor stay with me a while,
Then kiss my name before they leave
And vow to come to me again,
With broken heart and saddened glance
Unable there to smile.

If grass should grow upon my grave
And never tended by my love,
Nor pathway worn to seek my plot
Then I would never sleep,
Regrets would fill my empty days
For I should know that no one cares,
I'd feel my life had been for naught
And there my soul would weep.

A cold day in December

And as the snow lay on the ground
A mist did cloak the winter sun,
That tried to shine upon this day
But couldn't warm the chill,
My breaths made clouds within the air
As I did walk across the field,
And made new footprints as I went
Upon that morn so still.

I saw the children playing there
And stood and watched them for a while,
They brought some joy into my heart
When young I did the same,
I then continued on my way
Beneath the trees of hoary frost,
All frozen by the winter's night
That hid their bitter shame.

The cobwebs in the hedgerows gleamed
As droplets hung on silver threads,
From whence a lonely blackbird sang
The sweetest melody,
And yet he seemed as lost as I
As he did wait there all alone,
For only I could hear his voice
That longed for sympathy.

But then I watched him fly away
And wished that I could join him too,
To leave behind the memories
Of the sadness that I felt,
As through December's biting cold
I knew I had to carry on,
To seek another lonely soul
Who in the winter dwelt.

To England's fairest rose

To England's fairest rose I send
My deepest love with all my soul,
I pray my words you'll read with glee
And joy they shall impart,
For as they float on twilight air
Across the skies upon their way,
I hope that they shall reach you soon
And rest within your heart.

I can't exist to be alone
And live without your tender kiss,
The days are long the nights so cold
Just counting every star,
While wishing you were by my side
To keep me warm against the chill,
Although you're many miles away
My dreams can travel far.

If they should fall upon the stones
And fade into the distant past,
Then I shall keep the memories
Of those times that we did share,
Which now seem many moons ago
And yet I wait with bated breath,
For your reply but now I fear
That you no longer care.

No greater love

To see the rising of the dawn
The fire of morning skies,
As day begins with you I know
My heart forever lies,
For now my passion burns so strong
And never shall it end,
No greater love have I for you
My dear eternal friend.

The flowers never smelt so sweet
Before you came to me,
Nor did the birds all sing so loud
With joy from every tree,
I feel so blessed to be alive
And breathe the morning air,
No greater love have I for you
None other could compare.

For now the winter's at an end
And spring has come again,
The colours flow so gracefully
Where once the land so plain,
Now filled with golden daffodils
That ring from every tier,
No greater love have I for you
I long to hold you near.

So take my hand and let us walk
Beneath the blossomed bowers,
For we can see the beauty there
And rest amongst the flowers,
Then listen to the songbirds sing
Their melodies divine,
No greater love have I for you
So proud to call you mine.

The storm

And as the rain and bitter squall
Did drive throughout the winter's night,
With branches bending in the wind
And from my window stared,
I pitied those upon the sea
Whose vessels swamped by icy waves,
I hoped that they should make it home
And all their lives be spared.

And yet the storm would not relent
It gathered in its pace and power,
As I lay warm within my bed
I heard its chilling cry,
So fearsome as it cracked the tree
That fell with such unnerving force,
And echoed through the darkness
Of the bleak and clouded sky.

The ghostly gusts and howling gale
Continued as I tossed and turned,
I heard the sound of driving rain
That blew against the glass,
As fences creaked and strained to stand
For battered hard without remorse,
I lay awake I could not sleep
And prayed the storm would pass.

This song I play

This song I play nobody hears
And captures no elusive ears
My words do flow like falling tears
And sadness fills my heart,
My melody is plain but sweet
And yet my song is incomplete
For you I know it cannot greet
While we remain apart.

This song I play I wrote for you
With feelings that are deep and true
I didn't know what else to do
To show how much I care,
With longing eyes I watch the sky
As all the clouds go drifting by
And wonder how my dreams did die
Such hurt I have to bear.

This song I play with words I sing
Just like a bird upon the wing
And yet no fortune it does bring
For everything has gone,
The flowers wilt and bow their heads
As now my life's been torn to shreds
And as the thought of sorrow spreads
It's hard to carry on.

The song I played now at an end
I'm still alone without a friend
Yet if my wishes I could send
I'd wish for love this day,
But now I know it cannot be
For you shall never hear my plea
Or yield me any sympathy
Now hope has passed away.

The sunshine of morning will brighten my day

Now out of the sorrow a new dawn is rising
And drying my teardrops with colours and love,
The clouds passing by on the winds that are blowing
As hopes for the future are floating above,
While here I do stand with my thoughts that surround me
All winding in circles then carried away,
For darkness is over and I'm moving onward
The sunshine of morning will brighten my day.

The rain has stopped falling and shadows are lifting
And birds are all singing their songs full of cheer,
Their melodies float through the air full of wonder
And yielding such pleasure as skies start to clear,
The past lays behind me regrets now forgotten
And joy fills my heart and I know it will stay,
The blossoms of springtime will bloom on forever
The sunshine of morning will brighten my day.

Please let me see flowers descending from heaven
And if I should catch one I'll give it to you,
To show how I care for you mean the world to me
It's like every wish and my dreams have come true,
These romantic pictures with palettes of pleasure
So touching my soul with the finest display,
While green is the meadow and fresh are the daisies
The sunshine of morning will brighten my day.

Silent prayer

I need someone to help me now
The way ahead unclear,
My best days are behind me
And the future holds such fear,
I watch my dreams as they go past
And no one seems to care,
While carried on the springtime breeze
My wishful,
Silent, prayer.

If only I knew what to do
Yet no one answers me,
I'd find the road to happiness
A better place to be,
I'm trapped within these empty walls
With nothing but despair,
While carried on the summer breeze
My wishful,
Silent, prayer.

And yet my heart still waits for love
Abandoned to my fate,
A fruitless quest now all is lost
For life shall never wait,
The years go by so quickly
And each one so hard to bear,
While carried on the autumn breeze
My wishful,
Silent, prayer.

I feel the chill of loneliness
As snow begins to fall,
Upon the frozen land and sea
Still no one hears my call,
My voice grows ever weaker now
My hopes are fading there,
While carried on the winter breeze
My wishful,
Silent, prayer.

The call of the cuckoo

The call of the cuckoo that floats through the woodland
Does herald the springtime so sweet is the sound,
While soft-dappled sunlight does shine through the branches
And so gently falls on the fresh morning ground.

That's stained by the teardrops from showers of April
Where leaves of the autumn steadfastly remain,
So still they now rest lying scattered before me
And float in the puddles from yesterday's rain.

I speak of the dawning the colours of rainbows
The daffodils dancing as joy fills the air,
With strains sailing by on the breeze that is blowing
My words can't express all these visions I share.

The oceans of bluebells like waves of emotions
That spread to my heart as they roll to the shore,
As they bow their heads at the edge of the pathway
I feel I'm so lucky to see them once more.

So sing on sweet cuckoo with song so enchanting
Your voice speaks unto me like couplets of gold,
And rings through the treetops and sails to the heavens
As soft as the blossoms of spring that unfold.

The lark

The lark is now rising from out of the heath land
Ascending above to the beautiful sky,
And heads to the clouds and the blue of the morning
Whilst singing for joy through the air he does fly.

As higher and higher he's leading me further
Way over the scrub through the heather and gorse,
He tells of his presence displaying his glory
Wherever he guides I will follow his course.

As now he does soar in the gold of the sunlight
That's draping his wings which are beating so fast,
He sails over meadows where cattle are grazing
And into the heart of the woodland so vast.

His voice carries over the hills in the distance
Which shine now in green yet his notes remain clear,
They hang on the breeze that caresses the country
And still he sings on for my welcoming ear.

Old Barnaby's farm

Old Barnaby's farm is a part of the landscape
Adorned by the ivy that climbs the front wall,
Yet there at the edge of the road where it stands now
The clouds have all gathered and rain starts to fall,
The hand-painted signs on the boards and the placards
In hedgerows and entrance of worn pitted track,
Where stones and the straw and the puddles now lie there
Which slowly do grow in each crevice and crack.

As there in a field both the combine and tractor
Stand idle and silent for their jobs are done,
The weeks have gone by since the harvest and ploughing
So now they can rest for the winter's begun,
While stacked up and baled is the food for the livestock
And wrapped within plastic to keep it all dry,
With crops that are bagged and are stored in the barns there
Yet still the rain pours from the grey leaden sky.

No rest for the farmer and family who struggle
To strive and to strain in their hard lives of toil,
Still rising at dawn working late through the evening
For day after day they are slaves to the soil,
Just scraping a living as rents keep on rising
So tough to survive yet they still carry on,
While knowing they have little hope for the future
Their home and their livelihoods soon shall be gone.

A Christmas poem

Now here in the frosts and the chill of December
I stare from my window and look to the sky,
And see all the stars that are shining so brightly
Then think of the year that has almost gone by,
Of the chances I wasted and things I did badly
How I was a victim of life's bitter sting,
And as I gaze out on the cold-barren landscape
I think of the future and what it shall bring.

As there in the corner the candle burns lower
It flickers so softly then slowly does fade,
Until it is lost and the light is extinguished
With all dreams of love and the promise I made,
The street is so quiet and nobody is passing
So hushed is the night only silence I hear,
As I stay awake while the others are sleeping
No thoughts of glad tidings or festive good cheer.

For where are the angels with heavenly voices?
I wish they would come and then sing unto me,
To offer some comfort and light in the darkness
I can only hope that one day it shall be,
Yet soon in the frosts and the chill of December
The sun will appear on this cold Christmas morn,
And rise in the sky then in all of its glory
To shine on the day that my Saviour was born.

As mist does roll across the field

As mist does roll across the field
To cloak the lowly chestnut tree,
With silken gown while winter's chill
Now grips the frozen air,
And there the fallen amber leaves
Lay scattered where the wind did toss,
And rest upon the dampened grass
Beneath the branches bare.

Though stained with coat of mossy green
And lichen clinging to its trunk,
So broad and yet so frail to see
Bereft of life does stand,
No more the blackbird finds a perch
Or sings within its leafy boughs,
Forlornly now it waits for spring
When colours fill the land.

And as the evening does descend
Upon the lowly chestnut tree,
A silhouette against the sky
As nature now does sleep,
A breathless hush of sorrow mourns
The passing of the summer gone,
In stillness as the day goes by
The clouds now gently weep.

Apple blossom

Come soon apple blossom and shine like the snowflakes
In sunlight before me and herald the spring,
What joy you shall give to this heavenly morning
And thus warm my heart with the love that you bring.

I long to see buds on the twigs and the branches
To tell me that soon all the flowers will show,
For then I'll find solace in colours and pictures
All framed then in gold as the daffodils grow.

Please let me see tulips in all of their glory
That wave in the breeze for so pleasant their sight,
They capture my dreams with their hope for the future
So wake from your slumber and yield me delight.

Come soon apple blossom for you are the reason
I long for the springtime when you shall appear,
There's no better sight than to witness your beauty
I'll dream of the moment when you shall be here.

A part of me died with you

I still remember heartache
Like I'd never felt before,
With every hour that passes by
I miss you more and more,
It feels like only yesterday
I watched the stars so bright,
And a part of me died with you
On that cold and lonely night.

Now things can never be the same
A void so deep and wide,
An empty space that can't be filled
The loss I bear inside,
Still haunts me like the bitter wind
That chills me with its spite,
For a part of me died with you
On that cold and lonely night.

How cruel to me the hand of fate
That took my love away,
And left me here to weep alone
Where age and years decay,
Your image shall not weary though
A swan cut down in flight,
And a part of me died with you
On that cold and lonely night.

As from the chalky cliffs so sheer

As from the chalky cliffs so sheer
Where wind does cut across the waves,
Which break upon the shingle shore
With crowns of thudding surge,
No respite from the brewing storm
That inches closer to the land,
With clouds descending like a mist
As sea and sky now merge.

And soon the Needles' jagged rocks
Are swallowed by that gaping jaw,
But still the lowly lamp does shine
Across the murky plain,
And then the ghostly horn blows loud
That echoes through the silent air,
Resounding in the leaden mass
That carries forth the rain.

It sweeps across the verdant land
Adorning it with silken gown,
And with it brings an icy claw
That grips the grassy field,
And clings upon the climbing slopes
Then cloaks the crops the hedge and corn,
No longer now the way be seen
Until the storm shall yield.

Why I may kiss this scarlet rose

I stand and watch her from afar
With warm adoring glance,
And long the day our eyes shall meet
But know there's little chance,
For I'm so lowly and so poor
Unworthy of her trust,
And though I wish to be with her
My dream shall turn to dust.

Her beauty like no other so
I shan't forget her face,
Nor gentle words I hear her speak
And spoken with such grace,
Her kindly soul and tender smile
Could melt a thousand hearts,
And yet my hope to be with her
Has gone before it starts.

A single rose within my hand
That I can never give,
And yet I'll bear this deep regret
As long as I shall live,
For I will never come to terms
Or ever get to grips,
Why I may kiss this scarlet rose
But never kiss her lips.

Your hand of loving kindness

Your hand of loving kindness
Brought some comfort unto me,
It dried those lonely tears I cried
And helped me then to see,
Through silence of that darkened room
You opened up my door,
To yield a light into my life
And let me smile once more.

Your hand of loving kindness brought
A warm and tender touch,
That through the cold of winter nights
I'd always missed so much,
For when the dawn did rise again
And morn lit by the sun,
The feeling that I truly felt
My life had just begun.

Your hand of loving kindness brought
A gift I can't repay,
You filled my heart with deepest joy
That's with me every day,
And while you are beside me here
I know I shall walk tall,
For I will be with you my friend
Who I love most of all.

So still was morning's restful air

So still was morning's restful air
A dust of frost had coated trees,
And frozen hard the puddles lay
Upon the stony ground,
And there betwixt the fence and field
I stood and watched the misty hills,
And listened to the sparrows sing
So sweet their songs did sound.

Amongst the twigs of powdered thorn
That bore the scars of winter's bite,
Where cobwebs hung and threads adorned
The crofter's rustic hedge,
That made a home for all the birds
Who rested in the thicket dense,
And there they hopped along until
They found a kindly ledge.

As I walked on I gazed across
The furrowed earth now ploughed and turned,
That looked so bare yet for the crows
Who feasted on the seed,
And as the skies began to clear
And sunlight shone upon the ground,
I wandered down that narrow track
So overgrown with weed.

But soon I knew that spring would come
To fill the land with deepest green,
And yet that hope seemed far away
For I felt so forlorn,
I lifted up the rusting latch
And as I pushed the wooden gate,
I left behind those scenes amidst
That cold and frosty morn.

If love could fly upon the wing

If love could fly upon the wing
Across the winter sky,
And find a way into my heart
And not keep passing by,
For morning brings no fortune
And to loneliness I'm bound,
As a feather floats so softly
And it falls upon the ground.

And there it shall remain amongst
The fragments of the leaves,
That fell throughout those autumn days
And yet nobody grieves,
The air is still no wind shall blow
And frosted chills remain,
Amongst the boughs no bird shall sing
A comforting refrain.

No flowers to bring colour
To this stark and barren land,
For life has now deserted it
And trees forlornly stand,
Like stone they're gripped and cannot free
From ice the night had cast,
Until the sun shall rise again
And wintertime has passed.

If love could fly upon the wing
Across the winter sky,
And bring some warmth into my life
And melt these frosts that lie,
Then I should be a gladder soul
And see the way ahead,
But yet for now it cannot be
And hopes are all but dead.

Please paint me a beautiful picture

Please paint me a beautiful picture of springtime
When snowdrops and tulips and daffodils shine,
With pink cherry blossoms and hawthorn in flower
All mixed in a palette where colours entwine.

Please paint me a beautiful picture of summer
With emerald meadows where buttercups grow,
And hills that rejoice to the sound of the season
With cascading sunlight and rivers that flow.

Please paint me a beautiful picture of autumn
When trees in the forest are burning in gold,
As leaves gently float and then fall like a whisper
Then rest on the ground as the season grows cold.

Please paint me a beautiful picture of winter
With frost of the morning and chill mist that lies,
On snow laden plains where the scenery glistens
And capture the dawn with its apricot skies.

You are the reason

You are the reason why I carry on through all this heartache,
Not knowing if my pain will ever end,
You stood beside me when I thought I'd nothing left to live for,
And when I'd no one else you were my friend,
But even you deserted me and left me then with nothing,
I hadn't got a penny to my name,
I know I wasn't worthy and that I could never please you,
But I shall always love you just the same.

I feel I need you more and more with every day that passes,
Without you I am nothing but a shell,
I try my best and yet I seem to make so little difference,
I only wished that things would turn out well,
But no one wants to know me as I flounder on the wayside,
Each friend I had has left and gone away,
So helpless and afraid I walk alone into the sunset,
And close another chapter of a day.

I watch the stars shine brightly in the sky that holds no comfort,
The silence of the darkness hurts me so,
I listen for your footsteps but I know I'll never hear them,
I'll have to bear another night of woe,
I wait for dawn to rise again and offer new beginnings,
And look for morning skies to shine once more,
Then hope and pray that you shall come so we can be together,
To live again those times we shared before.

You are the reason why my days are now so cold and empty,
And why my dreams were never meant to be,
With no one to support me I'm so lost without direction,
Just like a boat that's drifting out to sea,
I'll never make it back to shore while trapped in stormy weather,
The waves will keep on crashing on the sand,
And winds shall blow me far away so I can never find you,
Or ever get to reach your loving hand.

Wind chime

As sun rose in the early dawn
And skies were lit with gold,
I saw the clouds go passing by
And watched my dreams unfold,
For as the morning breeze did blow
It softly spoke to me,
The wind chime played the sweetest song
A graceful melody.

I rested in the leafy shade
While there I thought of you,
I closed my eyes and there I wished
That you were with me too,
And as the noontime breeze did blow
Across the summer sky,
The wind chime played the sweetest song
That through the air did fly.

As shadows started falling
On the dark deserted ground,
I heard a gentle ringing then
So beautiful the sound,
For as the evening breeze did blow
And glowing sun did set,
The wind chime played the sweetest song
I never shall forget.

I watched the fading afterglow
That slowly slipped away,
Beneath the dark horizon far
To close another day,
And as the twilight breeze did blow
And stars did shine above,
The wind chime played the sweetest song
The sweetest song of love.

From whence that little robin came

From whence that little robin came
Who cast his caring eyes on me,
As he did fly upon the wing
To save me from my woe,
A spirit in a scarlet guise
Who sings with cheer from lofty bough,
A song that is so pure and sweet
Which sounds where'er I go.

And I shall hear that glad refrain
Until my days are at an end,
He found a place within my heart
'Twas such a noble deed,
He came to me as if the wind
That blew across the winter skies,
Until he found a lonely soul
Who was in deepest need.

All through the cold and darkest days
When love had so deserted me,
And I was lost nowhere to go
He acted as my guide,
He saw I never went astray
And lifted me from off the ground,
Where I had lain a broken wretch
Without an ounce of pride.

From whence that little robin came
To rescue me from my despair,
An angel sent from heaven above
Who sings with dulcet tone,
And like a shadow follows me
From dawn till dusk and now I know,
That I shall always have a friend
And never be alone.

While this ocean flows

As I stand upon this rugged cliff
And gaze across the sea,
I feel the winds that blow so strong
Are calling out to me,
Your name does sail above the waves
And through the longing air,
I know that while this ocean flows
That I shall find you there.

I watch the breakers crashing then
Upon the shingle shore,
And hope one day they'll carry you
To be with me once more,
For all the times I've dreamed of you
Yet still we live apart,
I know that while this ocean flows
You'll rest within my heart.

Above the shearing gulls now soar
Into the fading skies,
The evening's silence broken by
Their harsh and piercing cries,
While still I wait with open arms
Which long to hold again,
I know that while this ocean flows
My love shall not refrain.

I pray the winds shall never die
For in them I do trust,
That they shall bring you closer now
With every wishful gust,
I stand upon this rugged cliff
And gaze across the sea,
I know that while this ocean flows
That day will surely be.

A wonderful friend

Now winter has melted to springtime
And the flowers bring colours so bright,
Each morning I wake with the songbirds
Embracing my heart with delight,
I feel that a dream I am living
I pray that it will never end,
And I am so glad that I found you
For you are such a wonderful friend.

My heart once forlorn and so empty
Now flutters like butterfly wings,
It's filled with the love that you give me
And all of the joy that it brings,
Together we'll gaze at the sunrise
Then watch as the colours do blend,
And I know that I never will leave you
For you are such a wonderful friend.

The warm breeze so gentle does carry
The perfume of blossom so sweet,
That floats through the air of the morning
So making this moment complete,
I look to the clouds that are passing
My wishes of love they do send,
And I know they shall find their way to you
For you are such a wonderful friend.

Our lives are entangled

These circles lead nowhere
Our wires always cross,
In different directions
While sharing our loss,
To fly like a songbird
Or sink like a stone,
Our lives are entangled
Confused and alone.

No shoulder to cry on
No hand we can trust,
To offer us comfort
As dreams turn to dust,
Then carried on breezes
To places unknown,
As no one can save them
We both weep alone.

Now time is against us
So many days passed,
With hopes for the future
We knew couldn't last,
While memories keep fading
Our sorrow has grown,
Whilst feeling the sadness
We bear all alone.

And so we continue
Until our lives end,
We might find each other
Or gain a new friend,
Now as the dawn rises
No words can atone,
For all of our sorrows
We face all alone.

For every day without a smile

I wished that things were better
But the grey clouds up above,
Now spell the end to happiness
And any chance of love,
I can't be glad while I'm alone
And feeling so upset,
For every day without a smile
A day I must forget.

As raindrops now are falling
Making puddles on the floor,
I walk along these empty streets
But can't go on no more,
My sadness now shall never leave
While tears run from my eyes,
For every day without a smile
A day that someone cries.

My life flows down the gutter
And is heading to the drain,
With the fallen leaves of autumn
Which are remnants of my pain,
That never seems to leave me
So that burden I must bear,
For every day without a smile
A day of deep despair.

I hope that soon the sun will shine
To light the darkened gloom,
Then birds will sing within the boughs
And spring again shall bloom,
But no one does show pity to
This lonely soul in need,
For every day without a smile
A day my heart shall bleed.

As soft as a snowflake

Come winter relent let me hold her once more,
Let me feel all the joy that I had felt before,
Through the cold of December I wait here so long,
While these days are so empty I try to be strong,
As soft as a snowflake that melts in my hand,
Or settles upon all this still frozen land,
I pray that the tomorrow will spare me of pain,
And her warm kiss shall greet me again.

Yet I'll never lose hope all the time she is gone,
Through the grey skies that linger I shall carry on,
I don't want to wake up and face a new day,
While these thoughts do remain yet she's so far away,
As soft as a snowflake that melts in my hand,
Or settles upon all this still frozen land,
My tears gently fall for the sorrow I feel,
How I wish that my dreams could be real.

The chill wind is blowing no sign of her yet,
As another day ends and I'm feeling upset,
For the nights are the longest and so hard to bear,
And when I close my eyes I shall picture her there,
As soft as a snowflake that melts in my hand,
Or settles upon all this still frozen land,
I long for the springtime to bring me good cheer,
And the fresh wind to carry her here.

Now darkness has fallen but I'll never rest,
As I know that with fortune I've never been blessed,
While my sadness a shadow wherever I go,
And it seems never-ending my days filled with woe,
As soft as a snowflake that melts in my hand,
Or settles upon all this still frozen land,
I wish that the clouds now would break up above
And the stars guide the way to my love.

Hurt me most of all

Lost are the days of sunshine now
The skies are always grey,
For slowly we did drift apart
Then love did fade away,
There's nothing I could say or do
When words like stones did fall,
For spoken without feeling then
They hurt me most of all.

Now gone the times of laughter
And the joy that we did share,
My life is filled with deep regret
For you no longer care,
My dreams have sailed into the night
With words I can recall,
For when you said "it's over now"
It hurt me most of all.

Now I shall walk alone once more
For everything has gone,
And try my hardest to forget
But memories linger on,
I must look to the future
As the past now does appal,
And leave behind that time I knew
That hurt me most of all.

For every heart that's found true love

What is to become of me?
I'm trapped within these walls,
The sunlight slowly fades away
As now the darkness falls,
This day could never bring me joy
As sorrow's all I've known,
For every heart that's found true love
Another beats alone.

The silent night's so lonely
As the passing hours go by,
I look unto the stars above
Within the winter's sky,
My tears shall fall for evermore
I'll never smile again,
For every heart that's found true love
Another's filled with pain.

The moonlight shines so brightly now
It seems my only friend,
And tries to bring me comfort
But my hurt shall never end,
As frost now forms with deep intent
And yields a bitter chill,
For every heart that's found true love
Another never will.

Each night I pray unto the stars

Each night I pray unto the stars
My prayers though go unheard,
For lost within the darkness there
My every wishful word,
For times of joy deserted me
And friends I have not one,
I watched the years go passing by
And wonder where they've gone.

As I reflect on shattered dreams
I never did fulfil,
I tried my best to live them all
But know I never will,
For riches I did strive to earn
But ended up with none,
I think of all the things I had
And wonder where they've gone.

If someone should remember me
And proudly say my name,
Then maybe life's not been for naught
And one so filled with shame,
I'll leave behind my written words
To cast your gaze upon,
Please promise me to live each day
For soon they shall be gone.

In the shade of the green wood

In the shade of the green wood
The holly does grow,
While in soft rays of sunlight
The wild roses glow,
And I smell their sweet perfume
That gently floats by,
Past the trees strong and mighty
Which reach to the sky,
The pathway of gold
Autumn leaves still remain,
As I walk through the green wood again.

In the shade of the green wood
This bright sunny morn,
That's so cool in the shadows
A new day is born,
All the birds in the treetops
Are singing for me,
Sweet songs of the summertime
Which fill me with glee,
And I know from its treasures
I never shall part,
For the green wood does live in my heart.

In the shade of the green wood
A soft gentle breeze,
Now caresses the branches
And whispers through trees,
It's a sound reassuring
That carries me to,
All the scenes that exist
And each marvellous view,
For it's here that my spirit
Shall forever stay,
And the green wood is guiding my way.

Live out the rest of my days

I long to see flowers and blossoms of spring
And sing of their pleasure and joy that they bring,
The sights of the morning the pictures so sweet
Which carry me forth to new places to greet,
I'll roam through the meadows
With wondrous displays,
And live out the rest of my days.

I long to find beauty in all that I see
And know in my heart it's where I want to be,
When summer surrounds me with views to inspire
For there I'll discover all that I desire,
I'll roam through the country
When sunset's ablaze,
And live out the rest of my days.

I long to see forests of scarlet and gold
Which fade to the autumn as colours unfold,
When leaves gently float on the breeze as they fall
And birds in the branches shall gracefully call,
I'll roam through the woodlands
Where happiness stays,
And live out the rest of my days.

I long to climb mountains to look at the view
Of the snow-covered ranges of winter it's true,
Each breath that I take of that heavenly air
Shall herald their glory and welcome me there,
I'll roam through the valleys
And learn of their ways,
And live out the rest of my days.

A crofter's tale

I live in the highlands with valleys and mountains
And work on the soil where I spend all my days,
For this is my home I was born and was raised in
A crofter my father I learned from his ways,
I followed his footsteps like he had before me
Passed down generations from father to son,
I gathered the wisdom from all of my elders
And I learnt there was always a job to be done.

I toiled in the morning and toiled through the evening
I sowed and I planted and turned every sod,
When I was too tired to go on any longer
I sank to my knees and I prayed to my God,
To bring a good harvest to earn me a living
To clothe and to feed me so I could survive,
I prayed for my elderly mother and father
Until they were sadly no longer alive.

I married a lass she was sweet and so pretty
We raised a young family I taught them my trade,
My boys grew up quickly and as I grew older
I left them the reins and I lived in their shade,
And now as I look on the valleys and mountains
With my love beside me our lives almost done,
Our children have learnt all the ways of a crofter
And carry the torch now from father to son.

A thousand wishes

If I made a thousand wishes now for us to be together,
I know each one of them would not come true,
For since the day we broke apart I've fought for a solution,
And now there's nothing more that I can do,
For lonely hearts that need someone but cannot find an answer,
Shall have to go on beating all alone,
But still I can't forget the times we shared with such affection,
Till all my dreams of love sank like a stone.

My words can never say how much I'm missing you each day now,
I can't express the void that lies within,
The flame of passion now no longer shines and lost forever,
It's clear to me that losers never win,
And things are never going to be the same again without you,
The chasm that's between us is so deep,
I cannot bridge that sorrow for I always end up falling,
And yet I am still with you when I sleep.

If I made a thousand wishes now for love again to find me,
I still believe that it would pass me by,
For everything I need the most just never seems to happen,
And yet my only hope so I must try,
The dreams I had just blew away like leaves within the autumn,
And never seemed to settle anywhere,
If only one could find you now and melt the space between us,
And let you know that I still really care.

Some days

Some days I spend just gazing at the clouds as they are passing,
Which carry dreams that slowly disappear,
All through my life I've always been the one who's had to suffer,
The pattern of my life remains unclear,
I watch the sunlight falling as it fades into the evening,
Then as the stars above begin to shine,
I draw my curtains so to close another wasted chapter,
And then I pray that love shall soon be mine.

I'll never give up hoping while I breathe I still may find it,
And so I'll go on looking to the sky,
For I believe that lonely hearts were meant to be together,
And dreams won't always keep on passing by,
There are some days when I'm all alone and cannot face the future,
And some days when I really need a friend,
Some days I just don't want to live a single minute longer,
And some days I wished my loneliness would end.

I can't get over losing everything I ever wanted,
The wind can't blow the bitterness away,
And so I'm always left to cope with no one I can turn to,
And now it seems my heartache's here to stay,
I know that I've done all I can and yet I still got nowhere,
And so I face this harsh reality,
That I may never find the one for whom I have been longing,
So many years for love to come to me.

I know with every day that goes my chance is getting smaller,
I wish that youth and time were on my side,
But as the years now weary and I shan't grow any younger,
Those ravages I can no longer hide,
There are some days filled with sunshine that do warm the cold of winter,
Yet some days seem to be so full of rain,
And some days when I feel that love shall find a way unto me,
But some days I feel I'll never love again.

An acorn lies within the snow

Beneath this oak with branches strong
Where birds once filled each morn with song,
Through winter spring and summer fall
Their graceful tunes did softly call,
We saw the buds and then the leaves
But now for us December grieves,
For love that died so long ago
An acorn lies within the snow.

Through summer in its restful shade
So many vows and promise made,
That we would stay forever one
But now all hope of joy has gone,
With passing days when skies were blue
When flowers bloomed for me and you,
But as the icy wind does blow
An acorn lies within the snow.

When autumn came this oak stood bare
No longer did we linger there,
The circle of our love complete
That turned so sour no longer sweet,
No feeling left within each heart
We sadly drifted far apart,
Now all alone as tears do flow
An acorn lies within the snow.

Arise Sunday morning

Arise Sunday morning as sunlight's appearing
And shines on the meadow through silhouette trees,
The skies are aglow with a palette of colour
As whispers of cloud ride the cool gentle breeze,
Sing on for me songbirds your tunes are like silver
And welcome the new day with sweetness and love,
I open my window and breathe in the beauty
That carries me forth to the heavens above.

Look out on the country as shadows are fading
The hills in the distance and fields are of gold,
So true to my heart always yielding such pleasure
And capture the moment with sights to behold,
As butterflies sail through the gardens of flowers
A picture of summer with infinite grace,
That's flowing before me in streams so refreshing
So kind to my fingers and cool to my face.

Arise Sunday morning the church bells are ringing
And calling to worship they peal through the land,
I follow their way and rejoice with their sounding
For I have been blessed by my God's loving hand,
The swifts and the swallows are soaring up skywards
And into the blue of the vast atmosphere,
Celestial joy as the day is unfolding
With wonders that speak of this morning so clear.

I gaze at the sky

I gaze at the sky as I wake in the morning
And look from my window upon the new day,
The trees whisper softly the summer breeze gentle
As if to embrace me and show me the way.

I walk in the garden and smell the sweet flowers
The lilac so pretty the butterflies share,
And yielding such joy as they flutter about me
Their angelic wings in the silence of prayer.

While melodies float through the boughs up above me
From oak trees and ash sing the birds of the morn,
Their joyful refrains fill the air of the season
As if they rejoice for the new day that's born.

There's love all around me no need to look further
As nature now offers me all I desire,
For I have been blessed by these heavenly riches
Of songs so endearing and sights to inspire.

What hand now can marry my heart to my senses?
Such beauty befalls in the sights that I see,
That's leading me on through the arbour of roses
And knowing there's nowhere that I'd rather be.

For this is my home I shall rest in the shadows
So warm in the sunlight the shade is my friend,
I'm watching the day as it passes by slowly
And wishing it never would come to an end.

The last kiss I shall ever give

You gripped my heart with passion's fire
You filled my soul with true desire,
The first time that our eyes did meet
I felt my life was so complete,
I kissed your lips a sad farewell
But always in my mind you dwell,
For all the years I've left to live
The last kiss I shall ever give.

You made the light within me shine
You swore you'd be forever mine,
Back then we both did not foresee
How dreams were never meant to be,
I kissed your lips and you did leave
And now for you each day I grieve,
For all the years I've left to live
The last kiss I shall ever give.

You told me you would not return
You left me so but still I yearn,
To share again the life we led
But hopes of that are lying dead,
I kissed your lips my tears did flow
I never wanted you to go,
For all the years I've left to live
The last kiss I shall ever give.

Song thrush

The song thrush is singing sweet sounds of the morning
While perched on the bough of an old twisted tree,
Whose leaves have now withered and fall from its branches
And blow on the winds for soon winter shall be.

So hark to the call of her beautiful music
As sunlight does flicker through woodland surround,
And shines down before me and settles so gently
A blanket of amber now covers the ground.

Sing on for the autumn and glow of its colours
Your chorus of pleasure is filling my heart,
Like water that flows over stones in the valley
Each note is from heaven such grace you impart.

Please follow me song thrush I long for your comfort
Your voice reassuring, so fly on the wing,
I'll head on my way looking over my shoulder
While waiting for you and the joy you shall bring.

Your brazen heart shall never feel

Your brazen heart shall never feel
The hurt that burns inside me now,
Your words so cruel that cut me down
And left me there to bleed,
The torment of your wicked curse
That brought so many restless nights,
Will live with me for evermore
I never shall be freed.

For sadness now engulfs my world
And wrestles me from dusk till dawn,
I toss and turn I cannot sleep
My pillow damp with tears,
I shed for me and not for you
As there within my sorrow lies,
A shadow of the man I was
Who bears so many fears.

I so regret that fateful morn
Our paths did cross along that road,
I wished that I had carried on
And looked the other way,
For then I was so full of joy
But now I'll never smile again,
Until my mind can be erased
The pain shall always stay.

The wisdom of my youth

A child but I who had a dream
Above the hills and flowing stream,
A rainbow shone with colours bright
Against the clouds as black as night,
And where the arch did touch the ground
I hoped that treasure could be found,
I knew the way I knew the truth
It was the wisdom of my youth.

A child but I so weak not strong
The way was hard and very long,
I stumbled many times and fell
The rocky way as tough as hell,
Yet I got up and carried on
Until I found my fortune gone,
Too slow was I the price I paid
I watched the rainbow slowly fade.

A child but I could dream no more
As then the rain began to pour,
And I was lost nowhere to go
As icy winds did strongly blow,
I simply couldn't find my way
Beneath the skies of leaden grey,
I cried for help but no one heard
For gusts did smother every word.

A child but I who lay alone
And carved my name upon a stone,
Then placed it down beside my head
For knowing soon I would be dead,
And that no soul would find me here
And so I wept a lonely tear,
For I was lost without a friend
And that is where my life did end.

Upon the shaded riverbank

Upon the shaded riverbank
Where willows weep on water's edge,
And drape the sympathetic shore
Reluctant though to yield,
Some comfort while I sit and rest
And gaze upon the surface calm,
Reflecting on my bitter past
For now my fate is sealed.

I listen as the birds do sing
Upon the boughs that gently move,
Within the breeze that softly calls
Her sweet name unto me,
A breath so warm with tender touch
That melts the chill of lonely days,
But yet I know she'll not return
That day shall never be.

Upon the shaded riverbank
My only thoughts to be with her,
And I must bear the heartache now
Until I find relief,
The graceful swan who swims alone
In sadness now does bow her head,
As she does search in vain for love
I share her sense of grief.

A view from the park bench

Upon this old familiar bench
From which I've spent a time or two,
Just gazing at the sky above
And watching chestnut trees,
Which change throughout the seasons
Now their copper leaves do fall,
Which gather on this stony path
And tossed upon the breeze.

 For scattered far across the field
And through the air with random flee,
From every bough it seems to pluck
Until each one is bare,
Now soon the winter shall be here
With icy chills the frosts and snow,
When I'll not stop but carry on
And find no comfort there.

Upon this bench so old and worn
That's scrawled and etched on every slat,
And smeared with food from yesterday
Yet still to me so kind,
For here within my solitude
Away from all the toil and spite,
I'll take my time to look around
While others seem so blind.

Within this park the children play
Upon the swings the slide and frame,
And run around upon the grass
Just like I used to do,
But now so many years have passed
And older but no wiser I,
I wished I had my youth again
Reliving days I knew.

Upon this bench I sit and wait
And as the people pass me by,
Some of them do speak to me
Some look the other way,
Yet here the grass shall always grow
Beneath my tired and aching feet,
A friendly place I call my own
Where often I do stay.

I long for daffodils of spring
And watch them all come into flower,
When blossom blooms upon the bough
Such beauty there to see,
Then listen to the birds that sing
As if for me their sweet refrains,
And I alone shall hear them all
Each golden melody.

Upon this bench on which I rest
I think how many things have changed,
Yet here it almost seems the same
As times of long ago,
St. Mary's there still proudly stands
And in the morning sun does shine,
As ages passed it's witnessed all
And seen the village grow.

Now as I make my way back home
And walk along this stony path,
Adorned by scattered copper leaves
That through the autumn fell,
I know I shall return again
To lose myself within the view,
And watch the seasons changing
From the bench where I shall dwell.

Shannon's Mill

'Twas on that solemn August eve
When skies did glow like setting sun,
A time that no one shall forget
That tore the town apart,
The ruins smouldered through the morn
And smoke engulfed the locals who,
Surveyed the scene with disbelief
And sadness filled each heart.
The soul was gone
The spirit lost
We all had paid a dreadful cost.

The building stood yet but a shell
The landscape now forever changed,
For once so proud a remnant of
Those days of long ago,
The workers who had stitched the seam
And cut the cloth for many years,
Could not believe it all was gone
So many tears did flow.
They looked towards
The smoky sky
And there they stood all asking why?

The site now cleared there's nothing left
An empty void which can't be filled,
Another jewel been taken by
That undeserving hand,
For all those lives it helped to forge
Their memories now but ash and dust,
And blown upon the weeping wind
Across the barren land.
The stars did shine
The night was still
As flames engulfed old Shannon's Mill.

I kick the can

Frustration born of bitter hate
Of all the things that dragged me to,
The gutter where a can does lie
I kick along the road,
Not knowing where I'm heading now
I carry on upon my way,
Reflecting on those years gone by
And just what might have been.

I kick the can for all those tears
I wept when I was growing up,
For lovers lost the pain I bear
Shall haunt me to the grave,
The friends I had now scattered wide
Across the land I know not where,
I hope they all found happiness
Away from this old town.

I kick the can for all the times
I spent within those factory walls,
Each day I toiled for no reward
Upon that rusting press,
Just waiting for that bell to sound
The sweetest music to my ears,
I thought I was deserving of
A better life than that.

I kick the can for all the dreams
The branch of which did never bear,
The frost did kill the blossom long
Before the fruit did grow,
And so I'm left with nothing now
I wish I weren't so bitter but,
Alas now it shall never be
Again, I kick the can.

The son of a fisherman

Upon the bank a fisherman
Now looks across the river still,
While seated on his folding stool
With trusted rod in hand,
That's been with him since childhood days
A father's gift so long ago,
He treasures it just like a son
A memory of his life.

In days of old they shared such joy
Upon this spot they called their own,
Beside the bridge and 'neath the bough
That oak still firmly stands,
He learned the skills and learned the ways
The baits to use and where to cast,
The knowledge that has stayed with him
He never will forget.

For here within this leafy shade
A boy was raised to be a man,
Who grew to love the countryside
And found a sense of peace,
It's now the only life he knows
And every day he lives and breathes,
To watch the river gently flow
Along the valley green.

Yet now he fishes all alone
His father sadly passed away,
But proudly wears the cap he wore
That's pinned with feathered flies,
He often feels his presence here
A tutor's eye a guiding hand,
Where ashes spread his spirit lives
And dwells for evermore.

A frosty morn

A frosty morn I walk alone
I blow my hands to keep them warm,
As sunlight shines but weakly through
The lightly dusted trees,
The sky so blue like summer but
No warmth to melt the bitter chill,
And all around the land is gripped
By winter's cruellest freeze.

No song to fill the silent air
While faintest mist does firmly cling,
To branch and bough across the field
And to the thorny hedge,
Where silken webs adorn the twigs
Like veils upon the bridal gown,
With diamond dew and silver thread
They make their solemn pledge.

And as I walk along the way
My footmarks left upon the grass,
So crisp and white where autumn leaves
Make patterns on the ground,
I won't look back but look ahead
For spring awaits to bring me cheer,
As nature sleeps my heart is lost
For sorrow's all I've found.

I lean upon this tree so bare
Where once we rested in its shade,
But offers me no comfort now
Yet still seems like a friend,
I place my hand upon the trunk
But now its rough and pitted bark,
On which I carved my lover's name
Now marks my lover's end.

Cathedral bells

Hark I hear cathedral bells
Which fill the land this joyful morn,
From stony spire they ring with glee
And yield their rousing calls,
Above the tiled and slated roofs
On which the sunlight gently rests,
The peal does flow and echoes through
The streets of red bricked walls.

Again, again cathedral bells
Resound with all their strength and might,
They're stirring Christian souls to wake
And calling them to prayer,
Their sound does drift upon the wind
So far unto the woodland green,
Across the meadows and the fields
And through the morning air.

All now still cathedral bells
Have hushed and there is peace once more,
Save for the blackbird's sweetest song
With voice so pure and clear,
The stony spire stands silent now
While pointing to the skies above,
The cross it bears of burning gold
Will shine forever here.

For forty summers

For forty summers I have lived
And felt the sunlight on my face,
Within the meadows where I walked
And daisies always grew,
Beneath my feet amongst the grass
Like snow that rested on the ground,
And there the warm and gentle breeze
Once dried the morning dew.

And then beneath the woodland's green
I found the cool and leafy shade,
And rested there so many times
More than I care to know,
For every year I longed to see
The trees so broad and mighty stand,
I felt I was a part of them
And there I too did grow.

The birds once sang sweet songs of joy
And squirrels climbed the ancient oaks,
To gather stocks of winter food
They hid beneath the fern,
But autumn shall not come again
Nor shall the woodland turn to gold,
The creatures gone the birds have flown
And never will return.

For forty summers I have lived
To see the beauty of the land,
But now it has been cleared away
No longer shall I call,
To smell the flowers of the morn
And hear the songs from lofty boughs,
So plain the barren silence rings
A toll of death to all.

God bless the children

God bless the children who dwell in the desert
And bake in the heat under African skies,
For scorched by the sunlight the land lies infertile
So cracked and now empty their waterhole lies,
In drought they do thirst they are longing for rainfall
But each day they wake to the glow once again,
That slowly does rise through the shadows of darkness
And dwells on this vast and so desolate plain.

God bless the children have pity upon them
For naked and starving and wracked with disease,
Please dry mothers' tears as they're trying to comfort
Their young ones so precious they can never please,
They sing to them softly and cradle them gently
They yield what they have but they've little to give,
Forlornly they gaze to the heavens above them
Their sons and their daughters have not long to live.

God bless the children they do not deserve this
And nor should they suffer the way that they do,
They lie in the dust and nobody can save them
Our hands only able to pray for them too,
As life slips away in the blink of a moment
They watch as they die and are helpless to save,
Then wrap their frail bodies in rags while they're weeping
And place every child in a hole for a grave.

As dawn does stir the sleeping night

As dawn does stir the sleeping night
That gripped the woodland with its chill,
Through faintest mist and frosted trees
The ghostly sun does rise,
That creeps above horizon dark
Where shadows seem to linger on,
While branch and bough do reach unto
The pallid winter skies.

So still the air the gentle hush
As silver slowly yields to blue,
And clears the way for beams to shine
And frozen land to thaw,
The robin finds a lowly perch
And there forlornly casts his eyes,
Then turns the twigs and lifts the leaves
Which lie upon the floor.

With amber ferns now wilted there
Which line the winding wooded track,
And bow their crowns that glisten
In the early morning light,
Upon the way a puddle lies
And iced within a shallow mould,
All cracked and crazed too cold the morn
To free it from its plight.

I look towards the fallen oak
That fell yet but a month ago,
And there its mighty root exposed
To which the earth does cling,
And as it lies within its grave
Its leaves shall never turn to green,
Nor shall it bear its fruit again
Or see the coming spring.

For things will never be the same again

There lies a space within my heart that shall remain so empty,
As sadly now our days are at an end,
I know I never shall forget the time we spent together,
It is so hard to lose a special friend,
My words can never say enough or show the way I'm feeling,
So deep inside I try to mask the pain,
I cannot face tomorrow for the day shall be so lonely
For things will never be the same again.

I know you shall be happy when you walk into the sunset,
But pity those that you will leave behind,
Please don't look back to see my tears I wish that I was stronger,
And thus to all my sorrow I was blind,
So spread your wings and fly away above the dark horizon,
The wisdom of the stars you shall retain,
And as I gaze into the sky for me they shall be weeping,
For things will never be the same again.

As now I walk alone with just my shadow from the moonlight,
Yet that can never keep me company,
But still I know where'er you walk an angel shall be with you,
And there's no better place that you can be,
So live your dreams you dreamt of and do all that you have longed for,
Find freedom now across this barren plain,
And spend your days in happiness but you I shall remember,
For things will never be the same again.

Beside the frozen lake I stand

Beside the frozen lake I stand
And from the bank my eyes are drawn,
Across the surface still as glass
The blue of mirrored sky,
As ice does rest upon the swag
The lapwing walks the stony shore,
And turns the pebbles one by one
In search of worm and fly.

I hear the call of distant gulls
Afar a flock has settled where,
The cracks have formed and water seeps
And gentle sun does shine,
While mallards cast their longing eyes
Towards me as I throw some bread,
Then coots the swans and geese arrive
To form a grateful line.

And there they wait till I've no more
It breaks my heart to leave them so,
Upon the ice they vainly stand
And watch me walk away,
Then past the thorn and tree so bare
I cross the grass where shadows fall,
So long and dusted by the frost
That lingers through the day.

I'll walk with God

I'll walk with God to mountains high
And touch the clouds above,
While there with awe I'll look upon
The greatness of his love,
For where the peaks so mighty stand
And valleys lit with gold,
I'll find a place to call my home
And watch my dreams unfold.

I'll walk with God along the shore
And gaze across the sea,
The sand will be my carpet
And my spirit shall be free,
To watch the waves come rolling in
And as the waters part,
A beam so bright will guide my way
And joy shall fill my heart.

I'll walk with God through woodland green
Amidst its pleasing shade,
I'll see the wonders of my Lord
His beauty there displayed,
In every tree that firmly stands
And grows so tall and strong,
Then to the leaf the trunk and bough
I know I shall belong.

I'll walk with God beside the lake
That still and peaceful lies,
And see upon the water there
Reflections of the skies,
In every scene I witness
He shall always be my friend,
So I'll walk with God beside me
Till I reach my journey's end.

Where art thou pain?

Where art thou pain?
My joy can't last
For it was never meant for me,
I know my dreams
Shall fade and die
Like autumn leaves upon the tree.

Where art thou pain?
You must arrive
To douse the flame that burns within,
And nip the bud
Before it blooms
I know that I can never win.

Where art thou pain?
To break my heart
And tear my very soul away,
It always comes
And so I wait
For hopes of love can never stay.

Where art thou pain?
My joy to end
For I was made to suffer so,
My tears shall fall
I know not when
And bring again more days of woe.

Please let me rest

Please let me rest for I am weak
This weary road does never end,
Each day that goes does seem a year
No respite from the gale,
That cuts me through can barely stand
Or make my way to reach my goal,
For every step a struggle now
And I must surely fail.

Please let me rest and shelter from
The pouring rain and clouds above,
That follow me where'er I go
So cold those tears they cry,
What have I left to comfort me?
The leaves that fell so long ago,
Have blown away with all my hope
And dreams that passed me by.

Please let me rest I can't go on
To face the lonely road ahead,
I have my faith but nothing more
That urges me along,
So much I want to see and do
Before my time on earth expires,
And yet I get no nearer
For I know this way is wrong.

Brittle twigs

The brittle twigs upon the bough
So frail that surely time must break,
As now this elm bereft of life
Can't brave the winds no more,
The bark hangs limply from the trunk
With every gust a piece does fall,
For ridden with that cruel disease
The fungus beetle bore.

Yet in defiance it does stand
Alone within this furrowed field,
And casts its shadow on the ground
Although so faint and weak,
The view has changed since when a child
I gazed across this land before,
As now there's only emptiness
The scene so stark and bleak.

Its branches will not bud again
Nor shall its leaves of amber fall,
To gather on that barren ground
As summertime did fade,
Its shape and form that graced the way
Now stripped of all its dignity,
With nothing more to offer
But the memories that it made.

The victim of that dreadful plague
That spread throughout the countryside,
The scars of which shall never heal
And wounds will always stay,
As evening falls this tree remains
Its silhouette against the sky,
And dwells within the winter now
As bitter years decay.

For now as the dawning has ended the darkness

For now as the dawning has ended the darkness
I gaze at the scenes of these wondrous displays,
The hills in the distance the fields and the pastures
Where I long to dwell for the rest of my days,
For I am so happy and never felt better
To live through the seasons and share in their grace,
From blossoms of spring to the snows of the winter
My heart shall belong to this beautiful place.

The rivers and streams and their life giving waters
The trees of the autumn and woodlands of gold,
My dreams I shall follow wherever they lead me
To places where secrets now wait to be told,
So sing on sweet songbirds from out of the branches
And let all your voices rejoice now with glee,
Then fly over mountains that reach to the heavens
And sail over valleys that wind to the sea.

Please shine on me sunlight let flowers keep blooming
And may the breeze carry your scent on the air,
I live for these views and the gifts they has given
Wherever I look there is joy everywhere,
As colours entwine in a palette of riches
And spreading their greatness all over the land,
I know God is with me wherever I wander
And there through the country I'll walk hand in hand.

Footprints in the snow

The fire can't warm my lonely heart
Or stem the pain I feel,
This bleak December afternoon
My wounds shall never heal,
The door is closed a chapter ends
As now the cold winds blow,
The only thing that now remains
Your footprints in the snow.

The window pane looks out upon
The path that lies ahead,
Where thoughts of all my hopes and dreams
Shall fade until they're dead,
I long the thaw to come again
Shall winter never go?
To melt away these memories and
Your footprints in the snow.

But while the cold does linger on
I'll feel that bitter chill,
That offers me no respite
And I guess it never will,
For while it stays my days are filled
With emptiness and woe,
That shall not end while I still see
Your footprints in the snow.

The laden trees do bear the strain
But I can't do the same,
For as the day now turns to dusk
My soul still filled with shame,
As I await the night to fall
For darkness cannot show,
The sadness that now lies within
Your footprints in the snow.

As autumn leaves keep falling

I weep for all those summer days
And times that we did share,
Within the woodland's deepest green
We kissed and shaded there,
But now it's all come to an end
For love's deserted me,
As autumn leaves keep falling
And the winter soon shall be.

For now I walk a lonely path
Through scenery of gold,
The sun still shines so brightly but
The wind does blow so cold,
The branches now are growing bare
And bring more misery,
As autumn leaves keep falling
And the winter soon shall be.

Each one that falls does crumble 'neath
My feet where I do tread,
And turn to dust just like my dreams
Which too are lying dead,
With twisted root on frozen ground
No soul for company,
As autumn leaves keep falling
And the winter soon shall be.

No joyful songs do fill the boughs
The blue sky turned to grey,
For all the birds that welcomed me
Have left and flown away,
And from this emptiness I feel
I never shall be free,
As autumn leaves keep falling
And the winter soon shall be.

The water wheel

Upon the Palmers Brewery wall
The water wheel does gently turn,
Around, around the sodden spokes
In motion to the flow,
As there I stand upon the bridge
That spans the ebbing River Brit,
As peaceful waters glisten with
The sunlight's dawning glow.

The scent of yeast within the air
That floats upon this restless morn,
And clings unto the summer breeze
Like talons to its prey,
As grassy banks do bend and wave
With every gust that carries forth,
The linnet's song of sweetest joy
That sounds throughout the day.

Above the clouds do slowly pass
Across the peaceful Dorset sky,
That greets the pleasant countryside
Of rolling downs and fields,
While still the wheel does gently turn
Around, around the droplets fall,
Like silver raindrops they descend
Such grace their beauty yields.

Spiritual home

I feel I belong here I don't want to leave it
The sounds and the beauty of sights that I've seen,
Which capture my thoughts with a sweet understanding
And thus fill my mind with a peace so serene,
The walks in the country when sunlight is shining
The views of the landscape wherever I roam,
I found and discovered my destiny waiting
For this is my truth and my spiritual home.

The patchwork of colours the fields and the pastures
The way that the woodlands do speak unto me,
Forever they call by the wind and the breezes
That blow through their branches so restless and free,
The downs rise in emerald above they're surveying
The heavenly pastures and meadows before,
Serenity glistens in all of its splendour
It's all that I wanted I need nothing more.

As streams and the rivers now wind down the valleys
I taste their pure waters refreshing my soul,
I feel I'm at one with the land and its creatures
And know in my heart I've discovered my goal,
I gaze at the ocean as blue as a sapphire
The waves on the shoreline the surge of the foam,
I stand on the cliff tops and witness this wonder
For this is my truth and my spiritual home.

A beggar man

Within the dirty alleyway
That's strewn with paper cans and cups,
Beside the shops so brightly lit
A beggar man does sleep,
The bed of card he lies upon
Once packed the food he can't afford,
His blanket offers little warmth
A sad pathetic heap.

For here he sat throughout the day
With feeble hand he begged for coins,
From all the busy passers by
But mostly was in vain,
For there he was abused and kicked
As tears ran down his sallow face,
He shivered in the bitter wind
Tormented by the pain.

Yet in his dreams he can forget
And live the life of princely ways,
And be all that he longs to be
Until the dawn does break,
To face another weary morn
And gripped by harsh reality,
So cruel the hand of fate has been
He never wants to wake.

Rejected everywhere he goes
And moved along so hard to rest,
He carries his possessions
In a supermarket cart,
He drags his feet as he does walk
Along the street he calls his home,
Not knowing where he's going to
And sadness fills his heart.

The Penlee lifeboat disaster

December nineteen eighty one
Upon the nineteenth day,
The Union Star had floundered
In the stormy south west sea,
No power to drive the vessel from
The jagged rocky shore,
The Falmouth coastguard called to launch
The lifeboat from Penlee.

The Solomon Browne's eight crewmen
Were all Mousehole village men,
Who braved the mighty waves that night
Through winds of dreadful force,
And headed to Boscawen Cove
To where the ship did lie,
And fought with all their strength and skill
To keep their boat on course.

With disregard to danger
They pulled four from off the deck,
Yet four remained in peril
As the winds and ocean roared,
When they returned a massive wave
Engulfed the Union Star,
Which then capsized, the lifeboat lost
With all those hands on board.

When morning came a sense of grief
Did spread through village hearts,
When they awoke to hear the news
They didn't want to hear,
The splinters of the lifeboat lay
All washed upon the shore,
The search went on but futile
For no words did bring them cheer.

The Penlee shed lies empty now
Its doors stay firmly closed,
A tribute to those many souls
Who now are sadly gone,
The gallant crew who fought the seas
And braved the bitter storm,
Who gave their lives in service yet
Their memory shall live on.

Trainspotting

Upon the platform here I wait
And watch the rain come pouring down,
No other soul for company
To pass the time away,
The slatted bench on which I sit
With peeling paint all scrawled and etched,
Beside the bin that overflows
With litter and decay.

The hands upon the clock above
Seem frozen for so slow to move,
To click each minute passing by
It mocks relentlessly,
As puddles gather one by one
Beyond the shelter of the roof,
Where wind does blow the paper cups
And yields more misery.

I shiver with the bitter cold
And blow my hands to keep them warm,
Yet still I find no respite from
This bleak November's eve,
Deserted in the desperate throes
Of winter how I long to be,
Back home again yet still I wait
And wish that I could leave.

I look upon the silver rails
That wind into the distance there,
With sleepers stained so thick with oil
Yet still no train in sight,
While over on the other line
A Deltic trundles slowly past,
While pulling coal in blackened trucks
With all its strength and might.

With whistling wheels and buffer chinks
The diesel coughs and cackles by,
While points do clang and clunk so loud
And choking smoke of blue,
That drifts across these empty lines
I hold my breath until it clears,
And watch the train as it does go
Until it fades from view.

And as the hush descends again
Upon the empty platform here,
The circles in the puddles stare
With every drop that falls,
The red light shines from out the gloom
As I look down the track ahead,
And wait and wait but nothing comes
A captive of these walls.

The refuse collection

The winter's dawn at six a.m
Still dark save for the lamps that shine,
Two men do roll the dustbins down
Each pathway to the kerb,
One works the left one works the right
The wagon trailing far behind,
Yet inching ever closer
As the hush it does disturb.

Now side by side the bins in pairs
Do line the bleak and empty street,
Like statues forged of rusting steel
They stand as if in shame,
Each bears the number of the house
That's painted on their battered lids,
One bent so it now barely fits
Its poor misshapen frame.

They wait the brawny workers' hands
To lift them to their shoulders broad,
Then tip the waste into the truck
And place them down again,
The houses lit by amber light
That flashes on the driver's cab,
The wagon's engine roars so loud
While bin men toil and strain.

The crunch and crash as bottles break
And cans are crushed into a bale,
Within the strong and mighty jaws
Which chew the rotting cud,
One bangs the side it moves along
As bins are dragged back into place,
Then stops again to gather more
Discarded waste and crud.

My life

My life seems unimportant as I wrestle in the shadows
And feel that all my days have been a curse,
So little I've achieved and soon my words will be forgotten
And lost within the rhymes of clouded verse.

For no one shall remember me when I am here no longer
Nor place a single flower on my grave,
Then kiss the stone where I do lie or weep a mourning teardrop
A kindly word for me no one shall save.

The grass will grow around me there until my name is hidden
That over time will slowly wear away,
Until no one can read it then my stone will surely crumble
When ridden by the forces of decay.

Its dust shall blow upon the wind but never would it settle
Until my spirit found a welcome home,
I'd go on searching for the dream I never found when living
Across the hills and mountains I would roam.

Until I found a resting place where I could be so happy
And every day would be the first of spring,
As flowers bloomed I'd find a peace and I would weep no longer
For there my soul for joy would surely sing.

For when the light fills this darkness

I'm all alone in the evening
As the stars begin to shine,
Within the sky
They do lie
Where all my dreams did surely die,
I'm looking back to the morning
When my life was planned ahead,
And hope I saw
But yet no more
What does the future hold in store?

For when the light fills this darkness
And the day begins again,
Then I will see
Such misery
For now our love will never be,
And so the warmth of the summer
Shall never warm my heart,
As cold as ice
I rolled the dice
And I was left to pay the price.

As now the dawn is approaching
And the night is at an end,
The skies aglow
And yet I know
That my hurt shall never go,
Now the flowers are all weeping
And each dewy tear's for me,
For now they share
All my despair
And no one else does seem to care.

For when the light fills this darkness
As the sun does slowly rise,
To greet the day
And light the way
I wish that joy was here to stay,
For I know that in the evening
When the darkness comes once more,
The stars will shine
And yield a sign
The one I love shall not be mine.

On gentle breeze my love shall sail

I can but reach you in my dreams
The only way to love it seems,
But as I wake to find you gone
Each time I feel I can't go on,
I blow a kiss of feelings true
And hope one day it reaches you,
On gentle breeze my love shall sail
Across the dawning skies so pale.

Please float upon the blossom air
To end this winter of despair,
And carry all my wishes far
Across the lands to where you are,
I need you more than words can say
My broken heart does bleed each day,
In longing for my one true love
My thoughts shall ride on clouds above.

I call your name but no reply
Then watch the summer slowly die,
As leaves begin to turn to gold
The nights again do feel so cold,
And as they fall with every gust
My hopes do crumble into dust,
For as they rest upon the ground
I know my love could not be found.

As winter then does come again
And with it brings a lasting pain,
That lingers with the ice and snow
Of joy we shared so long ago,
And yet remains within the past
For love we had just couldn't last,
I wait for spring to yield a thaw
When flowers grow and bloom once more.

Those hands that gave (Easter Poem)

Those hands that gave and never took
Such miracles they did perform,
To make the crippled walk again
And blessed both man and child,
Those hands that caused no harm or pain
But only goodness did they yield,
So warm and gentle to the touch
So pure and undefiled.

Those hands that stilled the raging storm
And freed the muted tongue to speak,
That fed five thousand hungry souls
And made the deaf to hear,
Those hands that prayed to God above
And cast the cursed spirits out,
That cared for all those souls in need
And were so kind and dear.

Those hands so true gave only love
And always willing to forgive,
That turned the water into wine
And made the blind to see,
But yet they nailed them to the cross
And drew his sacred blood of grace,
I shan't forget my Saviour gave
His precious life for me.

How sweet her name does sound to me

How sweet her name does sound to me
What graceful music to my ear,
Like lark ascending to the sky
That sings for me a song so clear,
A phrase that echoes through the morn
That drifts across the hills and field,
And there unto my longing thoughts
With all the beauty it does yield.

How sweet her name does sound to me
A soothing stream that gently flows,
A soft refrain of silver calls
I'll follow her where'er she goes,
Melodic charms I shan't forget
Imprinted so within my mind,
And every day that I shall live
A love so pure I'll surely find.

How sweet her name does sound to me
Like waves that roll upon the shore,
And all the time I think of her
My joy shall last for evermore,
No word I'll find that may compare
For sun to shine and clouds to part,
A gentle wind that whispers through
The trees into my loving heart.

Eagle

You soar to the heavens and ride on the thermals
Then sail over valleys and into the sun,
To cast down your shadow on snow-covered mountains
Through radiant beams of the new day begun,
A symbol of freedom you fly without knowing
With awe we now greet you so humble we are,
Your grace and your poise as you circle in motion
Whilst holding a dream that will travel so far.

Please show us the way to the distant horizon
And spread out your wings as you glide through the air,
The wild-rugged landscape your home of such beauty
With hillsides of heather that welcome you there,
So lead and we'll follow wherever you guide us
For you are the master and lord of the skies,
The power and the strength in your talons so mighty
You look down upon us with predator's eyes.

Now caught in the sunset as evening is falling
Your dark silhouette on the canvas of gold,
Majestic and peerless so fly on forever
A sight to remember your story now told,
So rest in the moonlight at peace silent hunter
And sleep on the outcrop and wake with the dawn,
Then fly again raptor and soar to the heavens
And reach for the mountains and call to the morn.

Wishbone

The rivers run to nowhere
And their water's ceased to flow,
For lost within the wilderness
They have no place to go,
The days of summer disappeared
And with them skies of blue,
If I could break a wishbone now
I'd make a wish for you.

The leaves have fallen from the trees
And lie upon the ground,
The branches bare and stand forlorn
Such sorrow I have found,
For spring I know will not return
Unless my dream comes true,
If I could break a wishbone now
I'd make a wish for you.

The flowers have all wilted
And shall never bloom again,
Each day I live so cold and grey
Upon this barren plain,
No colours to bring happiness
No chance to start anew,
If I could break a wishbone now
I'd make a wish for you.

When April wakes the dawn shall sing

When April wakes the dawn shall sing
A graceful chorus sweet and long,
On blossomed boughs the birds shall rest
And fill the air with joyful song.

And when this pathless wood's adorned
With bluebells that shall ring for me,
Ten thousand peals unto my heart
The greatest sight a soul can see.

For here beneath these budding bowers
Their zestful shoots will bloom and grow,
And daffodils shall cast their spell
Upon the field where colours flow.

When sun does shine a ray of light
Then snow and ice shall start to clear,
The breeze will blow a warming breath
To fill the land with grateful cheer.

When April wakes the dawn shall sing
Each note will spell the winter's end,
For spring shall rise from slumbers deep
As if a long departed friend.

The piper plays a sad lament

The mountains dark that stand before
A home where he was born and raised,
This land that lives within his heart
And where he learnt to play,
A place that holds within each stone
The memories of the love he knew,
For here he knows her spirit rests
And thinks of her each day.
Upon the rock with sweet intent
The piper plays a sad lament.

For as he stands there all alone
The loss for him too much to bear,
And as he plays he knows full well
That his beloved hears,
His strains which sail upon the wind
Now all that he can give to her,
And yet can never bring her back
Nor dry his lonely tears.
Still grateful for the time they spent
The piper plays a sad lament.

As dawn does break a shaft of light
Does shine upon the heathered slopes,
From skies aglow in burning gold
And darkness then does flee,
Afar but yet his pain does stay
And never shall it leave his soul,
For him the sun won't shine again
Now love can never be.
As if a lasting compliment
The piper plays a sad lament.

Then at its end he says a prayer
That one day they shall meet again,
And walk the hills they used to walk
Together hand in hand,
For there in heaven she does wait
To greet the man she loved so much,
In life till death did take her from
This wild and rugged land.
The piper starts his long descent
From whence he played his sad lament.

When we were young

When we were young our lives ahead
We thought those times would never end,
Within the playground fun and games
Such laughter we did share,
Upon the swings upon the slide
The see-saw and the roundabout,
We stayed until the sun went down
For we so loved it there.

The cycle trips on summer days
When skies above were deepest blue,
We'd often travel from the town
To see the countryside,
Of Shenstone where the fields of corn
Did wave in gold and birds did sing,
From every bough along the way
Saw beauty far and wide.

Those April days in Cuckoo's Nook
We saw the bluebells there that flowed,
Beneath the trees and spread so far
Across the woodland floor,
Within the park we fed the ducks
And threw the bread and watched with joy,
On lazy Sunday afternoons
And yet we go no more.

The days seemed longer way back then
When playing games upon the field,
We'd run and run and never tire
And time was all our own,
Those days now passed so long ago
And we grow old yet young in heart,
We'll stay until our days do end
With memories carved in stone.

Your kiss so warm

Your kiss so warm you gave to me
Like none before I'd ever felt,
For then all time was motionless
As if it longed to stay,
An angel's voice spoke unto me
A whisper yet I heard it well,
The words of love upon the breeze
And yet they blew away.

Sweet music played within my mind
Which drowned the sorrow that I'd felt,
For all those years before we met
That I had grimly bore,
As if my hurt had truly gone
Dispelled into another land,
So far away that I'd not feel
That loneliness no more.

Yet it returned to haunt me so
Just as I knew it surely would,
Its talons gripped my aching heart
With all their strength and might,
I swore I'd never love again
Nor be a victim of its ways,
And yet I know your kiss so warm
Would melt the chill this night.

The rose shall never bloom again

The rose that shone within the sun
Has withered now its life is done,
Its head is bowed towards the ground
And here to sorrow I am bound,
As winter comes and cold winds blow
My days are filled with endless woe,
The rose shall never bloom again
Nor will it ever ease my pain.

O death so cruel that took from me
My love and all I wished to be,
And I remain yet but a shell
With lasting hurt I know so well,
And as I watch each petal fall
I know that I have lost it all,
And life shall never be the same
Yet in my heart there lives your name.

Abandoned to my bitter fate
I know I can no longer wait,
To see again your beauty fair
For gone the love that we did share,
So too the rose whose end is near
I wipe away a mournful tear,
And bid farewell to you my love
Then kiss the stars that shine above.

Awake the spring with happy cheer

Awake the spring with happy cheer
It is the best time of the year,
For when I see the flowers grow
It sets my longing heart aglow,
To see the snowdrops pure and white
I know there is no greater sight,
Than rows and rows of daffodils
Which stretch across the fields and hills.

When bluebells drape the woodland floor
I'll know that winter is no more,
As blossom blooms upon the bough
And corn shall rise behind the plough,
When meadows flow as if a stream
That time shall fill my every dream,
For then the view so fine to see
And all the land shall welcome me.

I know there is no finer place
And I shall walk within its grace,
To look upon the beauty there
Within the land beyond compare,
In every part along the way
A joy to savour through the day,
And when the birds so gaily sing
I'll know that then it shall be spring.

When shall my bitter days be sweet?

Too long my heart has loveless been
Too many wretched days I've seen,
And in self-pity I have drowned
For my true love I've never found,
I'm left alone but with my fears
For sorrow cannot dry my tears,
Yet love could make my life complete
When shall my bitter days be sweet?

For pain the wind can't blow away
Although the trees do bend and sway,
As leaves are falling one by one
I know my hurt shall carry on,
For while I live without a friend
My loneliness will never end,
Yet no one now does seem to care
To rid me of my deep despair.

So little now that I can give
Within the time I've left to live,
My fortune lost I have no more
No soul could lift me from the floor,
But now I fear it is too late
And so I must accept my fate,
That my true love I'll never see
And it was never meant to be.

Yet to the hope I'll always cling
That love shall fly upon the wing,
And find me then such joy I'll know
Then I'll forget these times of woe,
One day I feel a light may shine
And happiness will then be mine,
For love could make my life complete
When shall my bitter days be sweet?

As clouds shall float in skies of blue

This summer's day the sun does shine
And yet this lonely heart of mine,
That longs to love but never will
While hopes I have I can't fulfil,
I'll wander far and wander wide
May God then lead me to your side,
As clouds shall float in skies of blue
I'll find a way to be with you.

For many riches I have seen
Within the fields and hills so green,
So graceful as they tower above
And yet they cannot bring me love,
I close my eyes in silent prayer
That one day I should find you there,
And if I do so glad I'll be
Yet fate alone does hold the key.

I'll cross the rivers and the streams
For there the answer to my dreams,
Shall call to me and I shall go
Where'er the waters ebb and flow,
For there my love I'll surely find
And I shall kiss your hand so kind,
As we embrace you'll melt my heart
And from that day we'll never part.

And angel wings shall beat no more

For when two hearts do fall in love
The sun will shine in skies above,
When flowers bloom and colours glow
And crystal streams will gently flow,
The birds shall sing from every tree
Their songs will sail so gracefully,
The sweetest sound to lovers' ears
And bring the joy to dry all tears.

To see the emerald hill and field
When April comes with hope revealed,
A whispered breeze shall softly kiss
The lovers' lips with tender bliss,
And then caress the blossomed air
Their lives together they will share,
Each day shall be so warm and still
When angels fly it is God's will.

But when two hearts do break in two
The sun will set with autumn's hue,
And flowers then shall wilt and die
And crystal streams will all run dry,
No longer then the birds will sing
And only sadness they shall bring,
For silence then will fill the air
And tears shall well of deep despair.

Each hill and field shall then turn brown
When winter comes all hope will drown,
As cold winds blow and not abate
On lips of scorn so full of hate,
The blossom gone and leaves lie dead
When torn apart the lives they led,
Then storms will rage and rains will pour
And angel wings shall beat no more.

For I alone can say no more

Now all is still this silent night
There seems no end to this my plight,
Regretful words have all been said
And now all hopes are lying dead,
As clouds now gather up above
They signify our wasted love,
From stormy skies the rain shall pour
For I alone can say no more.

For this is not the time to plead
And yet my broken heart does bleed,
I cannot beg I've too much pride
But bear a constant pain inside,
That shall not fade till stars do shine
And you again forever mine,
But that I know just cannot be
For you shall never pity me.

As now the clouds so gently weep
I shall not rest I cannot sleep,
As puddles form upon the ground
The way to love cannot be found,
Now from the window I do stare
And pray to see you standing there,
If only wishes could come true
Then I would surely wish for you.

The stars have never shone so bright

A lover's hand a lover's eye
Has cast a spell upon the sky,
Where'er I go I think of you
A dream I wished has now come true,
I know my thoughts shall never stray
But rest with you and always stay,
The stars have never shone so bright
Upon this clear and crystal night.

For joy has filled the heavens above
And every star a star of love,
As if for me they all were made
I hope their light will never fade,
They glisten in their majesty
The greatest sight I'll ever see,
For I know now that while they shine
That I am yours and you are mine.

I wish this night would never end
For it bequeathed a lasting friend,
Yet know that soon the dawn shall rise
And sun will fill the morning skies,
But I will wake with happy cheer
For you my love shall still be here,
No dream at last this time for real
For love I know I truly feel.

O gentle voice

O gentle voice so deft the sound
That speaks to me with kindly word,
And tells me of your love so pure
The sweetest phrase that I have heard.

Your scarlet lips could give no more
Each word you say so pleases me,
They softly float upon the breeze
To soothe my ear so tenderly.

I shan't forget their grace and flow
Just like a stream that trickles by,
They shall remain within my mind
Until the day that I should die.

They yield a joy unto my heart
And sail like silver clouds above,
Where'er they go I'll follow them
For they shall lead me to your love.

O gentle voice please never cease
And tell me of your feelings true,
I'll listen with such glad intent
Then I shall always be with you.

The gate that leads unto the field

I walk the lonely way ahead
Along the path I often tread,
Beyond I know the golden corn
Shall wave upon this summer morn,
There is no finer place to be
As there within the hedge I see,
The gate that leads unto the field
For beauty there shall be revealed.

I lift the latch then open wide
The wooden gate then step inside,
And stand in awe as I do gaze
Upon the view where whispered haze,
Does linger on the distant hills
And to my soul such joy instils,
The sight that I know all too well
And I'm so happy here to dwell.

The mighty oak does firmly stand
And casts its shadow on the land,
I rest within its cooling shade
And know that here my fortune's made,
The lark does soar into the skies
And sings for joy as he does rise,
Into the air then disappear
Yet still his sweetest song I hear.

And there within the sunlight shine
The berries ripe upon the vine,
Where hawthorn and the holly dense
Do line the verge beside the fence,
With mayweed and the cowslip too
A palette of late summer's hue,
An image of the countryside
I look upon with greatest pride.

A little stream does gently flow
And ripples on the stones below,
With waters clear I take a sip
That's so refreshing to my lip,
And there I see a butterfly
I watch as it does flutter by,
Upon a flower it then does rest
As if for me a welcome guest.

I cross the stream then climb the stile
And then I linger for a while,
Beyond the meadow deep and green
Afar the woodland can be seen,
I venture on until I find
A tranquil spot and peace of mind,
And lean against my favourite tree
Then look upon the scenery.

For there I feel I do belong
Amongst the trees so tall and strong,
With twisted roots that rise and fall
A church without a spire or wall,
A holy place no bounds or ends
And where a reverent peace descends,
That fills my hopes my heart and soul
So calming that it makes me whole.

Although so much I long to stay
To live my life and spend each day,
I must return as sunlight falls
And echoes of the evening calls,
Again I cross the gentle stream
That flows as if a lasting dream,
The mighty oak still standing proud
Above the lark still sings aloud.

And then I reach the wooden gate
The skies aglow it's growing late,
I lift the latch then pull it to
And leave behind that wondrous view,
Before I go there's time to glance
To watch the corn in breezes dance,
The sights I've seen I'll not forget
As now the sun does slowly set.

My dearest friend

My dearest friend I speak with grace
Whene'er I say your name,
As if for me your love was meant
I know you feel the same,
The summer breeze does blow so warm
And carries me afar,
To some place where I want to be
And where you always are.

So deep within my humble heart
Such love I have for you,
And when I say that I am yours
No words could be more true,
When clouds do weep from stormy skies
The sunlight you will give,
And I shall be with you my dear
As long as I may live.

My dearest friend you are my rock
To which I always cling,
My hope and strength my lasting joy
You are my everything,
Our future's written in the stars
Which shine so high above,
And every one does show the way
To everlasting love.

A kindly word

A kindly word if you should please
Don't wave the blade without relent,
No hate or scorn that cuts me through
And has no space for sentiment.

The critic's hand although precise
Has often never held a quill,
And yet he always feels it fit
To savage and impose his will.

When rambling prose can reap reward
Against a finely crafted rhyme,
So easy to the ear and eye
Yet criticised as if a crime.

I shall not change my style or ways
To suit the mentors of this land,
And those who care to follow me
I'll shake them warmly by the hand.

For if to me her love belonged

For if to me her love belonged
I'd sing for joy this day,
And yet I know whate'er I try
It cannot be this way,
For now I have to spend my life
Admiring from afar,
But still my love shall never fade
And shine like yonder star.

Please pity me o God above
And spare me from this woe,
For she and I were meant to be
And yet it is not so,
For fate has been so harsh and cruel
And torn my life apart,
It cast my dreams like autumn leaves
And broke my loving heart.

What waits for me I do not know
Tomorrow could reveal,
The birth of spring and better times
And then my wounds may heal,
While winter bites its bitter cold
Shall chill me to the bone,
For every time I think of her
Reminds me I'm alone.

Please send me a postcard

Please send me a postcard or write me a letter
To tell me you love me and missing me so,
And seal it with kisses and post it this morning
For here I shall wait for your message to show,
Over the water the hills and the mountains
Please sail on the wind till it reaches my hand,
And then I shall read of your feelings towards me
In words that flow softly like waves on the sand.

The weeks have gone by and it seems like a lifetime
And hopes of the future are now hard to see,
For so far away is the chance to be near you
So spare me the sadness and come back to me,
The view from my window is masked by the raindrops
I hope the sun's shining wherever you are,
As thoughts of all romance now fade in the distance
I wish that my love now could travel so far.

Please send me a postcard or write me a letter
If I am forgotten I'll never forget,
For you are my world and so nothing else matters
If this spells the end I'd be hurt and upset,
If only I could I would send you a letter
And in it I'd say how I wish I was there,
To be by your side for I can't live without you
I so want to tell you just how much I care.

When Shire horses ploughed

When Shire horses ploughed all the fields of the farmland
And cut their deep furrows as straight as could be,
When they turned the soil in the sunlight of morning
Was no greater sight that a soul could then see.

When music once filled the sweet air of the country
To mark winter's end and the dawning of spring,
The sowing of seeds for the corn of the summer
And from lofty boughs all the songbirds did sing.

When landscapes were gold and would shine till the autumn
Then gathered for harvest and ground for the bread,
In the windmill that stood then so high on the hilltop
Yet gone are those days and the lives that they led.

When the food for the people was placed at the altar
And then unto worship the villagers came,
To sing and rejoice with their hymns of thanksgiving
And church bells would ring out in praise of God's name.

When Shire horses ploughed all the fields of the farmland,
Those days long ago now and dwell in the past,
As they pulled the blade that the farmer was guiding,
Then nobody knew that those days wouldn't last.

Away then fly yon bird of peace

Away then fly yon bird of peace
And spread your wings across the land,
So red with blood and scarred by shell
May you then greet each soldier's hand,
Your love all hatred could dispel
That rages through that weary line,
So arms be laid down in the mud
And then once more the sun would shine.

So sing for joy as you now go
And may your music fill the air,
For you alone can find the way
To end this sadness and despair,
Sail through the smoke the battles bore
Let peace descend from clouds above,
Then fall like rain upon those men
And show the way to lasting love.

Fly on! Fly on! My feathered friend
And over hills and mountains roam,
Until the guns lay silent fly
To make this land again your home,
For then the flowers will bloom once more
And blossom form upon the bough,
The winds of war shall then be stilled
And all shall heed your lasting vow.

The stained-glass window

Within this little country church
Above the tiny altar stands,
The stained-glass window that does shine
With colours deep and strong,
I look upon with reverent joy
As Christ is flanked by angels there,
A peace descends within my soul
And fills my heart with song.

And as I kneel and bow my head
Then close my eyes in silent prayer,
I turn my thoughts unto the Lord
For guidance I do pray,
I feel the window better plain
To look out on the hills of green,
That rise and fall 'neath skies of blue
Upon this summer's day.

For there's no scene that could depict
A better sign that God exists,
Than to survey that scene before
His hand created so,
Each tree and flower each blade of grass
Which thrive within his garden here,
Do pave the way unto his love
The greatest love I know.

I walk as dawn does slowly break

I walk as dawn does slowly break
Upon the hard and frozen ground,
So hush the morn for all is still
The languid sun does shine,
Betwixt the branches of the trees
Its beams do light the path ahead,
And yet shall never yield its warmth
Unto this heart of mine.

A whispered mist forlornly clings
And softly merges there beneath,
The periwinkle skies above
A ghostly shade of blue,
And as I go my shadow cast
Is all I've got for company,
No friend have I since yesterday
For lost my love so true.

The autumn leaves still rest upon
The undulating woodland floor,
So brittle there beneath my feet
Each step I fear to tread,
For each one takes me further from
The hand I wish to hold again,
And lips I long to kiss once more
But now those hopes lie dead.

As morning frost begins to thaw
The air still cold each breath a cloud,
I carry on reluctantly
With nothing but regret,
I wish that she could hear me say
I love her so and want her back,
For time we shared and days of joy
I never shall forget.

O love when shall you come to me?

O love when shall you come to me?
Such sorrow I have known,
The friends I had all settled down
Yet I remain alone,
What chance have I when all seems lost?
No future can I see,
I never longed to live this way
And yet it has to be.

O love when shall you come to me?
And not just pass me by,
I need you in my lonely life
To quell the tears I cry,
When will you bring me sweetest joy?
For sadness cannot last,
One day I hope that it shall end
Before my life has passed.

O love when shall you come to me?
I can no longer wait,
The pain I bear too much to take
It cannot be my fate,
When shall the days be brighter now?
And sunlight ever shine,
To find the one that I shall keep
Within this heart of mine.

O love when shall you come to me?
Take pity on me now,
As spring does make the blossom bloom
Upon the cherry bough,
When will you do the same for me?
I wish that you could tell,
For I shall never feel the warmth
While I in winter dwell.

Upon a lonely peak I rest

Upon a lonely peak I rest
With thoughts so many miles away,
I see that place I left behind
Within the distant haze,
I'll not return because I know
Those memories are too much to bear,
Each road and street reminds me of
Those joyful carefree days.

The thorny gorse upon the slopes
Lie tangled like my empty life,
That makes no sense and hurts me so
Whene'er I try to free,
So dense it grows and flowers shine
And yet I know they cannot last,
But prick the conscience of my dreams
That now shall never be.

Amongst the waving grass I sit
And pluck the seeds from off the stems,
Then throw them up into the air
And watch as they do fall,
Too heavy for the breeze to hold
They land beside my aching feet,
Where they shall grow and yet my love
Shall never yield at all.

I share the pity of that tree
Now withered in its brittle form,
Disfigured by the elements
And soon about to die,
For there as it does stand alone
With little hope I feel the same,
For our tomorrows stolen
And our yesterdays gone by.

Where'er the sweetest river flows

Where'er the sweetest river flows
I long that land to be my home,
Where I shall walk with my true love
Amongst the hills of green,
And there above the sun will shine
Within the skies of deepest blue,
And I shall never leave that place
Of beauty so serene.

Where we shall walk together through
The finest meadows hand in hand,
And stop to pick some daisies as
We rest beneath a tree,
And listen to the birds that sing
Within the boughs that cast their shade,
And there we'll stay till evening falls
And kiss so tenderly.

We'll stop to watch the stars appear
To share the silence of the night,
Then make a wish for love to last
So we shall never part,
We'll see the dawn then rise again
Above the hills that stand before,
To light with gold the way ahead
And joy will fill my heart.

Where'er the sweetest river flows
With waters pure I'll drink for thee,
Where blossom forms and flowers bloom
And spring shall never end,
Each day we live a treasured gift
But I know soon I shall awake,
Till then I'll rest within my dreams
With you my precious friend.

A dream I had so clear to me

A dream I had so clear to me
Of fields so rich and meadows green,
Embroidered woodlands blossomed with
The bluebells that did grow,
Beneath the boughs a peace therein
Did fill my heart with deepest joy,
That carried me along the way
To where a stream did flow.

But I awoke to find it gone
All that I'd seen had disappeared,
And left the stark reality
Of urban blight before,
What have we done? I asked myself
Where are the fields and meadows now?
Where too the woodlands and the stream?
No beauty anymore.

I tried to find a ray of hope
Somewhere within this barren land,
So filled with smoke from chimney stacks
That hung within the air,
And yet I felt it was too late
As I did walk the littered streets,
And past the blackened terraced walls
A sight I couldn't bear.

And yet I see each day I live
Within the town in which I dwell,
Imprisoned by my life of toil
I never shall break free,
For here the chains that bind me firm
Too strong and so I have to stay,
Yet when I sleep another world
Is calling out to me.

Four hearts she drew

The words she wrote did touch me so
I never shall forget,
For sweetness filled each flowing line
I live within her debt,
I am so proud to know her
For so honest kind and true,
She signed her name with deepest love
And then four hearts she drew.

I'll read her verse each day I live
It moves so gracefully,
And brings a tear unto my eye
Each time that I do see,
For her the sun shall always shine
And skies forever blue,
She signed her name with deepest love
And then four hearts she drew.

She gave me strength when I was weak
And so I carried on,
She was a friend when all alone
And I did need someone,
She spared me from my sadness
In the kindest way she knew,
She signed her name with deepest love
And then four hearts she drew.

What works of art and tender love (To John Constable)

What works of art and tender love
That touch my heart so deeply now,
And yield a sense of peace and calm
Whene'er I look and see,
For every stroke so bold and true
Adorned each waiting canvas there,
With greatness and the tales they tell
Shall always speak to me.

Those scenes of noble England green
And of its wondrous countryside,
The meadows and the fields of corn
Within the land so fair,
Amidst the views that have no end
So one can almost feel the breeze,
And hear the rustle of the leaves
As if you too were there.

With rivers and the silver streams
That yield a joy where'er they flow,
Reflections cast upon the lakes
And colours rich with hue,
They shall survive undimmed by time
Beyond a thousand years or more,
So all who seek will marvel then
And give their praise to you.

For every soul shall look upon
Your works with everlasting joy,
And see those skies of deepest blue
With clouds of light and shade,
As if a dream and yet so clear
While shadows rest upon the ground,
The sun will shine for evermore
And never dull nor fade.

O heaven is a lovely place

O heaven is a lovely place
Where graceful streams shall always flow,
And choirs of angels softly sing
As music fills the air,
The blossom hangs upon the bough
While flowers bloom as if the spring,
And sweet eternal love and peace
Is made for all to share.

When we shall walk into the light
And greet our long departed friends,
We'll have no fear for we shall be
Residing with our Lord,
Who'll welcome us with open arms
And keep us in his loving care,
In paradise we'll find our home
And rest in one accord.

O heaven is a lovely place
Where souls live on for evermore,
There blessed by youth restored again
And we shall not grow old,
The deaf shall hear the blind shall see
The crippled and the lame shall walk,
Unto our Lord we'll head upon
A pathway made of gold.

The rain runs down my window pane

The rain runs down my window pane
While weeping clouds above,
And all is lost but sorrow now
I have no one to love,
I long the skies to break again
And sun to shine for me,
But while the storm lies overhead
Then it shall never be.

As now the puddles form upon
The cold and sodden ground,
I think that once I shared her love
But now it can't be found,
For days of joy and happiness
Have all now sadly gone,
And I am left with nothing now
Yet memories linger on.

A wish can never bring her back
And yet I wish so hard,
But every prayer that I do say
My Lord does disregard,
Perhaps he's grown impatient now
And weary of my voice,
But still I pray and pray again
I have no other choice.

O speak to me now silent voice

O speak to me now silent voice
Your words I long to hear,
Please don't ignore my selfish plea
I miss you so my dear,
For hush now breeds these tears I weep
And while the night is still,
My dreams of love shall never be
Nor can my hopes fulfil.

The stars are bright within the sky
I watch as they do shine,
My thoughts do rest with you my love
And wish you were still mine,
I walk along these empty streets
With sorrow in my heart,
For I know when the dawn does rise
We still shall be apart.

O speak to me now silent voice
With words of precious gold,
I cannot bear to be alone
For now the night grows cold,
Upon the way ahead of me
I see the frost descend,
Yet cannot face the future
If our love is at an end.

Upon this rugged mountainside

Upon this rugged mountainside
My heart was lost to thee,
For once we stood together here
When you were part of me,
Where clouds now cloak the hidden peaks
I feel a lonely chill,
For as I stand my only wish
That you were with me still.

The wind does blow relentlessly
No shelter can I find,
And so I walk along the way
To leave that place behind,
Like rocks that fall then turn to dust
That's blown away so far,
I too shall never rest until
I find the place you are.

I'll not return with heavy heart
For memories linger here,
Of all the happy times we spent
I miss you so my dear,
And yet your spirit does remain
In every rock and stone,
And while that lasts I know that I
Shall never be alone.

The old antique shop

The boxes of china are laid on the footpath
Outside the antique shop with tables and chairs,
A weight props the door that's left wide for the public
Inside the old volumes are lining the stairs,
An oak English dresser is placed in the hallway
So narrow and cluttered I ease myself by,
And into a place where the walls are all whitewashed
Where gas lights and lampshades with ornaments lie.

The window is small and the glass is all dirty
The floor is of stone in this high ceilinged room,
I squeeze past the fittings the teapots and tumblers
And minding my steps in the mid morning gloom,
The scales in the corner remind me of childhood
The same used to weigh all my sweets from the jars,
I picture the scene now unearthed from my memory
Of pear drops and humbugs and penny chew bars.

Then back to the hallway a sideboard and mirror
A tea chest with bookcase and grandfather clock,
That's tolling the hour as it chimes through the silence
So proudly it stands there amongst all the stock,
The shopkeeper seated and reading his paper
While there in the glow from an old dusty light,
He casts but a glance as he peers round the corner
But stays ever watchful and keeps me in sight.

I bid him good morning he answers me softly
Goes back to his paper and news of the day,
I head past the boxes of tools and utensils
And taking great caution as I make my way,
By glassware so fragile that's crammed on each surface
And I hold my breath as I walk to the door,
As I bid farewell to the man in the corner
And head to the street where I entered before.

Spirits weep

Where to the songbirds flown away?
Where now the wonder of each day?
When meadows in their richness lay
And in the sunlight shone,
When bluebells graced the woodland floor
When rivers flowed but flow no more
Now spirits weep so softly for
The beauty that has gone.

Where now the blossom on each bough?
For spring does look so barren now
I don't know why nor don't know how
But winter shall not end,
So dull within this morning light
The dawn can't end the dark of night
And spirits weep now at the sight
Their pity they do send.

Where now the fruit upon the vine?
When berries made the sweetest wine
Where too the joy that once was mine?
Those times just couldn't last,
And how could this now ever be?
Once everything belonged to me
As spirits weep so tenderly
For all that now has passed.

Where now the waving fields of gold?
That every summer did unfold
Where too the hills that gently rolled?
But are no longer here,
Where too the hand of thee so fair?
And days of love we used to share
As spirits weep to show they care
I too now shed a tear.

The bleak and misty shore

I've never passed this way before
Upon this bleak and misty shore,
A sense of peace the air is still
A breathless hush descends at will,
The gentle waves that meet the land
Caress the damp and solemn sand,
And yet the tune that greets my ear
The sweetest sound a soul could hear.

So soothing to a broken heart
For they can mend each shattered part,
With music as each one does flow
To ease the hurt from long ago,
For now the shore is all my own
As I do walk here all alone,
For everyone's deserted me
My only friend is now the sea.

I cannot see the road ahead
The sunlight far away has fled,
No wind to blow away the cloud
Above the gull does cry so loud,
As if a call unto his mate
And yet for me it is too late,
For time has passed and still no sign
I know she never will be mine.

I cannot linger anymore
Upon this bleak and misty shore,
But there will come another day
A lonely soul shall pass this way,
To see the sights that I have seen
To tread the footmarks where I've been,
And listen to each gentle wave
For they a broken heart can save.

My love with deepest eyes of blue

My love with deepest eyes of blue
And kindly soul so warm and true
I long to give my heart to you
If you should give me thine,
My passion runs from every pore
For you my love whom I adore
And I'd be yours for evermore
I wish you could be mine.

And yet my life's the saddest tale
Whate'er I try I always fail
My days have now become so stale
I need to love again,
The nights are lonely and so cold
Your hand worth more to me than gold
And yet each dawn that does unfold
Just greets me with more pain.

And yet for you I'd catch the breeze
That whispers through the woodland trees
For any act I'd do to please
You mean so much to me,
I'll ride upon the clouds so high
And sail across the morning sky
And search for you until I die
Wherever you shall be.

The water from the river clear

The water from the river clear
Does quench my dry and thirsty lips,
As if from heaven it was sent
To find its way to me,
It shines within the rising sun
As ripples cross its stony bed,
So cool it feels unto my hand
And flows so gracefully.

I look toward the tangled bank
Where buttercups and daisies grow,
There sprinkled by forget-me-not
And dandelions of gold,
Amongst the grass some poppies too
Their scarlet heads do gently wave,
And dance within the summer breeze
As morning does unfold.

I watch the clouds that slowly pass
Across the wash of deepest blue,
Where land adorned with shadows
Till the light does shine once more,
I see upon the surface here
A mirror of the skies above,
A silver tide that flows within
Reflections cast before.

And here I'll stay and rest a while
Then to this scene I close my eyes,
And listen to the soothing sound
Of water ebbing by,
So sweet the music it does make
It fills me with a sense of calm,
That I could spend my whole life here
Until the day I die.

As here in the heart of the country I wander

As here in the heart of the country I wander
To witness the land and the streams,
And take in the greatness of all that surrounds me
I'll follow the way of my dreams,
Which carry me on to the fields where I linger
To gaze at the swallows that soar,
So high up above through the skies of the summer
A sight that I truly adore.

Where butterflies flutter and dance in the morning
I look on in awe as they go,
Their wings catch the sun and they glimmer like satin
Then rest on the flowers that grow,
While sheep safely graze in the heavenly pastures
I lie in the shade of a tree,
And know as I look to the hills in the distance
There's no better sight I could see.

The verges grow wild with the mayweed and parsley
And dandelion flowers of gold,
Entwined with the grasses that bend in the breezes
And poppies of scarlet so bold,
The birds sing for joy from the hedgerows and branches
The woodland's alive with their song,
And here I do listen to music so restful
That carries me further along.

As deeper and deeper they're calling me onward
Each scene is a picture of grace,
Wherever I look there is beauty unending
So happy am I in this place,
I live for its soul and its peace that surrounds me
To breathe all its life-giving air,
For this is my home and its spirit's within me
The heart of the country so fair.

Within the village churchyard I

Within the village churchyard I
Whilst on the sloping path I stand,
I read the names upon the graves
Amidst the waving grass,
Of Pickin, Banford, Butler, Lote
And some that I can barely read,
For worn away by time they rest
Forgotten now alas.

As there I stop a while to think
And look upon the lichgate there,
That urged me so to enter
And to walk this solemn way,
Unto the ancient church ahead
Where many feet have gone before,
To worship every Sunday morn
Yet no one comes this day.

While there beside the red bricked wall
A lonely yew does cast its shade,
Upon the stone before me now
With words inscribed beneath:
"Sacred to the memory of
Elizabeth the wife of Charles,
And daughter of John Arrowsmith"
I felt the hand of grief.

Around the graves the bluebells grow
The colour of the morning sky,
Where tussocks long have taken hold
And in defiance stand,
For as the spruce which tower above
The clustered nettles there below,
They cloak the stones all stained with green
Upon this sacred land.

While perched upon the needled bough
A crow does wait in silence there,
Unto the dark and weedy ground
He casts a reverent eye,
And clad in black the cloak of death
As if he waits another soul,
To there be laid within the earth
And watch the mourners cry.

As I look on with deep unease
I know that I must join them soon,
What waits ahead I do not know
Or when that time will be,
For all these souls who lie at peace
Within these grounds their names inscribed,
Will never be forgotten
Yet who shall remember me?

For what would be my epitaph?
My life to now so unfulfilled,
So much to do so little time
And yet I try my best,
Amongst these names I have no place
I have not earned my legacy,
What years I've left I must succeed
Or I shall never rest.

The mighty beech that line the path
Are slowly coming into leaf,
And soon will hide the church from view
Till autumn comes once more,
Within the village churchyard I
Now make my way towards the gate,
And as I leave I pull it to
Much wiser than before.

A walk along the Daw End canal

From Longwood I walk past the barges all moored there
Along the canal as I head on my way,
Thus leaving the noise from the traffic behind me
So glad to be part of this wonderful day,
I follow the path as it winds and meanders
I step around puddles that lie on the ground,
While verges are flecked by the dandelion flowers
With bluebells and daisies the nettles surround.

The Riddian Bridge with its narrow-bricked archway
Looks so picturesque in the pale morning light,
While casting its shade on the still and calm water
Beyond it the surface is shining so bright,
I'm lost in a place that all time has forgotten
Yet gone are the cargoes not seen anymore,
So too are the horses that trod the same towpath
Whilst pulling those barges of coal, lime and ore.

The hedgerow like snow as the hawthorn's in blossom
The bees and the butterflies make it their home,
So gaily they weave through the bright coloured petals
I watch as they wander and so freely roam,
Beyond lies the country the fields and the meadows
The cattle in pastures that feed on the grass,
I hear the sweet song of the chaffinch who sings to
Enlighten the season as slowly I pass.

While there in the reed beds the moorhens do linger
Their newly-hatched chicks staying close to their side,
I pause for a moment and then I continue
To gaze at the swifts who majestically glide,
As high up above through the air they are soaring
A picture of springtime before me now lies,
So warming my heart for a scene of such beauty
The land and the water beneath April skies.

The eye of the heron now peers from the bushes
With motionless stare he does patiently wait,
For ready to strike at the fish that swim near him
And shows all the skills of the hunter innate,
He lurks in the shadows to merge with the darkness
His plumage does blend with the light and the shade,
And hidden from view till he moves to the open
As then through the shallows he slowly does wade.

317

I head to the "Boathouse" the end of my journey
And stop for a drink as I rest by the wall,
I watch as two geese with their goslings are passing
And hear their soft voices as gently they call,
I gaze at the bank that lies over the water
So wild and untamed there the gorse bushes grow,
And cling to the land that does lie there before me
With flowers of gold in the sunlight aglow.

For as the final train appeared

For as the final train appeared
And stopped beside the platform there,
The last to journey disembarked
Then carried on their way,
Some stayed behind to watch it leave
With heavy heart and saddened tear,
They saw the guard with flag in hand
And looked on with dismay.
For as he closed each carriage door
Those days were gone for evermore.

The Beeching axe of sixty five
That tore the heart out of this place,
And left a void no soul could fill
The cruellest cut of all,
For when they closed the station down
Then cleared the site where it had stood,
A way of life was sadly gone
That few can now recall.
Those olden days of coal and steam
Alas but now a fading dream.

'Twas built in eighteen seventy nine
A building of such grace and charm,
That I remember all too well
When I was but a child,
I saw its windows boarded up
And then the slates fall from its roof,
And watched it when reduced to dust
Our village thus defiled.
Across the line a cold wind blows
For here now lie a thousand woes.

As one little snowflake

As one little snowflake does float down so gently
Then rests on the pavement so frozen and bare,
It dwells all alone through the depths of December
And toils through the hardship for no one does care.

Awaiting the springtime to melt in the sunlight
To turn into water and run to a stream,
For then it will flow to a river and ocean
And then shall feel wanted and part of a dream.

A sense of belonging to join in a union
And then form the waves that shall roll to the shore,
Whilst moving in motion will glisten like diamonds
And yet it must wait for the winter to thaw.

So there it must rest on the pavement unnoticed
Just watching the people each day passing by,
And longing for friendship it's not much to ask for
Yet nobody hears as it softly does cry.

Written on one starry night

The night so still
The air is cold
I look unto the heavens above,
And there I see
The stars that shine
And yet can never find me love.

I walk upon
The frosted ground
The moon does light the way before,
And yet so lost
I now appear
As night shall yield its joy no more.

When we first kissed
One starry night
'Twas if they all did shine for me,
And yet alas
Lie hidden now
For love was never meant to be.

Now sadness rests
Within my heart
That through my life shall always stay,
As long as I
Remain alone
Then love will never come my way.

I wish this night
Would quickly end
The memories now too much to bear,
My only dream
To be with you
And yet I only feel despair.

Unworthy of my Saviour's love

Unworthy of my Saviour's love
So poor a servant I have been,
I tried my best to follow him
But knew I never could,
I hope my Lord shall look upon
My life with sympathetic eye,
And judge me not upon my deeds
For they've been far from good.

Unworthy of my Saviour's love
I've let him down so many times,
Whene'er I found a soul in need
I looked the other way,
And so I must accept my fate
Whatever future waits for me,
I wish that I could live again
And start anew this day.

Unworthy of my Saviour's love
For such a lowly wretch am I,
Who has denied his faith to be
An unbeliever's friend,
I can but only now repent
And beg the mercy of my Lord,
Then try my best to change my ways
Before my life does end.

The wood ant mound

Upon a warm and sunny day
I headed on the woodland trail,
And listened to the songbirds sing
As I continued on,
Along the way with verges green
Of nettle fern and parsley too,
And there did bathe the butterflies
Where'er the sunlight shone.

Amongst the forest trees that grew
I came across a wood ant mound,
Beside the pathway that did wind
Through conifers so tall,
And there it stood a structure fine
For made of needles leaves and twigs,
So carefully arranged to build
A home so fit for all.

So many ants I couldn't count
Each seemingly a job to do,
They carried debris to the nest
And formed a steadfast line,
Unbroken there along the track
I watched them as they slowly passed,
To make their way unto the mound
And build their grand design.

As one by one they carried on
Unbothered by my presence there,
They worked and worked with all their strength
Their job was never done,
So captivated there I stood
I watched them weaving to and fro,
A sight that warmed my heart indeed
Just like the morning sun.

Bluebell woodland

New buds and the blossom are forming on branches
As April is turning to May,
I walk in the fields as I head through the country
And pause many times on the way.

I head past the new shoots of corn which are climbing
From out of the furrows I see,
While there in the distance my destiny's waiting
And where I know soon I shall be.

The hedgerows of hawthorn are lining the pathway
For now they are covered in white,
Then I come to the stile and the shade of the woodland
That so fills my heart with delight.

A carpet of blue that spreads out like an ocean
And flowing through trees as they grow,
While lit by the sunbeams which shine through the treetops
Inspired by their beauty I go.

As further and further my heart's captivated
To see all the flowers of spring,
Wherever I wander they wave all around me
I'm lost in the joy that they bring.

I follow the pathway that leads to the sunlight
And warmth from the coolest of shade,
I walk through the fields as I now leave the woodland
A journey I'm glad to have made.

Look to the sky

Look to the sky as the dawn does break
And the gold slowly turns to blue,
Look to the sky see the sun now rise
For it shines down for me and you.

Look to the waves as they ebb and flow
Hear the sound of the ocean roar,
Look to the waves watch them gently roll
Then fall upon the endless shore.

Look to the hills as they rise above
All the fields that are waving in gold,
Look to the hills at their shape and form
And gaze at the beauty they hold.

Look to the clouds of the sunset glow
As they're lit by the evening's fire,
Look to the clouds as their embers burn
For they yield all we now desire.

Look to the stars as the darkness falls
And the moon starts to shine above,
Look to the stars as we share a kiss
And wish for everlasting love.

You're always in my heart

You're always in my heart my dear
And always in my dream,
You guide the way unto the stars
That shall forever gleam,
Above me through the darkness
As each one does shine so bright,
I will be yours and you'll be mine
This everlasting night.

A lifetime spent in searching
Till my true love I did find,
You came to me as if a wish
When life seemed so unkind,
You lifted me and pulled me from
Those depths amid the mire,
And brought me untold joy because
You are my heart's desire.

I never thought it meant for me
Nor ever come my way,
And yet when hope was all but gone
I've greeted it this day,
A moment I shall not forget
As long as I do live,
For all the years that now remain
To you my love I give.

Beautiful grove

I crossed over meadows and fields of the springtime
As sunlight was shining the sky was so blue,
And there lay before me a patchwork of colour
I gazed then in awe at that marvellous view,
I stood on the bridge that was spanning the river
And looked at the water that gently flowed by,
Its music I heard was so soft and so soothing
As there on the surface reflections did lie.

From hedgerows of hawthorn that wore their sweet blossom
And draping the banks like a cascade of snow,
I paused for a moment to take in the wonder
As over the land then a fresh breeze did blow,
'Twas scented and laced with the perfume of flowers
As I through the heart of the country then strove,
An hour or so later I came to the woodland
Then rested within such a beautiful grove.

While there in the shade of the newly-leafed branches
I sat and I watched as the morning did pass,
Amidst all the bluebells so pretty together
And gracefully bloomed through the long waving grass,
Where gaily the butterfly flew from the shadows
When caught in the sunbeams its velvet wings shone,
I watched as it weaved and then fluttered about me
Then soared to the treetops and then it was gone.

I then closed my eyes and I listened to nature
The song of the blackbird embellished the air,
And then I did wish that this day last forever
And I should be part of that paradise there,
No dream could be finer than sights I had witnessed
Nor better the pattern God's tapestry wove,
For there I found heaven existing around me
And dwelling within such a beautiful grove.

Let my dreams

Let my dreams be of springtime with blossoms and rainbows
And of the lush meadows where flowers do grow,
With scenes of the country so green and enriching
And filling my sleep with its wonderful show,
I'll picture a stream as it flows from the mountains
And then rest beside it as morning goes by,
To take in the views and the sounds of the songbirds
And there I shall gaze at the glorious sky.

Let my dreams be of summer with visions so restful
Of warm days of leisure when sunlight does shine,
As butterflies dance in the wild waving verges
Where parsley and cowslip with mayweed entwine,
The landscape surrounding a patchwork of colour
The maize and the barley with cornfields of gold,
Which sweep through the valleys and dwell on the hillsides
And there I would watch every sunset unfold.

Let my dreams be of autumn when woodlands are glowing
In auburn and amber as if they were fire,
The hues of the season with crimson and ochre
When there lies before me all that I desire,
Just watching the leaves as they float down so gently
And then come to rest on the ground where I tread,
For there I would walk 'neath the boughs and the branches
And follow the pathway wherever it led.

Let my dreams be of winter the first glimpse of snowfall
When scenery glistens in purest of white,
And all that I witness lies dusted and frozen
So still and so peaceful a beautiful sight,
To gaze at the stars when they're shining so clearly
On cold frosty evenings that melt to the dawn,
When I shall awake to the call of the morning
My dream will then end as the new day is born.

And so shall the next wave?

As far as the ocean that spreads before me
And fades in the distance without sympathy,
While ebbing and flowing so graceful it lies
It clings to my dream but my dream always dies,
No promise it made as it rolls to the shore
And yet now I wish it would bring love once more,
But all of my wishes do seep through this stone
For it gives me nothing and I'm left alone.

While gulls seem to mock me I try not to hear
Their call unforgiving so loud and so clear,
 I wager that they never felt love and lost
Or thus paid the price of that terrible cost,
But here I shall wait till the sun starts to set
When I will return but I'll never forget,
For while I am living and breathing God's air
I will retain hope it shall end my despair.

With each day that passes my memories fade
As now I look back on mistakes that I made,
I wake every dawn and so empty I feel
For while you're not with me my wounds shall not heal,
And yet I still gaze on this ocean of blue
For there all its beauty reminds me of you,
But love is behind me and left in the past
And so shall the next wave be just like the last?

Hayhead Wood

In Hayhead the soft light of dawn gently rises
To shine on the woodland surround,
It falls through the trees and their silver white branches
As shadows are cast on the ground,
There dusted by frost on this October morning
And gripped by the onset of cold,
The birches so graceful do stand in the open
Still bearing their rich leaves of gold.

But soon they will fall as the winter approaches
And then shall be lost to the spring,
Yet I should be grateful now autumn is ending
To see the last colour they bring,
The pathway I follow is narrow and winding
And there twisted roots cross the track,
I look to the pond for its water lies frozen
But now is beginning to crack.

I walk through the woodland a peace there existing
A contrast of light and of shade,
But there in the glow of the hues of the season
My dreams of the summer now fade,
In Hayhead the soft light of dawn gently rises
So warming the chill of the air,
I pray for the springtime once more to deliver
And hope God shall answer my prayer.

The lilac tree

Each spring this lilac tree does bloom
As if an everlasting friend,
With scent so pure that carries far
And fills the April day,
I look upon those purple flowers
As if they opened just for me,
Beside the old and mossy wall
To make a fine display.

It warms my heart to see it so
When lit by morning sun it shines,
As butterflies and bumble bees
Now taste its nectar sweet,
For there until the leaves shall fall
And winter comes around again,
Then I shall look upon the scene
And feel my life complete.

I rest beside the lilac tree
Whilst in its cooling shade I dwell,
I listen to the songs that float
Within the blossom air,
What joy I feel to see again
The beauty that the spring's revealed,
To cast the greatest spell of all
Upon this land so fair.

The one that I love

I bid her farewell as she waves from the doorstep
My heart feels so heavy I so want to stay,
But there I must leave her till late in the evening
When I shall return at the end of the day.

I'm heading to work on a cold winter's morning
The sunlight does shine through the clouds up above,
Each step that I take is another step further
Away from the arms of the one that I love.

While there my mind wanders I'm thinking about her
Awaiting the time I can see her again,
As I count every second each minute and hour
Each day seems a lifetime of heartache and pain.

But then as I leave all my burdens seem lifted
I sail through the air like the clouds up above,
I'm flying for freedom and heading for home now
And into the arms of the one that I love.

The chestnut trees of May

Now spring has blessed this waiting land
I look upon the village Croft,
And see the chestnut trees of May
With blossom flowers of white,
As row on row they proudly stand
Adorned in all their majesty,
And all the glories of the earth
Could make no better sight.

The scent of new mown grass does float
Upon the early morning breeze,
As I now make my way across
This vast and shadowed field,
I rest upon a wooden bench
And all alone I calmly sit,
To take in all the beauty there
The season now does yield.

While birds do sing in dulcet tone
Within the mighty blossomed boughs,
I listen to each song of joy
That fills the sapphire sky,
Amid the chestnut trees of May
I find a peace that does surround,
As there I dwell a little while
And watch the day go by.

Swan pool

In the pale light of morning the water now glistens
As the sun softly shines on this wondrous display,
For here dreams are made by the languid reflections
Which lie on the surface and mirror this day.

As I rest on the shoreline so quiet and so peaceful
Yet disturbed by the sound of the gulls' distant cry,
I watch as the swans move with grace there before me
From the reeds on the bank where the shadows now lie.

So gentle the breeze that does whisper around me
Through the leaves of the birches its music does sound,
So warm and caressing the grasses and flowers
The love of a lifetime I know I have found.

As the smoke clouds are drifting across the horizon
And sailing afar on the canvas of blue,
The beams ebb and dance on the ripples like diamonds
And thrive in the heart of this magical view.

And here I will stay till the hush of the evening
Descends with the sunset and skies are aglow,
I'll watch as the embers then fade to the darkness
And wait for the moon and the starlight to show.

Please lend me your wings

Please lend me your wings let me fly over mountains
As night is now fading into the sunrise,
Above the horizon where cold rugged shadows
Now melt to the light of the glorious skies.

So high up above let me sail to the distance
And ride on the clouds that in scarlet do glow,
Then soar through the air with the beams shining brightly
That light up my feathers wherever I go.

I'll sense there the warmth of the dawn all around me
I'll float on the thermals and into the blue,
While feeling the freedom alone in the heavens
An ocean unending, a marvellous view.

And then I'd look down on the earth in its glory
That's lifting from darkness to herald the day,
And I'd never rest I would fly on forever
For there I would gaze at that wondrous display.

Please lend me your wings let me fly over mountains
As night is now fading into the sunrise,
For hope is eternal so I'll go on dreaming
And soar in the light of the glorious skies.

A misty day upon the moor

I wish the clouds would lift again
So sun could shine across the moor,
To light the purple heathered way
I trod so long before,
But dull as now the mist descends
Beneath the grey and drizzle skies,
I know that if the day be fine
What beauty there now lies.

Yet hidden from my gaze for now
I pray the wind to strongly blow,
Away! Away those leaden clouds
I wish that they would go,
But resolutely linger still
And so my eyes shall have to wait,
To see the wonder of this land
Lost to September's fate.

For there like ghosts the hills beyond
So faint that I can barely see,
Their form and yet my memory knows
They stand majestically,
But as for now lie cut in two
As falling mist does make me blind,
O Lord please let me see again
And thus refresh my mind.

Of all the grace that's held within
This land that sleeps beneath the sheet,
I wish that it would waken now
To make my life complete,
As mist does drift like smoke across
The hills and purple heathered moor,
I know that proud am I to say
I'd seen it once before.

If love should then belong to me

No blossoms brighter of the spring
No sweeter song the lark would sing,
When tulips, may and daffodils
Adorn the fields and distant hills,
When bluebells bloom within the wood
Their sight would never seem so good,
A better place the world would be
If love should then belong to me.

The summer sky no deeper blue
No greater scene or pleasing view,
When meadows in the sunlight shine
Should warm that lonely heart of mine,
And where the gentle stream does flow
My happiness would truly grow,
A better place the world would be
If love should then belong to me.

When trees of autumn did unfold
That never shone in finer gold,
Then make a carpet where I tread
To guide the way for me ahead,
The sight of heather on the moor
Would seem much greater than before,
A better place the world would be
If love should then belong to me.

And when the winter snows shall fall
Across the ground to cover all,
To paint a picture there complete
Where dreams were never made so sweet,
And in the sky that crystal night
Where stars had never shone so bright,
A better place the world would be
If love should then belong to me.

I love this world in which I live

I love this world in which I live
The land, the sea, the wondrous sky,
And though the years may weary me
I know this love shall never die.

For beauty lives within each flower
And every creature great and small,
Each one deserving of my love
So I shall always care for all.

For every one a gift from God
To live and grace his masterpiece,
With colours bright for all to share
And wonders that shall never cease.

A gift so great I can't repay
And I could never ask for more,
Than be a part of his great plan
Within this world that I adore.

So wise for one so young

He saw the rainbows in the sky
He heard the songbirds sing,
He loved the changing seasons
And the joy that they did bring,
He sang for peace when but a child
That song he always sung,
And everyone agreed he was
So wise for one so young.

He loved all creatures great and small
He loved the countryside,
Saw beauty there in everything
The land which gave him pride,
He sang for peace as he grew up
But few did heed his call,
For as he played the battles roared
And many souls did fall.

And so he played much louder
Than he'd ever played before,
And though he tried all that he knew
He could not end the war,
He sang for peace but words were lost
Upon the winds that blew,
Across the scarred and ravaged land
That he no longer knew.

He couldn't find an audience
To listen to his tune,
At dawn he played unto the sun
At night unto the moon,
He sang for peace till he grew old
And then so weak and frail,
Yet still no one did hear him sing
And so his song did fail.

Yet when he died the people mourned
Laid flowers on his grave,
And were so very grateful for
The lives he tried to save,
He sang for peace when but a child
That song he always sung,
When everyone agreed he was
So wise for one so young.

I cherish every day I live

There is no better feeling
Than to wake and see the dawn,
As when the beams of sunlight shine
To greet the brand new morn,
Then walk amongst the flowers
Of the spring when all aglow,
I cherish every day I live
And sad to see it go.

I love to see the blossoms
And the bluebells 'neath the trees,
That spread across the woodland floor
And dance within the breeze,
Then listen to the songbirds
As they sing along with cheer,
So grateful for the sights I see
And every sound I hear.

I love to see the mountains
And the hills that rise in green,
With valleys deep where silver streams
Meander there between,
And meadows as the daisies bloom
To light the grassy ground,
Each time I'll find a lasting joy
Whene'er I look around.

When evening then begins to fall
And daylight fades away,
I close my eyes and say a prayer
To thank God for this day,
Then watch the stars that shine above
Within the wondrous sky,
And dream about tomorrow
As the night time passes by.

The peace cairn

So high on the hillside not far from the village
A peace cairn is growing there stone upon stone,
While people are praying the war to be ended
They know God is with them and they're not alone.

And as they look over their poor ravaged country
That once held such beauty but now it's all gone,
They look to the heavens with dreams for tomorrow
And while there is sunlight their hope shall live on.

They carry a stone in their hand for a loved one
Their name etched upon it held close to their heart,
The victims of war and their dearly beloved
Of families now ruined and so torn apart.

Their eyes filled with tears as they come to the peace cairn
To place down their stone as the dawn greets the day,
But memories they'll keep and they won't be forgotten
And while war continues they'll come here to pray.

These stones are the future each urging the soldier
To lay down his arms and to join hands in prayer,
A lasting foundation that grows ever stronger
And shall yield a welcome to all that come there.

The skies ever-changing

The skies ever-changing the colours now blend
As sunlight is falling the day's at an end,
It shimmers on wave tops a pathway before
That leads over water and rests on the shore.

While moving and swirling the clouds lit with gold
A cascading collage does slowly unfold,
As skies turn to scarlet like embers of fire
Which burn in the hearth of all heaven's desire.

Then deeper and deeper to crimson they fade
So gently they drift as new pictures are made,
While doused by the fall and the breeze blowing too
They sink to the land and this ocean of blue.

As darkness approaches and moon starts to rise
The sea turns to violet so restless it lies,
While shining so softly the stars now appear
Like diamonds above as the clouds start to clear.

The skies ever-changing the moon is so bright
And casts on the water a pathway of light,
That leads to the dawning horizon aglow
The gift of creation's most wonderful show.

May you grow to find some wisdom

May you grow to find some wisdom
And to learn to love the land,
As you gaze upon its beauty
Let it take you by the hand,
And lead you through the meadows there
Unto the gentle stream,
Where you can find a peaceful place
To close your eyes and dream.

May you smell the sweetest blossom
That does bloom within the spring,
And hear the gracious melodies
Of all the birds that sing,
Their songs of joyful harmony
Which float upon the breeze,
And walk amongst the bluebells there
Which grow beneath the trees.

May you climb each hill and mountainside
Then look upon the view,
And feel a sense of warmth within
For God is there with you,
And see the clouds that sail above
Then watch as they go by,
And wish that you could join them there
To soar across the sky.

May you grow to find some wisdom now
As from your dream you wake,
To watch the golden sunset
As it shines upon the lake,
A mirror of the heavens there
As colours meet and blend,
A work of art that richly flows
And seems to have no end.

Farewell my love

Farewell my love for I must go
To walk that lonely road ahead,
But here my heart shall stay with you
While I alone must face that dread.

Please spare a kindly thought for me
As all my love to you I'll send,
For I shall always think of you
From dawn until each day does end.

Then on that dark and barren plain
I know the stars will always shine,
And as they do I'll make a wish
That one day soon you shall be mine.

Till then my love I'll not forget
For you shall never leave my mind,
And live within my lasting dreams
For there I know that you I'll find.

If I could only touch the clouds

If I could only touch the clouds
And soar above the land so free,
I'd ride the wind that gently blows
And spread my golden wings,
I'd look upon the fields and hills
And see the view for miles and miles,
But yet I know I'll have to wait
For what the future brings.

I long to sail with all my friends
So high into the wilderness,
Where freedom lives for evermore
And they would welcome me,
I'd join with them upon my way
For sadly I've been left behind,
And I must face a life alone
Until that time shall be.

So here I'll stay upon the ground
Until I heal or else I die,
I'll never grace the skies again
Until my woe does leave,
And I shall weep as I look up
To see my friends then head afar,
And wish that I could follow
Yet alone I now must grieve.

I walk within the shallows

I walk within the shallows
That now rest upon the shore,
Where land once met the ocean
Yet the waves do roll no more,
I look upon the surface there
So cool upon my feet,
Where weed does grip and tangled float
As waters now retreat.

Upon the beach the lug worm coils
Make patterns on the sands,
And sunlight shines on ripples
Forming scales of golden bands,
Which seem to hypnotise my mind
I watch each one that flows,
And yields to me an endless joy
That in my heart now grows.

I see the tiny fish that swim
All stranded by the tide,
And as I walk they swiftly dart
To find a place to hide,
Ahead the seagulls dip and feed
I hear each hungry cry,
They walk within the shallows there
And then away do fly.

The view amongst the pine

I look upon the mighty pine
So straight and true they reach above,
To point towards the hidden sky
And cast their shadow deep,
Across the land where I do walk
With scattered cone around my feet,
Each step I take in silence where
A floor of needles sleep.

For there an amber carpet lies
So barren save the holly bush,
With sharpened leaves of darkest green
Which through the dullness shine,
Ahead I go in dappled light
Where beams break through the canopy,
So densely packed yet thus reveals
The view amongst the pine.

The rows and rows of chiselled trunks
Beside the twigs and branches lie,
So brittle for they surely fell
A time so long ago,
And yet remain as years do pass
An eerie sight, a ghostly chill,
I feel as then an icy wind
Between the trees does blow.

I sail through the clouds

I sail through the clouds in my dreams of tomorrow
I'm leaving the shores of my past far behind,
Alone on a journey I burnt all my bridges
Not knowing the future or what I shall find.

My love might be waiting to welcome me home there
As sunlight is resting and skies turn to gold,
And then as it fades and is lost to the darkness
I know I shall sleep till the dawn does unfold.

I float on the wind while the stars shine so brightly
It carries me forth to a land far away,
As silence surrounds me a soft voice is calling
My name in the distance and greets the new day.

But then I awaken as beams of the sunlight
Now climb over hillsides and into the sky,
I've opened my eyes yet my dream it still lingers
For there lives my hope I shall never let die.

The Lime Pits

Unto the Rushall Lime Pits I
Now walk upon this lonely trail,
That winds through tangled thicket dense
Of nettle gorse and thorn,
That cramp the narrow way ahead
Where dampened grass and puddles lie,
Now littered by the fallen leaves
Upon this autumn morn.

So fresh the air does seem to me
So cool the breeze upon my face,
I look towards the skies above
Which now begin to clear,
As clouds do break and drift afar
To thus reveal the sight of blue,
As faintest shadows gently fall
And then do disappear.

As through the woodland I now go
Where ivy climbs embittered trunks,
The sun now shines through boughs above
And lights the sodden ground,
As over twisted roots I tread
Which cross the path that leads me to,
The picture of the mirrored lake
Where golden trees surround.

With grace their soft reflections rest
Upon the water calm and still,
Where mallard and the moorhen swim
Close to the reeded shore,
I linger for a moment there
To listen to the blackbird sing,
And cast my gaze across the scene
As leaves fall to the floor.

Amongst fern and nettles

Amongst fern and nettles the campion's waving
Its petals the hue of the clouds of the dawn,
They shine in the hedges and peer from the woodland
And rise to the call of the new day that's born.

The gorse casts a spell as it sprinkles the hillside
Now lifting from darkness with flowers of gold,
I climb to the skies through the grass and the clover
And watch as the morning does slowly unfold.

I see there before me the peak in the distance
Unveiled to my eyes as the clouds start to clear,
The summer air fresh yet it yields only silence
For only the sound of the wind do I hear.

I pause there to gaze at the view of the coastline
As mist is now lifting from over the sea,
I feel now as one with the whole of creation
In a land that's untamed and so wild and so free.

I wish I could fly on a journey to heaven
And sail on the wind as I soar through the air,
Far over the downs where the clouds leave their shadows
Upon the sweet meadows and fields lying there.

Amongst fern and nettles the campion's waving
And moves in the breeze as the evening does fade,
Whilst caught in the light of the sun that's now falling
Then sinks to the darkness and cool of the shade.

If I should through the woodland go

If I should through the woodland go
What scenes of joy would greet my eyes,
When I should rest beneath the oak
For there I'd surely see,
The glory of the wildest rose
That sweetly blooms within the sun,
With petals pink they'd warm my heart
So grateful I would be.

If I should through the woodland go
I'd find a peace amongst the trees,
To listen to the birds that sing
And glory at their sound,
Then I should walk the path of fern
Where twisted roots do cross the track,
And where the scattered acorns lie
Inert upon the ground.

If I should through the woodland go
I'd watch the squirrel gather nuts,
And store them 'neath the fallen leaves
As autumn time does near,
For soon the trees will turn to gold
Then winter winds shall cruelly blow,
And when the mighty boughs are bare
They shall bring little cheer.

If I should through the woodland go
To see the dainty butterflies,
Which flutter through the morning air
It would enrich my day,
To see the beauty as I walked
The winding track without a care,
Until I came unto its end
Then headed on my way.

I held a shell against my ear

I held a shell against my ear
Whene'er I heard the sea,
Its graceful sound did bring me joy
And thus did comfort me,
For every time I dreamed I stood
Upon that shingle shore,
And hoped the waves would you bring you back
So I could love once more.

I kept that shell so many years
It never left my side,
Through all those empty days that passed
In it I did confide,
For as I held it to my ear
I knew my love was true,
For every wave I ever heard
Did bring me close to you.

When time went by with all my hope
I locked that shell away,
And there it stayed within the drawer
Until this very day,
And as I hold it in my hand
It brings back so much pain,
And yet I wonder now if I
Could hear its sound again.

I hold the shell against my ear
And still I hear the sea,
Alas it brings a joy no more
And cannot comfort me,
For now it does remind me of
Those times that we did share,
And love I treasured for so long
That ended in despair.

And yet it shall remain with me
For I could never part,
From all those memories that I keep
Within my longing heart,
Still every night I dream of her
Then wake to find her gone,
This shell is all that I have left
To help me carry on.

The green hills

The green hills ascend to the clouds that are passing
And drift through the sky on that canvas of blue,
Then lost to the haze on the distant horizon
They drown in the water and fade from my view.

I climb as I go with my shadow beside me
The chalk-laden track worn by many before,
As higher and higher I head on my journey
The whispering waves gently roll to the shore.

The slopes are adorned by the gorse and the thistle
Which cling to the ground in the tormenting breeze,
They bend and they shake with each gust that is blowing
Exposed to their forces that will not appease.

It tosses the ocean that glistens in sunlight
And catches the crests that in silver now rise,
As over the hills where the view is unending
A buzzard does circle alone in the skies.

The flowers of clover enriching the grassland
With daisies and speedwell the buttercups shine,
I look on the scene and I take in its wonder
Where colours of nature so freely entwine.

As evening is falling with sunset of amber
A pathway of gold is now spanning the sea,
I still hear the sound of the waves that are rolling
As if their sweet music is calling to me.

The 1970 Isle of Wight music festival

The year of nineteen seventy drew
Six hundred thousand folk or more,
Who came to hear the music play
So many years ago,
They made their way to Afton Down
By foot, by road, by bus and car,
Then pitched their tents upon the slopes
Of "Desolation Row".

A purple haze there did descend
That filled the minds of every soul,
Its spirit drifted like a spell
Amidst the evening air,
Its essence carried on the breeze
And all it touched would not forget,
For they were left within a trance
And glad that they were there.

The music played and didn't stop
Five days and nights it carried on,
So many folk yet few did sleep
For all had so much fun,
The show did close as dawn did break
And lit with gold the waiting land,
The people joined in harmony
And sang "Here comes the sun."

And as it shone upon the down
They made their weary way back home,
And soon the place was empty
Only memories did remain,
The music ceased and all was still
A breathless hush did sweep the land,
For now the peace had been restored
The birds were heard again.

The cool island breeze

The cool island breeze blowing over the water
And into the morn as the sun starts to rise,
Caressing the waves as they head to the shoreline
And carries the clouds through the glorious skies,
As it sings then a song as it moves through the tree tops
With rustle of branches and flickering leaves,
Then touching the landscape it swirls in sweet motions
And then through the cornfields a pattern it weaves.

Then over the hillside it winds down the valley
And follows the river that flows to the sea,
It moves through the heath through the meadows and pastures
And there finds a home where it so longs to be,
As gently it whispers and calling so softly
The shadows grow longer as sunlight descends,
As skies turn to amber its embers are burning
A mixture of colour in palette now blends.

The cool island breeze blowing over the water
As seagulls so peaceful above me do glide,
For now as the sunset does rest on the ocean
It's fanning the flames of the still eventide,
The sun is now sinking beneath the horizon
And so brings the chill as the night starts to fall,
The afterglow fading and stars begin shining
Yet still I can hear as it softly does call.

No words to speak I'm so forlorn

No words to speak I'm so forlorn
For all seems lost to me,
No comfort in the rising dawn
That brings more misery,
The morning sky so peaceful yet
So restless is the breeze,
That chills my soul I can't forget
The hurt of winter's freeze.

The blossoms do not bring me cheer
Upon the cherry bough,
And all the flowers that appear
Yield only sadness now,
For as they shine within the sun
No joy does fill my heart,
Though colours bright and day's begun
My life's still torn apart.

No words to speak for no one hears
Or seems to care at all,
Now I alone must dry my tears
For soon the leaves shall fall,
And when the wood's no longer gold
A year should then have passed,
Since love and days did grow so cold
And I did see you last.

The weary traveller

O weary traveller rest thy feet
And stay here for a while,
For you have journeyed from afar
And walked so many a mile,
For with that Bible in your hand
You've preached the sacred word,
Been driven out from every town
But went on undeterred.

Be seated by the window here
And look out on the day,
Then listen to the birds that sing
Before you head away,
Please take this drink I offer you
I have not much to spare,
And with it take this piece of bread
That I'm so glad to share.

Take off your shoes and close your eyes
And sleep an hour or so,
For though you've come so very far
You still have far to go,
The road ahead is hard and long
I do not envy you,
But spread the word of Christ the Lord
For he was right and true.

You have such courage in your heart
A braver man than I,
As on your journey you must go
May fortune with you fly,
I shake your hand and wish you luck
As now I bid farewell,
And pray that soon within this land
That God again shall dwell.

Please take my hand my love I yield

Please take my hand my love I yield
I've nothing more to give,
No wealth or stock no home or field
No reason left to live,
Bring joy into my barren heart
Have sympathy for me,
I cannot bear to be apart
Yet seems my destiny.

Please have no fear my love is true
I'll never speak a lie,
This question now I ask of you
Be mine until I die,
Say yes to me my darling now
That word I long to hear,
As blossom waits to line the bough
For spring is drawing near.

As snow does melt upon the way
And winter's almost gone,
I long to wed this very day
Then we shall be as one,
Please end this bitter chill I feel
And rid me of despair,
For then a kiss would surely seal
The love we'll always share.

Please lift thine eyes towards that star

Please lift thine eyes towards that star
That shines for you and me,
For then my wish shall travel far
And fill my heart with glee,
For there within the darkness shines
An everlasting light,
That crosses seas and borderlines
To be with you this night.

Please lift thine eyes towards the sky
So we can be as one,
And watch the time go passing by
Until the night has gone,
For while it shines I feel your love
And never shall it fade,
For I believe in heaven above
Our love was truly made.

Please lift thine eyes though we're apart
And make my wish come true,
I have no room left in my heart
Such love I hold for you,
I hope that you now feel the same
And gaze unto that star,
When on the breeze I call your name
My voice shall travel far.

The daffodils in meadows shine

The daffodils in meadows shine
So beautiful to see,
The picture sweet the view divine
Now spring has come to be,
The day is warm the morning bright
No clouds within the sky,
I see the swallows of delight
As gracefully they fly.

The blossom on the cherry trees
With petals pink and frail,
Which float upon the April breeze
And through the air do sail,
Like snow they fall then gone so fast
For soon they're blown away,
I wish for once that they should last
And spring came every day.

I walk with you now hand in hand
The season's joy we share,
To see the wonder of the land
Upon this morning fair,
I gaze upon this work of art
For spring I do adore,
And yet can say with all my heart
I love you even more.

Where art you now where have you gone?

Where art you now where have you gone?
For I feel so alone,
I know that life must carry on
And yet my sorrow's grown,
The church bell tolls for love is lost
At empty fields I stare,
What price my heart what would it cost
To see you standing there?

I read the names that are engraved
In loving memory,
For all these souls could not be saved
And soon it shall be me,
I know as in your grave you lie
Beneath the twisted yew,
This love I keep shall never die
And will remain so true.

For I am certain while you sleep
My pain shall not be gone,
As on your stone I gently weep
Somewhere your soul lives on,
So rest in peace as I must leave
Though hurt shall not refrain,
For you my love I'll always grieve
Until we meet again.

The leaning tree

The leaning tree does vainly cling
To life upon the crumbling slopes,
With roots exposed it soon shall slide
Unto the depths below,
With every year that passes by
It inches closer to its death,
As it grows ever weaker now
And soon it will let go.

For every drop of rain that falls
Does wash away the fragile soil,
Where once it stood so proudly there
It now does stand forlorn,
Its leaves grow sparser by the year
And birds no longer sing amidst,
Its boughs so bare and helpless
With their bark all stripped and torn.

It may not greet another spring
Nor live to see the winter through,
So sad that this once mighty tree
Exists within this state,
Five hundred years it has adorned
The land that now has slipped away,
And now it seems prepared to face
The wicked hand of fate.

The leaning tree does creak and groan
With every gust of wind that blows,
Along the valley no escape
Or respite from its force,
So long ago the ground was safe
But time has seen it roll away,
Into the river's waiting grasp
Upon its winding course.

Hark the songbirds sweetly sing

Hark the songbirds sweetly sing
Their melodies for me,
With all the joy that they do bring
They fill the air with glee,
Across the meadows in the trees
Amidst the boughs above,
They sail afar upon the breeze
That yields to me such love.

The summer day so warm and bright
And brings me so much cheer,
The countryside a lovely sight
The view is crystal clear,
As over rolling downs that rise
Above the fields of corn,
Which wave in gold beneath the skies
Of blue upon this morn.

So proud am I to walk this land
No greater place on earth,
This sacred soil on which I stand
My homeland from my birth,
Now as the shadows start to grow
And sun begins to fall,
I'll stay to watch the stars that glow
The greatest sight of all.

A chill wind does blow

A chill wind does blow
From the northerly skies
As the wild sweeping rain starts to fall,
It's bringing the cloud
That descends on the land
As it rolls down the mountains so tall.

The scenery dulled
By the morning so bleak
And is cloaked by the shadows of grey,
For the winter is near
As the autumn does fade
And there's nothing to stand in its way.

For where now the peaks
Which are lost to the clouds?
And where are the songs of the dawn?
Yet somewhere they hide
In this September storm
Yet are pricked by cold of the morn.

The wind unrelenting
The force of a gale
And a torrent of anger it yields,
That's tossing the gorse
And is bending the boughs
And does buffet the grass in the fields.

Be still for me wind
Let the sunlight appear
May the rain cease to fall on this land,
Let the colour arise
From the mountains above
So again in their glory they'll stand.

The day when love was first revealed

The morning air was filled with song
I listened as I went along,
As spring had brought the colours bright
And hawthorn then was dressed in white,
The perfumed air did smell so sweet
Then by the river we did meet,
I walked with you across the field
The day when love was first revealed.

We saw the hills that rose so high
And almost touched the sapphire sky,
We looked across the land so green
The greatest sight we'd ever seen,
We saw the bluebells in the wood
The branches there were all in bud,
We felt the warmth that spring did yield
The day when love was first revealed.

We crossed the meadow there as one
Upon each flower the sunlight shone,
Where daisies graced the land so fair
The season's wonders we did share,
We headed far upon our way
To God were grateful for that day,
And when we kissed our fate was sealed
The day when love was first revealed.

What sorrow has befallen me

What sorrow has befallen me
No sun to light my day,
These clouds yield only misery
While joy has fled away,
Across the lands where no one goes
And all do fear to tread,
Where only fear and silence grows
And dreams are lying dead.

Now waves of sadness and despair
Do swamp my aching heart,
For no one now does seem to care
My life's been torn apart,
Regrets I shall take to my grave
My tears forever flow,
For all my hopes I could not save
And on the wind did blow.

And yet no malice do I keep
Nor hate towards my love,
I'll dream of her within my sleep
While stars do shine above,
And hope that soon the dawn shall break
Then shine just like before,
For now I know each morn I wake
I'll miss her even more.

As sadness blows the autumn leaves

As sadness blows the autumn leaves
Across the barren ground,
I know for me nobody grieves
Such heartache I have found,
For when the woodland turned to gold
My life did all but end,
I lost my love as days grew cold
And now I have no friend.

I see the branches standing bare
And winter soon shall be,
My sorrow now they seem to share
As if they wept for me,
Yet they shall see the spring again
While I must suffer so,
The tears I cry shall not refrain
And will forever flow.

As sadness blows the autumn leaves
Across the barren floor,
I know for me nobody grieves
Or cares for me no more,
I wait for winter's snow to fall
To face the bitter chill,
While knowing she will never call
And wished she loved me still.

That summer evening calm and still

That summer evening calm and still
I stood and looked across the sea,
And as the sun did slowly fall
It lit the waves in gold,
They glistened as they came to rest
Then seeped within the shingle there,
As if they fell like broken dreams
I could no longer hold.

Alone was I no other soul
To feel the breathless hush descend,
As I then saw the amber glow
That filled the skies with light,
The crimson clouds did drift away
Above the grey and barren sea,
That ebbed and flowed unto the shore
Then slipped into the night.

Yet no salvation did it bring
No respite from my lonely days,
My feelings burned much deeper than
The stones beneath my feet,
That summer evening calm and still
The moon did shine so brightly then,
And lit the way before me
As I watched the tide retreat.

And as the breeze now gently blows

And as the breeze now gently blows
Through waving fields of golden corn,
It weaves a pattern as it goes
Upon this bright late summer morn,
And as I rest beneath this tree
I hear the blackbird sweetly sing,
That fills my heart with tender glee
For so much joy his song does bring.

This aged oak that's blessed me shade
Will soon respond to autumn's call,
As warm days cease and slowly fade
Its amber leaves will gently fall,
Then rest upon this lowly ground
Beneath those mighty branches bare,
And barren fields will then surround
When winter's cold shall yield despair.

The afternoon does come and pass
I walk until the sun descends,
Now all seems hushed no songs alas
And darkness falls as evening ends,
I see the hills so far away
Their graceful slopes which fall and rise,
Which look so peaceful as the day
Now sinks into the setting skies.

I wake to see the rising dawn

I wake to see the rising dawn
The morning skies aglow,
The land so crisp and frozen white
Lies dusted by the snow,
The sunlight flickers through the boughs
Of still and leafless trees,
And rests upon the barren ground
The winter's night did freeze.

I wish that it were yesterday
My loved one by my side,
My wish shall not be answered now
All hope of love has died,
And as the cold of winter bites
It chills me to the bone,
For I am left with nothing
And must face my life alone.

A robin perched upon the fence
Looks longingly at me,
And there he rests and sweetly sings
As if in sympathy,
He waits a little longer there
And then does fly away,
To try and seek some respite
From this cold and lonely day.

The cobwebs grace the hedgerow
Which their silver threads adorn,
And glisten in the sunlight
On the holly, briar and thorn,
While shadows dark still linger
Where the sunlight cannot shine,
Nor can it warm my empty heart
Now she's no longer mine.

The dawning filled with birdsong

The dawning filled with birdsong now
My window's open wide,
The chaffinch sings upon the bough
With vigour and with pride,
Amidst the hedge beside the gate
So sweet the wren's refrain,
Who sings unto his lonely mate
There time and time again.

The blackbird too with gladdened cheer
From lofty perch does call,
His silken strains so pure and clear
The greatest song of all,
Upon the branch the robin sings
Within the cherry tree,
What graceful notes he always brings
Which fill the air with glee.

While sparrows chirp in thickets dense
Thus hidden from my gaze,
The song thrush sings upon the fence
With gentle golden phrase,
The dove coos from the roof above
The sound a soothing tone,
And there he sings his song of love
Unanswered all alone.

As peeping swifts now fill the skies
I hear the crows that caw,
The morning sun does slowly rise
To shine again once more,
The magpies chatter far away
While blue tits softly cheep,
The chorus of the brand new day
That stirred me from my sleep.

Fear not the fate befallen me

Fear not the fate befallen me
For I was weak of heart,
My eyes were blind I could not see
The time that we did part,
And with my tears I bade farewell
As I went on my way,
Your lips were hushed I could not tell
You wished for me to stay.

I walked the lonely road ahead
Not knowing where to go,
I longed to be with you instead
But then I didn't know,
As soon as I was out of sight
I stopped and turned around,
And there I waited through the night
Upon the barren ground.

The wind did blow an eerie tune
So that I could not sleep,
I gazed toward the chilling moon,
The pain I felt so deep,
For I knew then I had to stay
Without your love divine,
I could not live a single day
And prayed you would be mine.

So now my love I have returned
To try and win your hand,
I need you so my lesson learned
I hope you understand,
Please let me in your life once more
Forgive my foolish pride,
My darling now unlock the door
And let me come inside.

I've come to see my maiden fair

I've come to see my maiden fair
So long I've been away,
With her my life I want to share
For love shall be this day,
I've seen her in my deepest dream
That's now reality,
Betwixt the fields and gentle stream
Alone she waits for me.

Upon the breeze I call your name
And then we do embrace,
Though years have passed you look the same
No lines have aged your face,
For all the time we were apart
Your memory I did keep,
Each day you stayed within my heart
Each night as I did sleep.

Now I shall never leave your side
As long as I do live,
For with you now I shall abide
And all my love I'll give,
Please take this ring for it is thine
To treasure and adore,
For love this strong will always shine
And last for evermore.

The petals from my fallen rose

The petals from my fallen rose
Lie restless on the ground,
Then tossed upon the wind that blows
And wails a deathly sound,
No longer does my flower shine
Within the morning sun,
Nor does it warm this heart of mine
Now autumn has begun.

No longer can I smell the scent
Its life is at an end,
It bloomed in spring with good intent
In summer like a friend,
Yet now the scene that lies before
Has all but withered dry,
And there above I see no more
The swallows in the sky.

It seems there's nothing left for me
September days have passed,
And this the way it has to be
For joy could never last,
The petals from my fallen rose
Have now all blown away,
Until again this flower grows
My sorrow then shall stay.

I saw the newborn lambs that played

I saw the newborn lambs that played
Within the field before,
The sights of April were displayed
I could not ask for more,
I saw the daffodils of gold
As sun did slowly rise,
That warmed my heart against the cold
And filled the morning skies.

I saw the blossoms of delight
Upon the cherry tree,
The hawthorn too adorned in white
In all its majesty,
I saw the bluebells 'neath the trees
The gorse in flower too,
The meadow wave within the breeze
Where all the daisies grew.

I saw the swifts so high above
And heard the blackbird sing,
Each note to me a song of love
The joy that it did bring,
I saw the mayweed line the way
Within the country lane,
And I knew then upon that day
That spring had come again.

As softly as the stream does flow

As softly as the stream does flow
Down from the hills above,
The waters pass and yet I know
They shall not bring me love.

Its silver surface shines so bright
Within the morning sun,
Yet cannot free me from my plight
For life has yet begun.

As floating leaves begin to sink
My heart does sink with thee,
For as they drown it makes me think
That joy I'll never see.

The sound so sweet unto my ear
I walk its winding way,
Then look upon its water clear
And wish for love this day.

As softly as the stream does flow
Around the rock and stone,
I think of love so long ago
As I now watch alone.

When summer fades to autumn

What boundless joy does fill my gaze
For April's come to be,
What gracious sights do now surround
For all of us to see,
As flowers bloom from winter's rest
Such happiness they bring,
When summer fades to autumn
I'll await another spring.

I love to see the blossoms
Which do form upon the trees,
Then see their petals gently fall
Like rain upon the breeze,
And bluebells dress the woodland
While the birds so sweetly sing,
When summer fades to autumn
I'll await another spring.

As daffodils now light the land
And vibrant colours glow,
So glad am I to be alive
To marvel at this show,
As skies above are now abound
With birds upon the wing,
When summer fades to autumn
I'll await another spring.

I rest beside the golden corn

I rest beside the golden corn
Where wind does blow each waving ear,
So happy I to greet the morn
And dwell within its beauty here,
As swallows grace the sapphire sky
They bring such joy into my heart,
But soon away they all shall fly
And from these shores they then will part.

I see the hills that rise before
Which in their greatness there do stand,
It is a scene that I adore
To gaze upon this wondrous land,
At all the glory thus displayed
To listen to the birds that sing,
And know that here my fortune's made
With all the glory it does bring.

I'll savour every moment now
For soon the fields shall all be bare,
As harvest comes and then the plough
Then I shall see no beauty there,
As autumn fades to winter's cold
The spring will seem so far away,
And yet these memories I shall hold
Of scenes I saw upon this day.

I stay until the sun does fall
And shadows rest upon the ground,
As now the evening starts to call
The air is hushed there's not a sound,
I see the skies then all aglow
Which slowly slip into the night,
Yet still the corn does gently blow
Beneath the stars that shine so bright.

That fateful day

That fateful day I can recall
Was cold and dark and wet,
And lives with me for evermore
I never shall forget,
For on that chill November morn
The wind did blow so strong,
Then took away my precious love
And wailed a tuneless song.

Alone was I my tears did fall
And no one seemed to care,
I felt the pain of winter like
The trees that stood so bare,
As clouds did race across the sky
The storm would not relent,
It carried so much venom
And possessed a cruel intent.

I had nowhere to shelter
And each gust a mortal blow,
That struck me down and left me weak
And there my fear did grow,
For I knew then my love had gone
And never would return,
All hope was lost and yet for her
My soul shall always yearn.

That fateful day has scarred my life
Those wounds shall never heal,
Although the storm did slowly pass
Its hurt I'll always feel,
But as the sunlight fills the sky
And now the wind is still,
I love her so with all my heart
And know I always will.

Be still the chilly wind that blows

Be still the chilly wind that blows
Let sunlight come this day,
To thus remove a thousand woes
And take them far away,
Please let the darkest clouds now pass
Which yield this sleet and rain,
While sorrow pours no joy alas
And spring won't shine again.

Please may the air begin to warm
And end this bitter cold?
To let the cherry blossoms form
With daffodils of gold,
When palettes rich with colours blend
Beneath the sapphire skies,
I'll know that winter's at an end
When seas of bluebells rise.

Now for that time I shall await
With sad and longing heart,
And pray the wind will soon abate
Then from these shores will part,
When April comes the snows shall thaw
And melt unto a stream,
Then I will see the spring once more
And live again my dream.

My dreams of love may never be

My dreams of love may never be
My wishes not come true,
For all the beauties I did see
But none compared to you,
I long to live those days again
That sadly passed me by,
Yet but for now I hope in vain
As all alone I lie.

I bear such feelings in my heart
My spirit cannot rest,
For every day we spend apart
A day I do detest,
I hope that soon you will be mine
My dreams shall linger on,
So I will wait for love to shine
And won't accept it's gone.

My dreams of love may never be
While you are far away,
But still my heart shall rest with thee
And there forever stay,
I won't give up I cannot bear
The thought that it's too late,
Nor can I cope with this despair
And yet it seems my fate.

My lonely heart shall wait for spring

My lonely heart shall wait for spring
And winter's cold to go,
For then the birds for me will sing
As flowers bloom and grow.

Then I shall breathe the air of love
That found its way to me,
The sun will light the skies above
And shine eternally.

When leaves do form upon the trees
And yield to me their shade,
Then I will feel the warming breeze
And all my hurt shall fade.

I'll leave these lonely days behind
Forgotten in my past,
For then I know true love I'll find
That shall forever last.

My lonely heart shall wait for spring
And snow and ice to thaw,
I hope the blossomed boughs will bring
A chance to love once more.

That kiss shall keep you in my dreams

That kiss shall keep you in my dreams
I never will forget,
Though years have passed it only seems
Like yesterday we met.

With you the time has flown my love
Like clouds within the sky,
To yield the sunlight there above
Its warmth shall never die.

For there within my heart will stay
And it shall always shine,
I spend each moment of the day
So glad that you are mine.

That kiss we shared beneath this tree
Upon that summer morn,
Shall rest with me eternally
For here our love was born.

As sunrise brings the morning songs

As sunrise brings the morning songs
Of dawn I've waited for,
I know that here my heart belongs
And shall for evermore.

As light does shine upon the land
And skies are burning fire,
I know I have within my hand
All that I now desire.

For spring has come this joyful day
The snowdrops bloom in white,
Now wintertime has passed away
There is no greater sight.

For as the mist does slowly clear
Upon the hill and field,
The vision that I hold so dear
Then to my eyes revealed.

I push my window open wide
And breathe the morning air,
Then gaze upon the countryside
In all its beauty there.

As sunrise brings the morning songs
From every branch and bough,
They serve to right a thousand wrongs
And lift the darkness now.

As autumn comes with falling leaves

As autumn comes with falling leaves
And winter soon shall be,
The pattern that the wind now weaves
Does change relentlessly.

It blows through branches of the trees
Which bend within the gale,
And with each gust the beauty flees
Then through the air does sail.

Each leaf is like a broken dream
That crumbles in my hand,
Its dust shall fall into the stream
That flows across the land.

Down valleys steep and barren fields
Unto the distant shore,
The wind still blows and never yields
Till leaves remain no more.

As autumn comes and cannot wait
And evening fades to night,
Then through the clouds of scorn and hate
The moon does cast its light.

A scarlet rose for my true love

A scarlet rose for my true love
So sweet the perfume flies,
And drifts into the air above
Then through the longing skies.

I hope this love that I now send
Shall find a way to you,
With all my heart my dearest friend
Across the summer's blue.

The thought of you lies in my hand
Its beauty that you share,
Across the fields across the land
My love shall find you there.

Then I will yield this scarlet rose
It's all I have to give,
For you my love my passion grows
Each day that I shall live.

Farewell to England's pastures green

Farewell to England's pastures green
So sad to leave am I,
The wonders here that I have seen
Beneath the summer sky.

I breathe the air for one last time
And head upon my way,
Back to the town of dirt and crime
But how I long to stay.

Within the fields and meadows here
But time is at an end,
And so I wipe away a tear
For you my dearest friend.

As now towards my living hell
I know I must go back,
To live the life I know so well
Yet courage I do lack.

Farewell to England's pastures green
But soon I shall return,
To see again those sights I've seen
For which I'll always yearn.

Until he drew his final breath

Until he drew his final breath
He tried so hard to cheer,
All through his life until his death
His heart was kind and dear.

He lived by honest Christian ways
And tried the best he could,
Until the ending of his days
He fought to do some good.

This world will be a sadder place
Now that his life has passed,
He always greeted folks with grace
A saint unto the last.

So place a flower on his grave
And bid a kind farewell,
His life for peace he bravely gave
Yet here his soul must dwell.

Across the windswept downs I go

Across the windswept downs I go
Which lead unto the waiting sky,
And as the gusts do strongly blow
I watch the clouds go racing by,
Between their forms the sun does shine
Upon the slopes of yellow gorse,
With which the heather does entwine
To verge this worn and stony course.

Beyond I see each rolling field
A patchwork there of light and shade,
Unto my eyes are now revealed
The wonders that the Lord has made,
For there the ocean deep and blue
The rolling waves and cliffs of white,
And as I look upon that view
With awe I marvel at the sight.

So rich the green and pleasant land
That fills my heart with lasting pride,
To know that God's almighty hand
Has blessed this English countryside,
Across the windswept downs I go
And watch the bushes shake and bend,
As still the gusts do strongly blow
Where beauty knows no bounds or end.

Within the April woodland grow

Within the April woodland grow
The bluebells of the dawning spring,
A sea of blue like waves that flow
Upon the breeze they gently ring.

As now the boughs begin to leaf
The sun does shine with gentle beam,
To light the flowers there beneath
And glisten on the restful stream.

That through the woodland winds its way
And follows me where'er I tread,
For love has come to me this day
As to this land I now am wed.

My heart is filled with gladdened cheer
To see the sight and hear the sound,
To me the greatest time of year
When they adorn the barren ground.

Each one to me a lover's kiss
Upon my lips that waited long,
For now I feel a sense of bliss
That lifts me like the throstle's song.

Within the April woodland grow
The bluebells of the dawning spring,
A sea of blue like waves that flow
Unto the shore they softly sing.

If I should lose my heart to thee

If I should lose my heart to thee
Then all my woes I would forget,
A better man I'd surely be
To live each day without regret.

I'd love thee with a love so true
Away my lonely tears would fly,
For I would spend each day with you
Until the time that I should die.

My dreams of you would travel far
And while I breathe they would not fade,
But shine just like the brightest star
In all its greatness there displayed.

Each day to me would be the spring
And I should dance upon the air,
I hope tomorrow thus will bring
A love to end my dark despair.

If I should lose my heart to thee
Then we could live our lives as one,
A lasting joy would welcome me
And all my sadness would be gone.

As sheep within their pastures graze

As sheep within their pastures graze
Upon this summer morning still,
I see the sunlight's golden rays
Which shine upon the grassy hill.

No more my dreams go passing by
Like clouds within the skies above,
Instead with you shall always lie
For I have found my own true love.

Amidst the lands so peaceful there
I look upon this pleasant view,
For all my days I long to share
And spend my whole life here with you.

Beneath the trees my soul is free
To dance within the woodland's shade,
For here my heart's so filled with glee
My lasting joy shall never fade.

As sheep within their pastures graze
I hear the songs of morning sing,
Each flowing tune and gentle phrase
Do float with grace upon the wing.

The early morning lark did sing

The early morning lark did sing
To lofty heights from field did rise,
Then quickly soared upon the wing
So far into those summer skies.

The waving wheat that stood before
Within the restful breeze did blow,
And when his song I heard no more
I knew it time for me to go.

The path then led me far away
Unto a clear and gentle stream,
Then through the meadows I did stray
That in the sunlight there did gleam.

I walked within the woodland green
And rested in its cooling shade,
Against a tree I there did lean
Until the light began to fade.

Then as the sun began to set
And shadows rested on the ground,
I saw a view I'll not forget
For beauty shone then all around.

I went back on the way that led
Through meadows to the stream so clear,
And saw the waving wheat ahead
Again the lark I then did hear.

Where has the sun of morning gone?

Where has the sun of morning gone?
For bluest skies have turned to grey,
The scene so dull where once it shone
I wish the clouds would roll away.

To thus reveal the view I love
Yet while the wind does strongly blow,
It may then break the slate above
And force that darkened mass to go.

O sun please shine for me again
To light the hills with beams of gold,
The fields and meadows look so plain
As now the air does feel so cold.

While now the rain begins to fall
The hills lie hidden from my gaze,
No longer standing proud and tall
But cloaked within the mist and haze.

Where has the sun of morning gone?
That stirred me from my deepest sleep,
For now the land I look upon
So bleak as clouds now gently weep.

Please cease for me o restless breeze

Please cease for me o restless breeze
And let the day be still,
As leaves do fall from autumn trees
And scatter now at will.

So long it feels since summer glowed
And woodland was of green,
When daisies lined this winding road
And beauty here I'd seen.

When butterflies so gaily flew
And settled on the flowers,
Beneath the richest skies of blue
I spent so many hours.

Yet now the skies are filled with rain
So dull and overcast,
I wish I could relive again
Those memories of the past.

Please cease for me o restless breeze
For winter now draws near,
As leaves do fall from autumn trees
My hopes shall disappear.

The rose now blooms and shines so bright

The rose now blooms and shines so bright
On petals red the morning dew,
Does sparkle in the dawning light
With thoughts of days I spent with you.

Its scent does drift upon the air
And to the butterfly does call,
Who rests but for a moment there
With velvet wings revealed to all.

And then I watch it fly away
Upon the whispered breeze that blows,
Yet here I know I'll always stay
To look upon this scarlet rose.

For once this flower brought me love
And thus reminds me every year,
Like tears that fall from clouds above
I'll weep each time it shall appear.

The rose now blooms and shines so bright
Yet yields a sadness to my heart,
Although it makes a pleasing sight
It tells me how our lives did part.

All hope seems gone and lost to me

All hope seems gone and lost to me
As evening fades with thoughts of love,
I must accept it cannot be
Yet while the stars do shine above.

A chance may come if not too late
To bless me with that joy again,
But now I must accept my fate
And beg the winter to refrain.

Each night now holds a bitter chill
That cannot warm my aching heart,
Nor everlasting dreams fulfil
While we're two souls who drift apart.

For once our love was strong as stone
But now has crumbled into dust,
And all my trials I face alone
With no one now that I can trust.

As moonlight falls it softly casts
A spell upon the frozen land,
But never can erase the past
Nor guide me to your loving hand.

Awake sweet morn to end the night

Awake sweet morn to end the night
So sun can fill the dawning sky,
With pleasant songs of such delight
When wistful tunes above me fly.

As darkness ends and stars do fade
And clouds are breathing scarlet fire,
Above the land I thus persuade
To give me all I now desire.

Please let the still and frozen ground
Now melt to form the teary dew,
May silken threads then weave around
The hedges and the bushes too.

Then stir the blossom into flower
And urge the daffodils to grow,
Use all your mighty strength and power
To make this barren garden glow.

Please light the way so I can see
The petals as they start to shine,
A welcome sight shall always be
Unto these longing eyes of mine.

Awake sweet morn to start the day
And shake the darkness from its sleep,
Then greet the trees along the way
To rouse the spring from slumbers deep.

The mist does drape the distant hill

The mist does drape the distant hill
And grips the bleak and ghostly skies,
With silence for the morning still
Across the field and meadow lies.

For clinging to the darkness there
A cloak is cast upon the view,
Behind the trees so stark and bare
The sun is slowly breaking through.

The air is chill upon this day
November now begins to bite,
The swallows too long flown away
That once did bring me such delight.

The path ahead is so unclear
As features now are lost for me,
For all that I once held so dear
Lies hidden in the mist I see.

I walk across the lowly field
Where frost has settled on the grass,
And pray the spring again would yield
Its warmth to thaw this frozen mass.

So once again the stream could flow
Across the rich and emerald land,
Now veiled in white and thus could show
The hill within the distance stand.

While here remains my shattered dream

While here remains my shattered dream
Upon the fallen leaves,
I feel so low no self-esteem
For me nobody grieves.

Forgotten and unwanted I
No one to take my hand,
Beneath my feet my hopes now lie
In darkness where I stand.

The way ahead so bleak to me
I feel that all is lost,
I'd call but who shall hear my plea?
Instead I'll count the cost.

I hope that soon the coming spring
Shall light the way before,
And smile again then fortune bring
Some joy to me once more.

As through the autumn winds I go
The chill so hard to bear,
And yet a glimpse would end my woe
To see you standing there.

While here remains my shattered dream
That never shall come true,
And days that pass shall always seem
A lifetime without you.

My sweetest love beside me lie

My sweetest love beside me lie
And stay until the morn,
To see the stars within the sky
Then watch the breaking dawn.

I long for you to hold me near
And warm me from this chill,
With all my heart I love you dear
And know I always will.

For every day that I should live
I long to share with you,
My love is all I have to give
And yet so strong and true.

So please don't leave me now to fend
Throughout this night alone,
Then love we share shall never end
And will be set in stone.

My sweetest love beside me lie
As darkness starts to fall,
Let's gaze upon the starry sky
The greatest sight of all.

I wish I were that butterfly

I wish I were that butterfly
That goes from flower to flower,
Then sails into the morning sky
To seek the blossomed bower.

I wish that every day the spring
And I could follow thee,
If I could fly upon the wing
So happy I would be.

I wish to taste that nectar sweet
And flutter through the air,
For every bloom that I should greet
I'd find a welcome there.

I wish this place could be home
Where all my days I'd spend,
For over fields and hills I'd roam
Until my life did end.

I wish I were that butterfly
Upon the breeze I'd ride,
Above the land within the sky
To view the countryside.

So green the land that I can see

So green the land that I can see
The hills and fields before my eyes,
Which blend with joyful harmony
Beneath the peaceful summer skies.

I breathe the morning air so sweet
So glad to be alive this day,
To see the new shoots of the wheat
And hedgerows now adorned with May.

Along the country lane I head
Not caring where it leads me to,
I know wherever I am led
I'll always find a pleasing view.

Beneath the bridge a river flows
Where ripples dance and brightly shine,
Like diamonds as the water glows
And winds unto this heart of mine.

The sweeping slopes of light and shade
Where clouds now cast their shade before,
With all the beauty there displayed
No man could ever ask for more.

So green the land that I can see
With gladdened soul I now do roam,
And as I go I say with glee
Fair England always be my home.

I touch the morning of the spring

I touch the morning of the spring
And breathe its giving air,
Then listen to the birds that sing
Those songs they love to share.

I hold the blossom in my hand
Upon the cherry tree,
Then look across this April land
No better place to be.

As bluebells grace the woodland floor
So wondrous is their sight,
And glad am I to see once more
The hawthorn dressed in white.

With all the yellow daffodils
Which in the meadow shine,
And there beyond those emerald hills
Which warm this heart of mine.

To me each one such joy does give
No better time of year,
These are the days I'm glad to live
For now the spring is here.

My aching heart does need you so

My aching heart does need you so
To fill my empty days,
And rid me of this dreadful woe
With all its hurtful ways.

Each morn I wake I feel so sad
For you are never there,
I wish the chance to make you glad
And show you that I care.

While I'm resigned to misery
My tears shall never dry,
I must accept what's meant to be
No longer live a lie.

My thoughts of you shall never fade
But linger through the night,
As to the stars I often prayed
Until the morning light.

For in the Lord I put my trust
My prayers though went unheard,
My hopes all crumbled into dust
For crushed my every word.

And so alone I must go on
To face the road ahead,
For now the chance of love has gone
And all my dreams are dead.

The summer breeze that gently blows

The summer breeze that gently blows
Shall never send to me her love,
With every gust it yields more woes
Across the lonely skies above.

Which seem to bring me only tears
For they shall fall and never dry,
Until again my love appears
This sorrow will not pass me by.

My loving heart I pledged to you
Upon that fateful autumn day,
Alas in vain a cruel wind blew
And thus my dreams did blow away.

So when it comes and leaves shall fall
A wretched year should then have passed,
That's been the hardest time of all
Since I did weep and saw you last.

The summer breeze that gently blows
Shall carry now my longing prayer,
For every day my sadness grows
And every dawn does yield despair.

I love to walk upon the hills

I love to walk upon the hills
And breathe the cool refreshing air,
Then find the peace the land instils
Where I may rest in comfort there.

I'll sit beneath a tree to shade
And write of all the sights I see,
For in that place my dreams displayed
And everything they mean to me.

I'll watch the birds upon the wing
Within the morning skies of blue,
Then listen to the songs they sing
And look upon that wondrous view.

Then I'll return with gladdened cheer
With memories I shall always keep,
For in my mind the picture's clear
Of which I'll dream within my sleep.

I love to walk upon the hills
Where I can roam and wander wide,
For they could cure a thousand ills
And yield a lasting joy inside.

O radiant stars that shine above

O radiant stars that shine above
And fill the evening sky,
Please offer me a sign of love
Or else just fade and die.

Cast down on me a beam of hope
To which I may now cling,
For I am lost and cannot cope
Glad tidings may you bring.

Shine on for me until the dawn
When sunlight shall appear,
I long to greet the rising morn
And find my loved one here.

For in them all my fortune's told
If they could speak to me,
Yet frost descends the night grows cold
And darkness all I see.

O radiant stars that shine above
Yield joy into my heart,
Please offer me a sign of love
For soon you shall depart.

Your loving hand

Your loving hand has blessed me so
And holds me in your care,
For when I call I always know
You hear my every prayer.

Someone I trust with all my heart
When in my deepest need,
And you and I shall never part
A kindly friend indeed.

Please guide me through my life ahead
And show me how to live,
Throughout the times of fear and dread
To me some courage give.

Please take my hand and lead the way
And always be my guide,
My Lord be with me every day
And never leave my side.

When swallows grace the morning sky

When swallows grace the morning sky
Of April's deepest blue,
As through the air they deftly fly
I'll always think of you.

Though years have passed now long ago
The times we shared true love,
When here we watched the flowers grow
And gazed at skies above.

And now that spring has come again
I know they'll soon be here,
But they shall only bring me pain
Until they disappear.

As now the land begins to bloom
From winter's deepest sleep,
I know that it can't lift the gloom
While still my eyes do weep.

Each spring that comes does wound me still
And fills me with regret,
That stays with me and always will
For I just can't forget.

Until the leaves from boughs shall fall
And swallows fly away,
I'll love you so and give my all
To be with you this day.

When swallows grace the morning sky
And winter's at an end,
I'll watch them as they deftly fly
And think of you my friend.

Sweet thrush if I could sing like you

Sweet thrush if I could sing like you
Upon the bough of that old tree,
Then I would sing the whole day through
And fill this land with melody.

Sweet thrush if I'd your wings to fly
I'd soar into the summer air,
Then chase the clouds as they went by
And all your freedom I would share.

Sweet thrush if I did have your grace
And wore your clothes of speckled white,
I'd move along from place to place
And folks would marvel at my sight.

Sweet thrush if only for one day
I could be you instead of me,
I'd find a branch and there I'd stay
To sing with joyful harmony.

My lonely heart can never love

My lonely heart can never love
Cruel fate's befallen me,
Away hast flown my dream above
Now it will never be.

No hand shall ever rest in mine
No lips shall kiss my cheek,
My eyes shall never see a sign
Nor find the joy I seek.

And so I now must look ahead
And never look behind,
Where hopes I had are lying dead
For love I could not find.

Yet still I call but no one hears
Too far away to care,
So I shall drown within my tears
Alone with my despair.

My lonely heart can never love
My passion has run dry,
For like the clouds that sail above
The chance has passed me by.

The school tree

The year was nineteen seventy three
At school we set a sapling tree
Back then it was as tall as me
But now it towers above,
My classmates there did gather round
Upon the shaded grassy ground
As birdsong then did sweetly sound
It stood for peace and love.

I can recall that I was seven
And saw it grow until eleven
I was so young and life was heaven
And joy filled every day,
But now so many years have passed
My childhood dreams just didn't last
And time went by so very fast
I'm left now in dismay.

 For now my school is sadly gone
The land been cleared it stood upon
Where children played there now are none
And chilly winds do blow,
As now I look upon that tree
That once did stand as tall as me
I shed a tear of sympathy
For now the truth I know.

Upon the blackened canvas

Upon the blackened canvas
Of the cruellest April sky,
A flash of light a thunder roll
And startled birds do fly,
As raindrops now start falling
From those anvil clouds of spite,
For now the storm lies overhead
And day becomes the night.

The rain does fall in torrents
Forming puddles on the ground,
The birds have flown upon the wing
And shelter they have found,
As rivers run in gutters now
The drains are swamped by force,
Unable to subdue the flow
Nor halt them from their course.

Another flash does light the sky
As still the rain does pour,
Another roll of thunder
Like a lion's mighty roar,
When suddenly a beam of light
Breaks through the evil cloud,
And there a rainbow slowly forms
An arch of colours proud.

The sunlight shining brightly
As the hail begins to fall,
The sound of distant thunder now
Seems like a clarion call,
Another far off rumble
As the storm does move away,
The dark clouds have passed over
And the night has turned to day.

The birds are singing once again
With joyful songs they share,
Each one does sound so sweetly now
To grace the evening air,
The rooftops steam within the sun
For they so quickly dry,
As colours of the rainbow fade
Within the April sky.

At the bottom of the garden

At the bottom of the garden now
Our apple tree stands bare,
Through all the years I can recall
I've known it standing there,
Although its shape has altered
In the time that has gone by,
For once it was a sapling
Now it's old and withered dry.

Yet through my life it's borne much fruit
And blossomed every spring,
But now each branch lies empty
And no apples shall they bring,
I'll miss the joy it gave to me
Since I was young and small,
For there I watched it grow each year
Until it stood so tall.

It is forever winter yet
No frost does grip each bough,
For it shall never leaf again
Or rise from slumber now,
It seems like I have lost a friend
And things don't seem the same,
It faded in the autumn time
And spring just never came.

Summer dreams

My summer dreams I'll not forget
Those memories I shall keep,
The sights I saw and cherish most
Stay with me in my sleep,
I saw the leafy woodlands spread
Far over land and dale,
Then roamed upon the downs and hills
And saw the clouds there sail.

I sat beside a restful stream
So soothing was its sound,
Then closed my eyes for in that place
Serenity I found,
I leaned upon a tree to shade
And then I carried on,
Through meadows green where flowers grew
And in the sunlight shone.

Saw waving wheat within the fields
Of burning gold that grew,
And watched the patterns that it made
With every gust that blew,
As swallows soared so gracefully
Within the sapphire sky,
I saw them head upon the wing
And watched the day go by.

I gazed upon the ocean
As the fiery sunset glowed,
And glistened on the water
As the waves then gently flowed,
Unto the shore where I did stand
Within the fading light,
And looked upon the evening
As it sank into the night.

Love

Love can bring you pleasure
But can also bring you pain,
For skies of blue and sunlight
Can so quickly change to rain,
Yet love can bridge the water
And can touch each lonely heart,
Then bring you back together
When you'd drifted far apart.

Love can paint a picture
Of the sweetest sights to see,
Can fill your life with happiness
And end all misery,
For love can make the flowers bloom
And shine in colours bright,
Can come within the daytime
Or upon a starry night.

Love is a gift to treasure
For it doesn't come to all,
As some will never find it
And like leaves their dreams shall fall,
Then rest upon the autumn ground
Where they will wither dry,
For them the spring shall never be
As joy has passed them by.

I'm crossing the causeway

I'm crossing the causeway that leads over water
The path is so narrow and straight as can be,
Its verges are lined by the grasses and flowers
Which dance in the breeze blowing in from the sea.

I walk past the boats that are moored in the harbour
As gently they sway on the incoming tide,
The sunbeams are shining and glisten so brightly
And rest on the ripples like diamonds they ride.

As over the bridge I now make my way onwards
The same lies behind me as what lies before,
As further I go then I pause for a moment
To watch as the waves slowly head to the shore.

And to gaze at the woodland adorning the coastline
While seagulls are calling above as they fly,
The swans move with grace as they pass in the distance
And sail on the Mill Pond as blue as the sky.

The softest reflections are cast on the surface
Whilst moving and swirling they ebb and they flow,
The patterns keep changing and colours keep merging
As with every gust a new picture they show.

I'm crossing the causeway so hushed and so peaceful
I come to its end as it reaches the sand,
Then over the dunes as I head to the Duver
And then greet the Solent dividing the land.

When frozen streams shall flow once more

I wish the cold would melt to spring
When colours of the season bring,
A joy that autumn took away
And left me there alone that day,
For while the land so bleak and plain
I'll never feel that joy again,
Forever winter it shall be
Until that time releases me.

From this my sentence that I live
So much I have but cannot give,
For no one now does seem to care
Imprisoned by my own despair,
A light may gleam within the sky
And yet it soon shall fade and die,
Not strong enough so it could last
Nor wipe the memories of my past.

Surrounded now by ice and snow
Those happy times seem long ago,
While land is gripped and all is white
It cannot save me from my plight,
Nor ease the hurt that I now feel
The wounds of which shall never heal,
Until the spring again does come
I shall remain so cold and numb.

For winter seems to have no end
Nor offers me a lasting friend,
While wind does blow a bitter chill
The restless air is never still,
I wish for me the sun would shine
To warm this lonely heart of mine,
As I await the ice to thaw
When frozen streams shall flow once more.

O lasting love that knows no bounds

O lasting love that knows no bounds
Why do you never come to me?
To spare me from these lonely days
So bitter and so cold,
For me the winter shall not end
No birds will sing within the boughs,
Till joy shall fill my empty heart
The spring will not unfold.

As life goes on without me now
I feel that I've been left behind,
No friends have I to share my grief
Or pain I've borne so long,
So all alone I face my fears
And yet no courage I possess,
My will grows ever weaker now
I wish that I were strong.

O lasting love that knows no bounds
Why do you never come to me?
For still you keep on passing by
As if you do not care,
Yet here you'd find a welcome home
Where you could bloom for evermore,
Then every day would be the spring
And joy we both could share.

The sound of wind within the trees

The sound of wind within the trees
Like falling waves upon the sand,
It rushes through the boughs and leaves
Amidst the woodland green,
Across the skies the clouds do race
As morning yields the golden beams,
That lights the land and all around
With summer's finest sheen.

The sound of wind within the trees
A symphony that grows then fades,
And calms until it gusts again
As loudly as before,
The music sweet unto my ear
So soothing till it builds again,
A gradual climb that rises like
The lion's mighty roar.

The sound of wind within the trees
Those restless leaves in harmony,
So sing a million voices there
As if they were as one,
They never cease until the air
Is still and peace does reign again,
As evening draws its final breath
A whisper, then it's gone.

The Airston wool shop

The Airston wool shop long ago
Once stood beside this busy road,
The name has changed the people too
'Twas such a friendly store,
A child was I and yet recall
Those times we spent with fondness there,
A jewel within the village then
That sadly is no more.

So clearly I remember well
The rows and rows of woollen balls,
With every colour you could think
Stacked neatly in a line,
The ribbon bows the ties and pins
Elasticated cords and bands,
The zips and fabrics beads and lace
With sequins that did shine.

The buttons sewn upon the tags
Adorned the creaking swivel stand,
Beside the wooden counter there
And made a fine display,
The knitting needles large and small
With pattern books and tapestries,
The twine and darn with silken thread
And cottons in a tray.

It doesn't seem that long ago
But many years have passed since then,
My thoughts though all come flooding back
Each time that I go by,
I think of all my childhood days
With fondness but they can't return,
So much has changed so much been lost
Yet memories shall not die.

The rusting old bucket

The rusting old bucket now stands by the shed
In the heart of the damp cobbled floor,
As raindrops are falling from dark leaden skies
But they gather within it no more.

For the bucket now holed by the years of its toil
That did once carry coal to the fire,
As proudly it stood by the poker and tongs
With its clean and its shining attire.

Now it lies there unused in the dirty back yard
And its last days are fading away,
As it stands in the cold of the wet winter's morn
And now riddled by signs of decay.

The handle that bore all the weight that it held
Is so twisted and bent on the pail,
And is now only used as a perch for the birds
On that bucket so battered and frail.

The gift of love

No soul can live without it
For it's such a precious thing,
That's born out of compassion
With the joy that it does bring,
Throughout the world it's needed
So then heed its mighty call,
The gift of love for certain
Is the greatest gift of all.

So if you have a bit to spare
Then send it on its way,
To places where they need it most
And make things change this day,
For if you do ignore it
And decide to make it wait,
By the time you go and do it then
It may be just too late.

So send your love upon the wind
For God shall make it blow,
Across the lands and oceans wide
So quickly it shall go,
To find each heart that's lonely
And is wracked by hurt and pain,
You have the power and the strength
To make them beat again.

While many souls do suffer
Caught within the pangs of war,
Don't keep your love unto yourself
For they do need it more,
To all those who are starving
And through daily hardship strive,
The gift of love of which you send
Will help them to survive.

Nobody has the answers
So you can but only try,
Just go ahead and do it now
And never question why,
Throughout the world it's needed
So then heed its mighty call,
The gift of love for certain
Is the greatest gift of all.

If I should find no answers there

If I should find no answers there
Where should I go instead?
To search for what I need the most
When hopes are lying dead,
It only takes a moment
For a leaf to gently fall,
Yet where it lies I too shall grieve
If I have lost it all.

If I should find no answers there
Then maybe I'll return,
A better, wiser, stronger man
For lessons I did learn,
It only takes a moment
For the clouds to blow away,
And life shall seem much better
When the sun shall light my day.

If I should find no answers there
What kind of fool am I?
To let the chance of precious love
So cruelly pass me by,
It only takes a moment
For that grief to disappear,
The way unto your loving heart
Does make my choice so clear.

Getting ready for apple picking

As now the fruit has grown and formed
So round upon the laden boughs,
The colour of the evening skies
And summer's end does near,
The apples ripe and so they must
Be picked and then all gathered in,
Before they fall down to the ground
And autumn time is here.

The months have passed since blossom formed
It's hard to think where summer's gone,
It seems but only yesterday
When daffodils spread wide,
But now as August days do fade
I'll take the basket in my hand,
And twist the cores until they break
Then place each one inside.

Too many there for me alone
I'll share them with my feathered friends,
To thank them for the chorus
Every morning they do sing,
So they will stay and dine with me
And never fly to pastures new,
When branches bare I can but hope
To see another spring.

Portland stone

The quarry men of long ago
Within the mines of Portland isle,
Once split the rock with wedge and scale
And swung their hammers down,
Time again with all their might
Until the stone was cut in two,
Then shipped afar to distant shores
Away from this old town.

Chink a chink the quarry sound
The ringing echoed through the air,
The toil of men so greatly skilled
Who grafted every day,
With honest sweat on honest brows
Their brawny arms and calloused hands,
Were hardened from their labours yet
They earned so little pay.

Chink a chink from dawn till dusk
They chiselled through the limey seam,
A band of brothers side by side
Each one a trusted friend,
Their skills were passed on down the line
For fathers taught their sons the trade,
Their sons did teach their sons the same
Until the work did end.

For times have changed in Portland now
So few survived to show the way,
How things were done before machines
Replaced the workers there,
The fruits of which adorn the lands
And grace the towns and cities far,
Across the seas for evermore
Those epitaphs we share.

The washing line

The clothes now wave which hang upon
This tired old line that stretches from,
The house unto the garden's end
In winds that blow so strong,
With every gust there yields a chill
Of winter that does cruelly bite,
The bitter air is never still
And wails an eerie song.

Each garment there is pegged and spaced
Upon the line that bows and sags,
Beneath the weight of dampened sheets
And every sock and shirt,
Which dry within the morning sun
That shines between the racing clouds,
Yet there does lie a handkerchief
Of white within the dirt.

Now fallen from the line it dwelt
And stained with mud where once it held,
My tears I wept now washed away
Yet I remember well,
The cause, the pain, the grief and hurt
The scars of which shall never heal,
The memories fresh I'll leave it there
Exactly where it fell.

The potter

Within the cobbled back streets
Of the town where he was born,
The potter walks the lonely path
Amidst the breaking dawn,
Unto his workshop he arrives
To start another day,
Puts on the light and then he dons
His apron stained with clay.

His arms are strong his chest so broad
A mighty man is he,
And yet his fingers nimble
And so blessed with artistry,
With greying beard and tresses long
His face the years now show,
For lined with age he bears the strain
Of times so long ago.

He opens wide the kiln door
Where he fired his work last night,
Now cooled and so he checks each one
To see that all is right,
No cracks nor flaws no chips or scuffs
Perfection to his eye,
Then placed upon the shelf to glaze
He stirs the barrelled dye.

With hands so skilled he takes some clay
And spots it on the wheel,
That slowly turns then gathers speed
So deftly he does feel,
His work that he then shapes into
A vase he makes with ease,
For made a thousand times or more
And always seem to please.

He carries on he does not rest
Until his work is done,
While through his dirty window pane
Now shines the morning sun,
Some children watch him working yet
He doesn't seem to mind,
Just waves and smiles then carries on
He mustn't fall behind.

As all day long he hardly stops
It's all he has in life,
His home is cold and empty since
He lost he dearest wife,
And so he strives from break of dawn
Until the sun does set,
And keeps his mind upon his job
To help him to forget.

When evening comes his work complete
So ends another day,
He yields a sigh and then removes
His apron stained with clay,
Turns off the light and as he leaves
He locks his battered door,
Until tomorrow when again
He shall return once more.

The early morning mist and dew

The early morning mist and dew
The faintest sunlight shining through,
The branches of the languid trees
That slowly forms this autumn frieze,
With subtle shades as leaves now turn
And fiery glows of amber burn,
That warms the chill of breaking dawn
Upon this late October morn.

The silver birch in primrose stands
Its trunk is flecked and striped with bands,
While bracken frames this stony course
That winds its way through thorny gorse,
A carpet made of leaves and twigs
While berries ripe on holly sprigs,
Glow scarlet in the shade of night
And almost hidden from my sight.

The air is still so hushed the sound
As leaves are falling to the ground,
Like raindrops from a passing shower
They gather there beneath the bower,
A squirrel roams the woodland floor
While searching for some food to store,
Amongst the span of empty husk
He seldom moves from dawn till dusk.

When evening falls and shadows rest
And sunlight sinks within the west,
Then soon descends the cold of night
Beneath the stars that shine so bright,
A frost does form as winter nears
That glistens like the fallen tears,
Of autumn for its end is nigh
As if to say its last goodbye.

To me you are the sunlight

To me you are the sunlight
That does fill my every day,
The warmth you have the joy you give
Each smile a golden ray,
You rise within the morning
And you shine through clouds above,
From dawn until the stars aglow
I'll be with you my love.

To me you are the river
That does wind towards the sea,
Where'er you go I'll follow
For it's where I long to be,
So pure unto my wanton lips
Abandoned now to you,
The heartbeat of each ripple
Casts a spell on all I do.

To me you are the mountains
For so beautiful your sight,
To see you stand before me there
Does fill me with delight,
Your shape and form your grace and poise
You soar unto the sky,
A vision that shall live with me
Until the day I die.

To me you are the moonlight
That does rest upon the lake,
So softly through the darkness there
Until the dawn does break,
When once more you shall rise again
And colour you will bring,
For when you shine across the land
The birds for love shall sing.

I feel a joy now spring's begun

I feel a joy now spring's begun
As shadows lift the breaking sun,
Does shine upon this land so fair
Caressing now the morning air,
As flowers all around me grow
The blossom on the wind does blow,
For now the May is dressed in white
I know there is no greater sight.

Among the boughs the birds do sing
And fly with grace upon the wing,
I hear them as the morn they greet
With silken songs so pure and sweet,
Which echo through the woodland trees
Across the meadow on the breeze,
Unto my beating heart they call
The sound that I love most of all.

As from the hills a gentle stream
Meanders like a distant dream,
I watch the ripples dance and play
As down the valley make my way,
I follow on its winding course
Past slopes adorned by clumps of gorse,
With petals of the finest gold
And see the season there unfold.

Through pastures rich where grazing sheep
With newborn lambs in safety keep,
And daisies light the sacred ground
A heaven on this earth I've found,
Such beauty here I gaze upon
But know that soon it shall be gone,
And I must wait another year
For spring to yield its merry cheer.

Till God does find another path

Till God does find another path
For me to tread I'll carry on,
And walk where'er life takes me to
And climb each rock and stone,
My destiny cannot be changed
Yet my sweet Lord shall guide my steps,
And angels lead me on my way
I'll never be alone.

I shall not stray from what is right
Until I breathe my final breath,
And meet my Lord and Saviour
Then that paradise I'll see,
To join with those who've passed before
In peace within the garden there,
And I'll rejoice when I have found
The greatest place to be.

Till God does find another path
For me to tread I won't complain,
The course is mapped for me to go
For everything is planned,
If therefore I must suffer now
I know that there's a reason why,
If hidden it shall be revealed
Then I will understand.

All is silent

All is silent all is still
A breathless hush does sigh until,
The shadows of the night do fade
And morning glow does cast its shade,
Across the land this winter's morn
As sunbeams greet the rising dawn,
Through branches of the frozen trees
To light the way as darkness flees.

The icy claws that grip the air
Now reaching from the woodland bare,
For leaves did fall so long ago
On autumn winds they then did blow,
Like statues there the trees now dwell
For only spring can break the spell,
And come as if a welcome friend
To breathe new life at winter's end.

All is silent there's no sound
As snow does rest upon the ground,
And undisturbed it there does lie
So pure and white beneath the sky,
Of gold that slowly turns to blue
Awakens all God's creatures too,
As birds begin to sing with cheer
With pleasing songs unto my ear.

And as the winter's moonlight falls

And as the winter's moonlight falls
Upon the crisp and frozen ground,
We share the night beneath the stars
Which shine so high above,
For as we walk the empty streets
We gaze unto the evening sky,
To see their greatness there displayed
And thank them for our love.

Although the night does feel so cold
While you are there I shall be warm,
And sense those lonely times no more
Nor feel that bitter chill,
With memories left within the past
I look towards the future now,
Then hope each day shall bring me joy
And pray it is God's will.

The puddles iced beside the kerb
Are cracked like many dreams before,
But they will thaw as morning sun
Does greet the coming dawn,
Yet as the winter's moonlight falls
The way ahead seems crystal clear,
I feel the stars were made for us
For love this night was born.

The trawler

The trawler now tied up in port
So long since she last sailed,
The peeling paint upon her hull
A sign that all has failed,
The barren seas that line the coast
Far from the eastern shore,
Now means this boat can't ride the waves
To fish there anymore.

So here beside the quay remains
As months turn into years,
A mist descends upon the town
So filled with bitter tears,
The crew that served so faithfully
All left and moved away,
To find some work as jobs were lost
They could no longer stay.

Her nets now tangled holed and torn
Across her deck they lie,
For never to be used again
Those days have all gone by,
Now rust has gripped the wheelhouse
Where the skipper steered her course,
Abandoned to the elements
Which offer no remorse.

The trawler now tied up in port
In such a sorry state,
For now unsafe to go to sea
Abandoned to her fate,
Her name has gone her number lost
She soon will meet her end,
An empty space shall line the quay
And all will lose a friend.

I found it in the morning

I found it in the morning
As the dawn began to rise,
It drifted like the autumn mist
That hung within the skies,
It caught the beams of sunlight
That did shine upon the land,
Then found its way into my heart
So I could understand.

I found it on the mountain
For it lay within the view,
The scene was one of wonder
And it taught me all I knew,
For there within the valleys lay
A land so rich in gold,
And I could see the future there
With all that it foretold.

I found it in the forest
As I walked within its shade,
I heard the whisper of the leaves
And knew my fortune made,
I felt the spirit move within
The branches of the trees,
That lifted me unto the clouds
Upon the summer breeze.

I found it on the shoreline
As I gazed across the sea,
For there I felt a sense of peace
And deep serenity,
The waves did glisten brightly
And the skies were all aglow,
For as the sun began to fall
I saw that wondrous show.

On the sixteenth day of August 1977

On the sixteenth day of August
Came a newsflash on TV,
"The King of rock and roll has died
In Memphis Tennessee,"
The cause of death his kindly heart
So generous and true,
His life cut short within his prime
At only forty two.

As thousands gathered at the gates
Of Graceland they did cry,
In disbelief and horror
He was far too young to die,
They prayed and they lit candles
And the flames did burn so bright,
They glistened like the stars above
And shone throughout the night.

They sang his songs together
As his music filled the air,
They knew that he was with them
And they felt his presence there,
The people stayed and would not leave
And still their tears did flow,
Upon that fateful August day
So many years ago.

The timber trail

I trod the dusty trail ahead
That wound its way through evergreen,
But there beside the fern did lay
The timber cut that morn,
It hurt me so to see them there
Those lifeless trunks no root nor bough,
For I remembered when they reached
Unto the skies of dawn.

For once they graced the place they stood
That silhouette forever changed,
And I'll not live to view again
The sight that used to be,
As I approached with heavy heart
I saw the scars that they had left,
Upon the land that now stood bare
With nothing left to see.

Their cones lay still upon the ground
And scattered far from where they fell,
As I then stooped beside the trunks
To count the rings they bore,
Their age was great for I did make
One hundred years I tell no lie,
A part of this great forest yet
They sadly were no more.

I carried on along the way
The sunlight shone upon my face,
Where once I had been cast in shade
I could not hear a sound,
The birds had flown the deer had fled
Now hushed the saw the damage done,
Yet stumps remained like stones within
A church's sacred ground.

The ancient pearl

Unto the depths of sadness lost
And shall not see the light again,
The pearl does rest upon the bed
Amongst the shipwrecked graves,
Once treasured now unseen by all
For out of reach of human hand,
It now does lie so still beneath
The motion of the waves.

The cause of so much hurt and pain
Perhaps it's wise it should be left,
There undisturbed for evermore
Far from those jealous craves,
They fought with cutlass sword and blade
And blood was spilt to gain this stone,
That now does lie so still beneath
The motion of the waves.

It ruined many greedy lives
For all who clenched it in their grasp,
Did never find the joy they sought
And were but merely slaves,
The last did throw it overboard
So from that curse he could be free,
Where it remains so still beneath
The motion of the waves.

My heart is yours for evermore

The stillness of the morning rise
Its greatness that I see,
The peace existing in my soul
Shall last eternally,
As shadows fade and colours glow
And faintest sun does shine,
My heart is yours for evermore
And yours is always mine.

Each day to me brings happiness
So glad to be with you,
I feel my life has just begun
Each moment fresh and new,
Whilst knowing now that I do share
A love that's so divine,
My heart is yours for evermore
And yours is always mine.

To hear the birds so sweetly sing
In shade of woodland's green,
And look upon this gracious land
Such wonders I have seen,
The views so captivating
Where the fields and hills entwine,
My heart is yours for evermore
And yours is always mine.

Another day is ending now
As light begins to fade,
And shadows grow and darkness falls
Until I'm cast in shade,
And as the clouds begin to glow
Above God's grand design,
My heart is yours for evermore
And yours is always mine.

Put aside your differences

Put aside your differences
Forget about the past,
Forgive those who've upset you
And don't let bad feelings last,
A time to come together
With your family and your friends,
And those for which you care the most
On whom your life depends.

Take care of all your neighbours now
For some may be alone,
And spend a little time with them
Don't have a heart of stone,
Please see they don't go hungry
And then warm them if they're cold,
Then give them all that you can spare
For one day you'll be old.

If Christmas brings no presents
And rich gifts you can't afford,
Instead of feeling sorry then
Find comfort in the Lord,
Give all that you can offer
In the name of God above,
The greatest gift costs nothing
For it is the gift of love.

A misty light

A misty light this ghostly dawn
Does flicker as the day is born,
For still and gentle not a sound
I gaze across the frozen ground.

As sun now glimmers through the trees
The fiery sky above the freeze,
As birds do wake from slumbers deep
The frosted boughs begin to weep.

And as they drip like gentle rain
Upon the grass of white they stain,
That soon shall thaw as sun does rise
Into the glowing amber skies.

As mist now drifts and fades away
And birds begin to sing this day,
I look towards the woodland there
That once stood green but now so bare.

My love shall flow like gentle streams

My love shall flow like gentle streams
Along their winding course to you,
Forever in my lasting dreams
I know one day they shall come true,
For then with you my heart will rest
And through my life will never stray,
From north to south from east to west
I know that it shall find a way.

My love for you will bloom and grow
As if each morning of the spring,
When blossom falls like flakes of snow
Then all the birds for joy shall sing,
Each night you're with me as I sleep
But then I wake to find you gone,
And yet these thoughts I always keep
That one day soon we'll be as one.

My love shall flow like gentle streams
And never will those waters dry,
Forever in my lasting dreams
Until the day that I shall die,
I shan't forget those times we shared
And wish that you were still my friend,
For then from sadness I'd be spared
And all my pain would surely end.

I shall forever think of you

I shall forever think of you
Your memory will not fade,
I'll keep a thought within my mind
Of all the joy you made.

You always gave to others
Asked for nothing in return,
And gave your time for everyone
No matter what concern.

While your spirit lives with me
I shall try to carry on,
Yet my days all filled with sadness
And my zest for life has gone.

Yet I know you are in heaven
Looking down from high above,
And with me every day I live
And sending me your love.